DATE DUE

AUG 0 9 2000	
AUG 1 9 2000	

GAYLORD

PRINTED IN U.S.A.

Fallen in
Battle

FALLEN IN BATTLE

American General Officer Combat Fatalities From 1775

RUSSELL K. BROWN

Greenwood Press

New York • Westport, Connecticut • London

Library of Congress Cataloging-in-Publication Data

Brown, Russell K.
  Fallen in battle.

  Bibliography: p.
  Includes index.
    1. Generals—United States—Death.   2. United
States—History, Military.   3. United States—Armed
Forces—Officers—Death.   I. Title.
E181.B886   1988   973   88-5644
ISBN 0-313-26242-X (lib. bdg. : alk. paper)

British Library Cataloguing in Publication Data is available.

Library of Congress Catalog Card Number: 88-5644
ISBN: 0-313-26242-X

First published in 1988

Greenwood Press, Inc.
88 Post Road West, Westport, Connecticut   06881

Printed in the United States of America

(∞)™

The paper used in this book complies with the
Permanent Paper Standard issued by the National
Information Standards Organization (Z39.48-1984).

10 9 8 7 6 5 4 3 2 1

Copyright Acknowledgment

The author and publisher gratefully acknowledge permission to reprint material
from "Fallen Stars" by Russell K. Brown, which appeared in *Military Affairs*,
February 1981. Copyright 1981 by the American Military Institute.

To My Father

Contents

Acknowledgments

This volume is dedicated to the memory of my father, James Lewis Brown (1906–1975), whose depth of knowledge and delight in studying U.S. military history far exceeded the limits of his formal education or his ability to pursue his interest. Among the many things for which I am indebted to him is the encouragement to continue with this work from its inception.

A study of this nature and magnitude, spanning fifteen years of research and writing as it does, results from the assistance and goodwill of many people who have contributed time and information. Of course, it is also a distillation of the research and scholarship of those who have written on the same topic in the past. Those printed sources which have been used are acknowledged throughout the text and are listed in the bibliography. A complete listing of other people who have contributed time or information would be too long for inclusion. All of them have my heartfelt thanks but only a few can be mentioned by name.

I wish to take special note of the help provided by John Slonaker of the U.S. Army Military History Institute and Kenneth Rapp of the U.S. Military Academy Archives for this and other of my literary ventures; Detmar Finke and Dr. Robert R. Smith of the Office of the Chief of Military History (now the Center for Military History); and Ken Paulsen of the National Personnel Records Center in St. Louis. Also of immeasurable assistance were Linda Orn and Fred Danes of the Woodworth Memorial Library, Fort Gordon, Georgia, who cheerfully and diligently pursued my endless demands for arcane volumes through interlibrary loan. I must take note of the considerate attention paid to my calls for help by Edward M. Coffman, Shelby L. Stanton, and Robert M. Utley, all three experts in their own areas of military history. No acknowledgment would be complete without a reference to the letters of encouragement provided by Major General William A. Burke, U.S. Army, retired, who also gave me valuable insight into the emotional burdens of the battlefield commander. Some of General Burke's thoughts are quoted in my introduction.

The assistance of Dr. William Felker, who read every page of my original manuscript, is gratefully acknowledged for his valuable corrections and suggestions. To Faye Beasley I am indebted for the cheerful typing of innumerable pages of that original manuscript and its corrected typescript. My thanks, too, to the American Military Institute for permission to use copyrighted materials which first appeared in my article in *Military Affairs* in February 1981.

Through the better part of two decades and while living on two continents I have made full use of all the talent, information, and support which family, friends, and professional experts made available to me. I have benefited greatly from their advice and have profited shamelessly from their contributions; however, I alone am responsible for any facts of error or interpretation which may be found.

Introduction

This is a story about death. It is also about courage and glory, incompetence and vainglory. It is the story of American generals who have given their lives while leading their troops. It reveals them as a heterogeneous group of human beings with all of the strengths and weaknesses, fortes and foibles one expects of the human race. It is a litany of leadership demonstrated in no other profession in our nation's history.

No other figure in the American pantheon of heroes is more honored than the military commander at the head of his troops. The cause may be futile, the tactics may be faulty, but the leader who gallantly risks his own life while asking his men to do the same deserves whatever praise he may receive. Johann deKalb at Camden, George Custer at the Little Big Horn, Stonewall Jackson at Chancellorsville, each demonstrated a willingness to lead by example and made the supreme sacrifice to achieve the results desired. Thousands of captains have shared that risk over the years and thousands more have paid the final price. The fortunes of war make no odds over fame or obscurity, high rank or low, but the focus of history is on those few hundred who took the gamble and lost and who were distinguished enough or lucky enough to be wearing the stars of general or flag officers when they did so.

In 1978, Richard Gabriel and Paul Savage published a study impugning the ability and the willingness of the U.S. Army officer corps to *command* their troops rather than manage them.[1] Gabriel and Savage did an impressive amount of work to prove that the Army officer in the Vietnam era did little or nothing to motivate his men or to bring his unit that sense of pride and cohesiveness so essential for high morale and combat effectiveness. Much of what they wrote was valid; despite offended denials, much that the army has done for organizational effectiveness in the past ten years was in response to the shortcomings pointed out by Gabriel and Savage.

Indeed, there is a trend away from physical *leading* toward remotely *managing*. One would be wrong, however, to interpret this wholly as a function of lack of leadership. As the dimensions of the battlefield have been expanded, as means of transportation and communication have improved, and as the size of units commanded by general officers has increased, the necessity or ability to be everywhere, or to be seen by everyone, has decreased. A Civil War division commander had 5,000 men under his control, could watch their deployment from a hilltop, faced no weapon with a greater range than a mile or two, and conducted most of his battlefield communications by word of mouth or written message. His counterpart in World War II directed 15,000 men, controlled a front of several miles length, used and defended against weapons with effective range of dozens of miles, and communicated by radio most of the time. By sheer, overpowering physical circumstances, it was less possible for the World War II division general to communicate with or be seen by his followers than it had been for his Civil War counterpart. Certainly, in this regard, the physical presence dimension of leadership was removed.

In Vietnam, the butt of most of Gabriel and Savage's fulminations, the advances of communications and transportation, made it possible for the commander at all levels to preside over a battlefield from relative heliborne comfort, placing between himself and his troops an additional barrier of lessened vulnerability to danger. The helicopter has greatly enhanced a commander's ability to view and control operations. It has done little for his personal relationship with troops in battle, although it has made it possible for the commander to make more frequent visits to more remotely located units.

Despite criticisms of a change in the culture of command over the years, the testimony of actual participants may be more telling than the carping of the critics. Better than the culture of command, one might say that the culture of war has changed, as noted above, while the duties and responsibilities of the commander, although greatly expanded, remain unchanged. Certainly, industrialization has removed whatever glamor war might have possessed, as the *levee en masse*, or national conscription, has brought war into the home of every citizen, removing participation in hostilities from the exclusive domain of the professional cadre. Even so, each modern commander suffers the same agonies as did his predecessor of one or two hundred years ago.

In 1864, Colonel (later Brevet Brigadier General) Daniel Chaplin of the 1st Maine Heavy Artillery experienced such a flood of anguish over the heavy losses of his regiment at Spotsylvania and Cold Harbor that he went into a fit of depression which lasted until his own death in action two months later.[2] No different from Chaplin's is the concern expressed by a Vietnam era division commander, Major General William A. Burke of the 4th Infantry Division, who succinctly states:

There were a lot of generals in Vietnam who groveled in the mud and saw their responsibilities from the soldier level. An idea which [should be stressed] is the absolute loneliness of the combat commander, *particularly of general rank*. The Army's discipline/rank structure never allows the commander to discuss his wraths, fears, or emotions with anyone. He is alone with his own conscience and can never relieve himself in any way of the heavy weight of his plans to send his troops into a situation at risk, or of the feeling afterward when the casualty figures come in. Taking counsel of his fears and personally questioning his decisions within himself are crosses he must bear and which become heavier as time goes by. I have never overcome the effect of what the lonely commander goes through.[3]

Separated by the years though they may be, General Burke and General Chaplin would certainly understand each other's emotions despite the changed face of war or modes of command. Critics may point up the increasing remoteness of the commander from his troops; the responsibilities and burdens of command have not changed.

Contrary to a view commonly held, more general officers were killed in Vietnam as a percentage of total combat deaths than in World War II. In the latter war, twenty-five Army generals suffered death at the hands of hostile forces. This was in a total of over 230,000 combat deaths. In Vietnam, five Army generals died of hostile causes out of a total of slightly more than 30,000 combat deaths. The ratio of general officer to total combat fatalities was approximately one third greater in Vietnam than in World War II. Precise ratios are found in Table 2 of Appendix A.

One is compelled to recognize the different circumstances under which these deaths occurred. In World War II, twenty-four of the twenty-five generals died in the presence of their troops or followers. Even the Army Air Force generals were killed while flying combat missions. In Vietnam, three of the five killed were heliborne and were shot down; the other two had just alighted from their helicopters. Although this can be interpreted as evidence of the remoteness of the modern era general, it can also be seen as a factor in the enhanced mobility of the commander on his expanded battlefield.

The work of Gabriel and Savage may be valid insofar as small unit commanders having an effect on the cohesiveness of their commands is concerned. Their findings do not seem to apply to the professional general officers who fought a limited war fraught with social and political overtones. These were the same generals who recognized the need for change in the post-Vietnam era and oversaw the rebirth of the U.S. Army. These are the officers who are the professional descendants of earlier, prouder times. It is the basic purpose of this study to identify and recount the careers of those men who have given their lives while serving as general officers and who established the tradition of self-sacrifice and professional conduct in the face of the enemy, a tradition which their modern-day counterparts will be expected to emulate. Not every officer whose career is reviewed herein showed the greatest of good sense or all of the principles of leadership when faced with command in battle, but none of them exhibited any degree of unwillingness to shoulder his burden, to face death, or to provide anything but a positive example to his followers. The reader may determine for himself the value of these examples and their impact on American fighting forces through the years.

In 1970, Colonel Robert D. Heinl, the Marine Corps historian, wrote a column for the *Armed Forces Journal* in which he attempted to trace the history of general and flag officer combat fatalities in American wars.[4] His brief article contained a number of factual errors as well as being short of the mark in giving an accurate account of those killed. However, it was sufficient to create the germ of an idea which has come to fruition in this compilation. Subsequent inquiries were to prove that the respective branches of the armed forces, which were his sources, had no more idea of the numbers Colonel Heinl was looking for than did he.

The death of Richard Tallman, the "last" general officer combat fatality, in the early summer of 1972 was further impetus for an investigation of the numbers and identities of his peers and predecessors. If he was the last, who was the first? How many were there in between? Where and how had they fallen? Were there common denominators to their lives and deaths? Where could this information be obtained?

The answer to the last question was the easiest: nowhere, or rather, from no single source. Extensive inquiries to a number of military agencies produced fragmentary results. The Office of the Chief of Military History provided a valuable but unreliable list of general officers killed in World War II,[5] and statistics on general officers killed in World War I and Korea.[6] The casualty branch of the Adjutant General's Office provided names of general officers killed in Vietnam.[7] The Military History Institute at Carlisle could only confirm the other two sources.

The Navy Office of Information had no idea how many admirals had died of combat-related causes but consented to provide biographical sketches of any who had. The Marine Corps and Air Force Historical Divisions knew that their first combat fatalities had occurred in Vietnam but the actual identities were uncertain.

This was the extent of official information. Everything else had to be obtained through painstaking research through unit histories and newspaper accounts, archives and libraries, correspondence and conversations with fellow service men and family members.

From the outset, the criterion for admission to this Roll of Honor was inclusion in all of the following three categories:

a) Held at time of death, had previously held, or was posthumously promoted to general or flag officer rank, including brevet.

b) Served in an *American* military force: Continental Army or militia; U.S. Army regulars, volunteers, or militia; Philippine Army during World War II; U.S. Navy, Air Force, or Marine Corps; Confederate Army or Navy.

c) Died at the hands of an enemy force or while on *combat* operations, except through clearly accidental causes: killed in action; missing in action, declared dead; died of wounds; executed or died while a prisoner of war.[8]

The general purpose of this categorization is to provide broad enough parameters to include any individual who might be considered eligible for inclusion by another statistician or historian. However, as will be discussed below, certain officially listed or generally recognized combat deaths have been deliberately omitted after an examination of the cause of death and in the interest of consistency.

Also omitted were officers who became generals in American forces but were killed in combat while fighting with foreign forces, and Americans who were generals in foreign forces. Two examples were Confederate brigadier Mosby M. Parsons, who was killed while fighting with the republican forces in Mexico in August 1865, and Frederick Townsend Ward of Salem, Massachusetts, Admiral-General of the Imperial Chinese Service, who was mortally wounded at the siege of Tsekie and died at Ningpo in September 1862.

The period of the American Revolution provided a starting point of this study. Some consideration was given to including general officers of British provincial troops in America during England's imperial wars with France during the seventeenth and eighteenth centuries. However, these officers do not fit the criterion of having served in an American military force, so they were excluded. An examination of all the officers identified by Heitman and Boatner[9] as generals in the Continental or state service, including those promoted by brevet at war's end, produced a list of twelve names for inclusion. Nine of these were straightforward combat fatalities and three died as prisoners of the British, one from his wounds.

The next period of military activity was the collective Indian Wars, which lasted on and off for over 100 years. The principal sources in this case was Heitman's other collection[10] plus a variety of works on the Indian Wars. This time four persons were identified, all of whom were genuine fatalities of Indian action, but one of whom was a civilian at the time of his death. This was Wiley Thompson, the Indian commissioner murdered by Osceola in 1835. Thompson has been included here on the basis of his service as a general in the Georgia militia from 1817 to 1824.[11]

The War of 1812 and the Mexican War provided no dilemmas of categorization. Two generals were killed in the former, none in the latter. The service of all generals in both wars was verified in Heitman.[12]

The battles of the Civil War caused general officer fatalities larger in number on each side than all other American wars together. Northern and Southern losses were equal when brevet generals of the Union forces are included. This is a testament to the bravery of both sides, but when one considers the smaller number of Confederate generals commissioned during the war the ratio of losses becomes unbelievably disproportionate.

Of 583 Union generals[13] and nearly 1,400 generals by brevet,[14] eighty, or 4 percent, were combat fatalities. On the other side, the Confederate government commissioned 425 generals and another dozen were appointed by local commanders.[15] Of these, eighty, or 18 percent, were fatalities. The disparity is obvious. McWhiney and Jamieson's examination of Southern military tactics largely explains the reason for this wanton loss of life.[16] As Freeman said, "[They] seemed to have been promoted solely to be slain."[17]

The identification of Union full-rank and commissioned Confederate generals was relatively simple. Warner's two volumes were essential tools for these cases. Appointed Confederate generals were checked against Clement Evans's compilation with good results.[18] Union brevet generals posed a greater difficulty. Phisterer's list of fatalities is useful but incomplete and somtimes inaccurate. A review of all officers identified by Boatner as brevet generals yielded several changes to Phisterer.[19] Additional research produced the final results contained herein.

One case which posed special problems was that of Colonel John Taylor Hughes of the Missouri State Guard and later, of the Confederate Army. After fighting in Sterling Price's army both east and west of the Mississippi, Hughes was sent back to Missouri in the summer of 1862 to raise a new brigade. In the capture of Independence on 11 August he was killed while leading an attack on the Union defenders' camp. At least two sources list him as a Confederate brigadier. In addition, during the dedication of a memorial in Hughes's honor in Independence in 1963, the principal speaker mentioned that Hughes had been a brevet general. Of course, no such rank ever existed in the Confederate service. Records of the Missouri Adjutant General indicate that Hughes died a colonel, the highest grade he ever achieved.[20]

The wars of America's expanded interest in international affairs produced their own share of fatalities, two in the Philippine Insurrection and one in the Boxer Rebellion. Heitman's identification of regular army officer casualties and volunteer general officer appointments up to 1903 provided the basic information required for further research in this area.[21]

The first of the two world wars had relatively little impact on U.S. general officer fatalities, but there were some. The late entry of the United States into combat operations as well as the nature of the warfare in which most higher commanders were remote from the battlefield produced only one general officer death. In addition, one former general who chose service as a battalion commander was killed.[22] A review of the twentieth-century general officers listed in the *Army Almanac*[23] was the starting point for identifying those men.

As mentioned above, beginning with World War II, the various military departments have maintained sufficient data to help the serious student start on an identification of general and flag officer fatalities since 1941. Unpublished documents, published registers, and frequent press releases are available for the knowledgeable researcher. A serious drawback is that research in official records is hampered by the National Archives rule which limits the release of information on people who have been dead less than seventy-five years. Even today, data on World War I combat casualties officially may not be available and information on fatalities from World War II will be restricted for many years to come.

A word of explanation about "bona fide" is appropriate at this point. The categories of fatalities mentioned earlier include two, died of wounds (DOW) and missing in action, which are subject to some interpretation. Several instances exist from the Civil War period which could be construed as DOW but are not and vice versa.

Edward N. Kirk, wounded at Stone's River in December 1862 and died in Chicago, July 1863; Stephen G. Champlin, wounded at Fair Oaks in May 1862 and died in Grand Rapids in July 1864; Stephen Elliott, Jr., wounded at the Petersburg Crater, July 1864 and died in Aiken, South Carolina, in March 1866; and Cleveland J. Campbell, also wounded at the Crater and died in New York in June 1865, are the examples of officers whose deaths occurred long enough after their wounding to make the causes suspiciously remote. In the case of Campbell, the official cause of death given by the attending physician was "consumption and chronic diarrhea."[24] Phisterer shows Kirk, Champlin, and Campbell dying of other causes.[25] However, most sources agree that all died of the debilitating effects of their wounds. This study supports those conclusions.

On the other hand, at least three Union generals and one admiral who were wounded and later died are universally reported as victims of natural deaths. These were T.E.G. Ransom, wounded three times but died of exhaustion and typhoid; Joseph Plummer, severely wounded at Wilson's Creek but died of exposure; Andrew Foote, wounded at Fort Donelson but died of kidney disease; and John Buford wounded at Second Manassas but died of exposure. Surely, the wounds helped to break down the health of these men, but the historical records say otherwise.[26]

The case of Confederate brigadier James J. Archer also bears explanation. Captured at Gettysburg in an enfeebled condition, Archer languished in a Union prison for over a year before being exchanged in the late summer of 1864. He was with the Army of Northern Virginia only a few months before dying. Most authorities cite ill health; *Confederate Military History* says his death was the result of wounds and imprisonment. No other source indicates that Archer was wounded. In this case, the majority opinion rules.[27]

A corollary issue is that of officers whose deaths, while attributable to their wounds, occurred long after the end of hostilities. They deserve to be mentioned here, although not afforded full sketches. They were:

Brevet Brigadier General George Baylor, wounded as a colonel in September 1778 at Tappan Zee, New York; died in Barbados in March 1784;

Brevet Major General Alexander S. Asboth, wounded September 1864 at Marianna, Florida; died in Argentina in January 1868;

Brigadier General James L. Kiernan, wounded as a major in May 1863 at Port Gibson, Mississippi; died in New York City in November 1869;

Brevet Major General Robert O. Tyler, wounded June 1864 at Cold Harbor, Virginia; died in Boston, Massachusetts, in December 1874

Also in this group was Brigadier General Arthur M. Manigault, CSA, who was wounded in 1864 and died in 1886, supposedly of his wound. All of these officers have been excluded from the basic list. Only those generals and admirals whose deaths occurred within approximately two years of their wounds have been included.[28]

During World War II the designation missing in action (MIA) was rather liberally applied and some of the cases do not bear up under examination. The first was that of Clarence Tinker, whose plane was lost on a bombing raid to Wake Island in June 1942. Although his flight seems to have suffered from pilot error,[29] and although there is no evidence of any contact with enemy aircraft, the record has been accepted as written because of the combat nature of the mission. Such seems not to have been the case in the loss of Asa Duncan off the coast of France in November 1942, and Millard Harmon and James Andersen in the Pacific in February 1945. In fact, Harmon's and Andersen's losses were later conceded to be merely a case of a missing aircraft.[30] As for Duncan, he was a staff officer on an administrative, not an operational, flight, and the evidence does not exist that his loss was due to combat causes.

One other World War II air loss not accepted as combat related is that of Brigadier General Alfred J. Lyon. While flying as an observer on a mission over Germany, Lyon manned an open turret machine gun after the gunner was wounded. As a result of his exposure he died of pneumonia in December 1942. He was never wounded and his case is less compelling than those of Ransom, Plummer, and Buford.[31]

Possibly through a desire to glamorize their deaths, two generals who died in Korea, Walton Walker and Bryant Moore, were carried by the Army as combat-related fatalities.[32] Of course, it somehow redounds to the credit of the service to have its commanders killed in combat and there is no doubt that both were brave leaders, but the truth is Walker was killed when his jeep was run off the road by a Korean army truck and Moore died of a heart attack after his helicopter crashed.[33]

The Vietnam era fatality claims produced a dilemma for U.S. propaganda purposes. Almost all general officer losses of the war were related to aircraft downings. On the one hand the attribution of these losses to enemy fire showed that the generals were sharing the risks of the troops. On the other hand, the same claims pointed up the prowess of Viet Cong gunners, a less than desirable admission. Each announcement of a general lost in an aircraft was followed by a claim from the Viet Cong of having shot it down.[34] Four of these claims, involving five generals, have been validated. One, the case of George Casey, lost in July 1970, has been designated an air crash.[35]

Air Force Major General William Crum died in a mid-air collision of two B-52s over the South China Sea in July 1967. Although he was involved in an operational mission, his loss was clearly attributable to pilot error, unlike that of Clarence Tinker. Therefore, the Defense Department claim of combat loss is not accepted.[36]

Appendix C lists wartime general officer losses from non-hostile causes. Integrating this list with Appendix B, Combat Fatalities, will give a complete picture of all wartime fatalities. Appendices D and E list generals wounded and captured by hostile forces. This rounds out, as nearly as possible, the all-time roster of general officer combat fatalities.

Confederate general officer statistics in the two latter categories are less reliable than those of their Union counterparts, largely because of the dearth of Confederate records extant. For example, in April 1865, General Joseph Wheeler wrote a synopsis of his final campaign in which he mentioned the names of six of his generals who had been wounded a total of ten times. The Official Records has information on only five of these wounds. Indeed, Wheeler claimed to have been wounded four times himself during the course of the Civil War but only two of these wounds are authenticated by his biographer.[37]

The variety of ranks held by generals who died in combat requires some definition.

During the American Revolution two types of commissions were recognized: those issued by the states and those issued by the Continental Congress. The latter were issued to officers of the "regular" or Continental Army; the former, to officers commanding state troops or militia. It was possible for an officer to hold both types of commissions simultaneously. David Wooster never relinquished his commission as a Continental brigadier but was appointed by Connecticut as major general of state troops, the position in which he was serving when he died. William Lee Davidson was separated from his Continental regiment while it was marching to Charleston in 1780. Subsequently he became brigadier general of North Carolina state troops.

At the end of the war, as a paltry reward for faithful service, Congress authorized a brevet promotion of one grade for all officers below major general who had served in the same rank since 1777. By this act, eleven brigadier generals became brevet major generals, twenty-three colonels became brevet brigadier generals, and hundreds of lower-ranking officers were similarly advanced. George Baylor was so honored and thus became eligibile for consideration as a combat fatality.[38]

The commissioning of Richard Butler as Major General of U.S. Levies in 1791 was a one of a kind appointment. Levies were short-term volunteers, raised and controlled by the federal government for a specific emergency or time period. After the Indian campaign of 1791 no similar type force was raised until 1898 except for the "galvanized yankees" of 1864–1865.[39] Butler's position was roughly analogous to the generals of volunteers of the Mexican, Civil, and Spanish Wars.

Numbers of militia generals took an active part in the Indian Wars. Few, if any, were casualties; none were fatalities. Wiley Thompson, the Indian superintendent in Florida, had resigned his Georgia commission long before his murder by Osceola. His inclusion here is more by courtesy than conformity.

Both generals killed in the War of 1812 were regularly commissioned. Volunteer rank did not exist. Some militia generals served but without loss.

The complexity of general officer rank in the U.S. forces in the Civil War deserves a volume of its own. In fact, a volume has been written to describe the intricacy, impact, and perniciousness of the system of brevets.[40] Basically, generals were commissioned in the regular U.S. Army (USA) or in the U.S. Volunteers (USV) for war service only. During the course of the war only twenty-four officers held full rank as generals in the U.S. Army, excluding staff department heads.[41] All other generals were appointed in the volunteers. Many U.S. Army officers of lower grades held volunteer general commissions without relinquishing their regular rank. Many hoped to be generals in the regular service as well.[42]

Brevet rank was conferred on officers for special noteworthy acts or for long meritorious service which did not deserve full promotion. A discussion of when and how brevet rank took precedence over regular rank would be a needless digression from the purpose of this work. Suffice it to say brevets were a source of bitter jealousy and endless controversy as long as the system lasted.[43]

During the Civil War roughly 1,400 officers were made general by brevet in either the U.S. Army or the U.S. Volunteers. Another 300, who were already generals, were breveted to a higher grade in one service or the other. Some officers held as many as three ranks at one time. Edward Canby was a major general, USV, a brevet major general USA, and a brigadier general USA, his permanent grade. George A. Custer was a permanent captain and a major general by brevet in the regular army. At war's end he was commanding a cavalry division in his volunteer grade of major general. For our purposes all general officer appointments are designated either USA or USV to indicate regular or volunteer commissions.

Rank on the Confederate side was only slightly less complicated. From the start of the war the Confederate government recognized four grades of general officer. It also differentiated between those commissioned in the regular Confederate States Army (CSA) and those in the provisional Army of the Confederate States (PACS), which was the equivalent of the U.S. Volunteers. During the course of the war only six generals were confirmed in the CSA, all full generals.[44] One of them was Albert S. Johnston, killed at Shiloh. Other than those six, most generals were commissioned in the PACS. These were further subdivided into regularly authorized, temporary, and special appointments. In addition, there were a few generals of C.S. Volunteers and several appointed by local commanders without approval of the central government.[45] One of these appointees, Horace Randal, was killed in combat as was one volunteer and several who held special or temporary commissions. Because all the C.S. generals listed here were Provisional Army except A.S. Johnston, the familiar shorthand "CSA" has been used throughout. In the category of state-commissioned officers in the Confederacy, Alexander E. Steen was the sole fatality who did not also hold a CSA general's commission.[46]

The outbreak of World War I found the United States woefully deficient in trained manpower for an effective military effort and in the large officer corps required to lead it. The solution was a National Army, raised by conscription, to be added to the existing regular army and National Guard.[47] Many officers of the regular army were commissioned at higher rank in the National Army, much as had been done with the volunteer forces in the Civil War. Edward Sigerfoos was one of these. At his death, he still retained his regular commission as lieutenant colonel.[48] The other World War I fatality, Henry R. Hill, was a National Guard officer given a commission when his brigade was federalized in 1917.[49]

Since the end of World War I, the U.S. Army has recognized two types of rank for its officers: permanent and temporary. Whether in the regular army, the National Guard, or the Army Reserve, each officer progresses up two concurrent promotion ladders. Temporary promotion normally comes first, followed by the slower, permanent promotion, which occurs at stated time intervals and as vacancies are available. For World War II and Vietnam, most general officers were serving in temporary, Army of the United States (AUS) grades. Only a few were in permanent, U.S. Army (USA) grades. It should be noted that with a few, personalized, exceptions, the highest permanent grade authorized by law is major general. Generals above that rank normally hold indefinite but temporary commissions. No effort has been made here to distinguish between the two types because as a practical matter it makes no difference.

The ranks of commodore and rear admiral in the U.S. Navy were created in 1862.[50] Before that time commodore, or flag officer, was a courtesy title given to officers commanding squadrons. No flag officers were lost in action before World War II and none since. During the 1941–1945 war, five U.S. admirals lost their lives to enemy action, all in the Pacific. It has been suggested that one other flag officer may have been a combat-related death. Rear Admiral Forrest B. Royal died of a heart attack attributed to overwork and strain while aboard USS *Rocky Mount* en route from Borneo to Leyte in June 1945. Reflection suggests that this case is not different from those of Civil War generals Ransom and Buford or General Moore in Korea.[51] Two pre-Civil War commodores are listed among the wounded in Appendix D and one among the captured in Appendix E.

The U.S. Air Force traces its rank structure and history back to the Army Air Force. Only two Air Force generals have ever been combat losses, although the junior service counts Army Air Force losses as its own. The U.S. Marine Corps commissioned its first full-rank general officer in 1867.[52] The death of General Bruno Hochmuth in Vietnam is their single instance of a combat fatality.

Information in the biographical sketches presented here is arranged to show the same basic data for each officer: full name, year of birth and year of death, place of birth and state from which entered service, branch of service, and place of death. The entry includes a brief synopsis of preservice and service career and a more detailed account of the cause and circumstances of death. The highest rank held with date of commission and specific date and place of death are given for each officer. The entry closes with a list of sources, identified by short title.

The full names of all but two of the officers are given. These two show middle initial only. Exhaustive attempts to find the elusive middle names have been unsuccessful although the information is undoubtedly recorded somewhere. The date or approximate date of birth is shown for every officer except one. James Hogun's date of birth and age at death are now lost to history. The only indication of his age is his marriage in North Carolina in 1751, suggesting that he must at least have obtained his majority by that time.

Tables contained in the appendices sort the officers in a number of ways. Based on these tables, a composite profile of the average general can be drawn. First and most apparent, he is a white male. The only exceptions to this rule were the two Oriental generals of the Philippine Army. Second, he is an American by birth, generally of western European ancestry. His normal occupation is professional military, with law being predominant among the non-professional officers. He is forty years old, a college graduate, and a brigadier general of infantry.

Some minor variations exist between the information presented here and that set forth in an earlier magazine article on the same subject.[53] Additional research, further refinement of data, and stricter adherence to criteria for inclusion are the reasons. I freely admit and take full responsibility for the arbitrary nature of the decisions to include or exclude any particular officer. Recommendations from readers for other names to be included are welcome, as are comments on factual error or more complete information on any person already listed.

Abbreviations used throughout either are commonly understood or are explained in the text or bibliography.

Since the adoption of uniform regulations by the Continental Congress in June 1780, the traditional insignia of rank for American generals has been a silver star or stars, copied from the French custom. In the U.S services, one, two, three, four, or five stars represent, respectively, brigadier general, major general, lieutenant general, general, and general of the army or air force. Their naval equivalents are commodore (recently restored to the Navy's rank structure), rear admiral, vice admiral, admiral, and fleet admiral. Even in the Confederate service three gold stars surrounded by a wreath was the insignia of rank for generals of all grades. In modern times the pressures of jungle or guerrilla warfare have led to the use of subdued coloring for rank insignia but under normal circumstances every general or admiral proudly wears his silver stars. They are the symbols of his rise to the pinnacle of military authority and success. Retirement does not dim their luster, nor does death. Indeed, especially of those who have made the ultimate sacrifice in battle might it be said that their stars, though fatal, continue to shine.

Postscript

As *Fallen in Battle* goes to press, we are grieved to learn of another potential candidate for inclusion. On 17 August 1988 a Pakistani Air Force C-130 crashed after take-off from a remote airfield in the south of that country. More than thirty people died in the crash. Among them were the President of Pakistan, Mohammed Zia ul-Haq, U.S. Ambassador Arnold Raphel, and the U.S. Defense Attaché, Brigadier General Herbert M. Wassom. Results of an investigation into sabotage as a possible cause of the crash were still pending as this epilogue was being written. Should sabotage or the act of a hostile element be proven, then General Wassom deserves recognition as a Fallen Star, as much a victim of enemy action as any wartime fatality. A brief sketch of Wassom's life, taken primarily from news reports, is as follows.

WASSOM, Herbert Marion, 1938–1988, Tennessee, U.S. Army, killed 17 August 1988 in the crash of a possibly sabotaged airplane at Bahawalpur, Pakistan.

Herbert Wassom, who was called a "very capable guy" and a "comer" by his colleagues, was born in Rockwood, graduated from Western Kentucky University, and entered military service as an ordnance officer with an ROTC commission in 1961. In 1965 he transferred to the artillery as a regular army officer and served thereafter with artillery and missile units. He had a tour of duty in Vietnam, and served with the 101st Airborne Division during the 1970s. Wassom attended the Command and General Staff College at Leavenworth and the National War College. While at the latter he also earned a master's degree in international relations from George Washington University. In 1980, as a Colonel, he became commander of the 528th Artillery Group, part of the U.S. Army's Southern European Task Force in Italy. In 1981 he was assigned to the office of the Army Chief of Staff in Washington, and in 1983 he became chief of staff of the 101st Airborne. Wassom was promoted Brigadier General in September 1985 and advanced to become assistant division commander of the 101st. In July 1987 he was appointed Defense Attaché at the U.S. Embassy in Islamabad, Pakistan. On 17 August 1988, Wassom accompanied Pakistani President Zia ul-Haq, U.S. Ambassador Arnold Raphel, and a number of Pakistani generals on a flight in a C-130 to inspect tests of the U.S. M-1 tank, which Pakistan was considering buying. Shortly after the plane took of from a small airfield at Bahawalpur, it was said by some witnesses to waver in the air and suddenly disintegrate in a ball of fire. Others said the plane did not explode until it hit the ground. The wreckage was spread over an area only 100 yards in circumference, supporting the latter report. In any event, there were no survivors.

Army Register, 1965–1986; *Atlanta Constitution*, August 18, 1988; *New York Times*, August 18 and 19, 1988.

Notes

1. Richard A. Gabriel and Paul L. Savage, *Crisis in Command* (New York: Hill and Wang, 1978).

2. Horace H. Shaw, *The First Maine Heavy Artillery, 1862–1865* (Portland, 1903), p. 141.

3. Major General William A. Burke to the author, June 23, 1987, emphasis added.

4. Robert D. Heinl, "They Died with Their Boots On," *Armed Forces Journal*, April 11, 1970, p. 14.

5. U.S. War Department, *U.S. Army General Officer Casualties*, 7 December 1941–2 September 1945 (Washington, D.C.: War Department Public Relations Division, 1946).

6. U.S. Army Department, *Battle Casualties of the Army* (Washington, D.C.: Office, Assistant Chief of Staff, G-1, 1954); U.S. War Department, *Report of the Secretary of War to the President, 1926* (Washington, D.C.: Government Printing Office, 1926).

7. Chief, Adjutant General Casualty Branch, to the author, April 27 and August 9, 1973.

8. Russell K. Brown, "Fallen Stars," *Military Affairs*, Vol. 45, No. 1 (February 1981), p. 9

9. Francis B. Heitman, *Historical Register and Dictionary of the Continental Army* (Washington, D.C.: National Tribune, 1914); Mark M. Boatner, *Encyclopedia of the American Revolution* (New York: David McKay, 1966).

10. F.B. Heitman, *Historical Register and Dictionary of the United States Army* (Washington, D.C.: Government Printing Office, 1903).

11. Congress of the United States, *Biographical Directory of the American Congress* (Washington, D.C.: Government Printing Office, 1968).

12. Heitman, *U.S. Army*.

13. Erza J. Warner, *Generals in Blue* (Baton Rouge: Louisiana State University Press, 1964).

14. Frederick Phisterer, *Statistical Record of the Armies of the United States* (New York: Scribner's 1883; reprint: New York: The Blue and the Gray Press, no date).

15. Erza J. Warner, *Generals in Gray* (Baton Rouge: Louisiana State University Press, 1959).

16. Grady McWhitney and Perry D. Jamieson, *Attack and Die, Civil War Military Tactics and the Southern Heritage* (University, Ala.: The University of Alabama Press, 1982).

17. Douglas S. Freeman, *Lee's Lieutenants*, 3 vols. (New York: Scribner's, 1943), Vol. 3, p. 581.

18. Clement A. Evans, ed., *Confederate Military History*, 12 vols. (Atlanta: Confederate Publishing Company, 1899).

19. Mark M. Boatner, *The Civil War Dictionary* (New York: David McKay, 1959).

20. R.S. Bevier, *History of the 1st and 2nd Missouri Confederate Brigades, 1861-1865* (St. Louis: Brand, Bryant & Co., 1879), pp. 123-124; Evans, *CMH*, Vol. IX (Missouri), p. 97; University of Missouri Library, Western Historical Manuscript Collection, "Dedication of Monument in Memory of General (*sic*) John T. Hughes"; Records of the Adjutant General of Missouri, "John T. Hughes."

21. Heitman, *U.S. Army*.

22. See "Henry Root Hill," *infra*.

23. U.S. Armed Forces Information School, *The Army Almanac*, 2nd ed. (Harrisburg, Pa.: Stackpole, 1959).

24. National Archives, Military Service Record, Cleveland J. Campbell.

25. Phisterer, *Statistical Record*, pp. 318-322.

26. Boatner, *Civil War*, under separate entries.

27. *Confederate Military History*, Vol. II (Maryland), p. 171; *Dictionary of American Biography*, 10 vols. (New York: Scribner's, 1943); Freeman, *Lee's Lieutenants*.

28. *Dictionary of American Biography*; Warner, *Generals in Blue* and *Generals in Gray*.

29. Samuel E. Morison, *History of United States Naval Operations in World War II*, 15 vols. (Boston: Little, Brown, 1947-1962), Vol. 3, p. 151; Gordon Prange, *Miracle at Midway* (New York: McGraw-Hill, 1982), p. 356.

30. *Assembly*, Vol. 7 (April 1948-January 1949), pp. 12-14, 16-18.

31. *General Officer Casualties 1941-1945*, *New York Times*, December 2, 1942.

32. *Battle Casualties of the Army*, 1954.

33. *New York Times*, December 24, 1950 and February 26, 1951.

34. See, for example, the Viet Cong claim to the death of General Bruno Hochmuth. *New York Times*, November 17, 1967.

35. Adjutant General Casualty Branch Letter, August 9, 1973.

36. *New York Times*, July 8, 1967.

37. *The War of the Rebellion, Official Records of the Union and Confederate Armies*, 128 vols. (Washington, D.C.: Government Printing Office, 1880-1901), Vol. 47, part 1, p. 1132; John P. Dyer, *"Fighting Joe" Wheeler* (Baton Rouge: Louisiana State University Press, 1941).

38. Heitman, *Continental Army*.

39. Richard H. Kohn, *Eagle and Sword* (New York: The Free Press, 1975), pp. 109-110.

40. James B. Fry, *The History and Legal Effect of Brevets in the Armies of Great Britain and the United States* (New York: D. Van Nostrand, 1877).

41. Phisterer, *Statistical Record*, pp. 247-248, 262-263.

42. See Bruce Catton, *Glory Road* (Garden City, N.Y.: Doubleday, 1952), pp. 16-17 for a discussion of the relative merits of regular and volunteer rank.

43. Reference the case of Winfield Scott vs. Alexander Macomb or that of David Twiggs vs. William J. Worth in Fry, *History of Brevets*.

44. Warner, *Generals in Gray*, p. xxiv.

45. Francis T. Miller, ed., *The Photographic History of the Civil War*, 10 vols. (New York: The Review of Reviews Company, 1911), Vol. 10, pp. 318-320.

46. See "Alexander Early Steen," *infra*.

47. Harvey A. DeWeerd, *President Wilson Fights His War* (New York: Macmillan, 1968), pp. 208-209.

48. U.S. War Department, *Official Army Register*, 1918.

49. See "Henry Root Hill," *infra*.

50. U.S. Navy Department, *Civil War Naval Chronology, 1861–1865* (Washington, D.C.: Government Printing Office, 1971), p. II–83.

51. S. E. Morison, *The Two Ocean Navy, A Short History of the United States Navy in World War II* (Boston: Little, Brown, 1963), p. 581; Morison, *History of United States Naval Operations in World War II*, Vol. XIII, *Liberation of the Philippines* (Boston: Little, Brown, 1947–1962), p. 266.

52. Robert D. Heinl, *Soldiers of the Sea, The U.S. Marine Corps, 1775–1962* (Annapolis: U.S. Naval Institute, 1962), p. 87.

53. Brown, "Fallen Stars."

A

ABBOTT, Henry Livermore, 1842–1864, Massachusetts, U.S. Volunteers, killed in action 6 May 1864 in the Wilderness, Virginia.

Abbott was the epitome of that class of young intellectuals who rose to arms in the spring of 1861 to preserve the shattered Union. Born in Lowell, the son of a lawyer and sometime judge, young Abbott was a Harvard graduate who was studying law in 1861. He first entered service that May as a private of Home Guards. By July he had accepted a commission as a 2nd Lieutenant of the 20th Massachusetts. His regiment was engaged at Ball's Bluff and in the Peninsula campaign, where he was wounded twice. He was promoted 1st Lieutenant in November 1861 and Captain in December 1862. At Gettysburg, Abbott succeeded to regimental command after Colonel Paul Revere was mortally wounded and the lieutenant colonel was wounded. He was present when Pickett was repulsed on 3 July and led the regiment through the fall and winter of 1863–1864. At Bristoe Station on 14 October, when the II Corps smashed A.P. Hill's attempt to cut off Meade's withdrawal, Abbott's 20th Massachusetts captured two guns. He was promoted Major on 10 October. In the Wilderness, on 6 May 1864, Abbott, still leading the regiment, was ordered by General James Wadsworth, commander of another division, to have the 20th leave their works in order to support his (Wadsworth's) left. When Wadsworth was refused, he accused the men of being afraid and led them forward in a charge during which Abbott was shot in the abdomen. He was carried to the rear, where he died in a hospital tent within a few hours. Abbott was posthumously breveted Brigadier General USV, to rank from 6 May. In their official reports, the corps and division commanders, Generals Hancock and Gibbon, both cited him as a brilliant officer with the highest reputation as a soldier.

Boatner, *Civil War*; Palfrey; Rice; *B&L*, Vol. 4; *OR*, Ser. I, Vols. 29, pt. 1; 36, pt. 1; Military Service Record.

ADAMS, Carroll Edward, Jr., 1923–1970, Rhode Island–Massachusetts, U.S. Army, killed in action 12 May 1970 near Pleiku, Vietnam.

Carroll E. "Hap" Adams was the only U.S. Army officer killed in action in Vietnam to be posthumously promoted Brigadier General. Scion of a military family, he was born in Pawtucket, attended Brown University for two years, and then received an appointment to West Point from Massachusetts. He graduated in 1945 and went immediately to the Pacific theater but saw no action before the end of World War II. Returning to the United States in 1948, Adams obtained a master's degree from the Massachusetts Institute of Technology, and then served in a variety of engineer posts. He was with the New England Engineer Division, on construction duty in Canada and Iceland, and at the Ballistic Missile Construction Office in Los Angeles. He attended the Command and General Staff College, the Army War College, and the Industrial College of the Armed Forces. In 1963, he earned a second master's degree from George Washington University. Promoted Lieutenant Colonel in 1962, Adams spent two years in Europe, 1965–1967, as engineer battalion commander and as combined headquarters staff officer. From 1967 to 1970 he was engineer for the Norfolk District in Virginia and was cited for his work there. In February 1970 he volunteered for duty in Vietnam and was assigned as commander of the 937th Engineer Construction Group. On 12 May 1970, while he was riding in a helicopter in the Central Highlands with Major General John A.B. Dillard, the aircraft was shot down by enemy ground fire near Pleiku. Adams was killed in the crash. He was posthumously confirmed as Brigadier General to rank from the date of his death.

Army Register, 1970; Cullum, Vol. 9; *Assembly*, Spring 1971; *Congressional Record*, 91st Congress, 2nd Session; *Boston Globe*, May 14, 1970; *New York Times*, May 17, 1970.

ADAMS, John, 1825–1864, Tennessee, C.S. Army, killed in action 30 November 1864 at Franklin, Tennessee.

John Adams was one of six Confederate generals killed within a few hours at the battle of Franklin, one of the bloodiest and most useless engagements of the Civil War. The son of Irish immigrants, Adams was born in Nashville. After graduation from West Point in 1846, he served in Mexico, where he won one brevet for gallantry. Thereafter he served on the frontier as a dragoon officer, was aide to the territorial governor of Minnesota, and eventually resigned his commission of Captain in May 1861. Appointed Captain in the regular Confederate cavalry, Adams served at Memphis and Jackson (Mississippi) and in western Kentucky. He was promoted Colonel in May 1862 and Brigadier General on 29 December 1862. He led a brigade under Joseph Johnston in the Vicksburg campaign and under Polk in the Army of Mississippi. Adams was with the troops from Mississippi who joined the Army of Tennessee at Resaca, Georgia, in 1864 and he fought through the Atlanta campaign. After the fall of Atlanta he accompanied Hood on the latter's disastrous Tennessee campaign in the fall of 1864. Adams was killed at Franklin after he had ridden his horse onto the parapet of the Union earthworks and attempted to capture the colors of the 65th Illinois. His body was recovered from the ditch in front of the works the next morning.

DAB; Boatner, *Civil War*; Warner, *Generals in Gray*; McDonough and Connelly; *B&L*, Vol. 4; *CMH*, Vol.VIII.

ANDERSON, George Burgwyn, 1831–1862, North Carolina, C.S. Army, died 16 October 1862 of wounds received 17 September 1862 at Antietam, Maryland.

Anderson was one of those Old Army officers who resigned his commission to follow his home state out of the Union in 1861. A native of Hillsboro, he graduated first in his class at the University of North Carolina at age seventeen, and then went on to graduate from West Point in 1852. For nine years he was a Lieutenant of dragoons on the Plains, in Utah, and on recruiting duty. After his resignation in April 1861 he became Colonel of the 4th North Carolina. Arriving at Manassas shortly after Bull Run, he became and remained post commandant there until March 1862. At Williamsburg in May 1862 his personal bravery while commanding Featherston's brigade was so outstanding that President Davis, who witnessed the fight, appointed him Brigadier General to rank from 9 June. In that action Anderson's own regiment sustained casualties of 89 percent. He continued in command of the brigade during the Seven Days battles, being wounded at Malvern Hill. Conspicuous again at South Mountain in September 1862, Anderson took his brigade to Antietam Creek, where, on 17 September, while observing his line from a slight elevation, he was painfully wounded in the ankle. At first it was thought he was not in serious danger. He was evacuated to Richmond and then to Raleigh, where his foot was amputated. He died on 16 October after complications set in.

Boatner, *Civil War*; Cullum; Warner, *Generals in Gray*; D.S. Freeman, *Lee's Lieutenants*, Vol. 2; *B&L*, Vol. 2; *CMH*, Vol. IV.

ARMISTEAD, Lewis Addison, 1817–1863, North Carolina, C.S. Army, died 5 July 1863 of wounds received 3 July 1863 at Gettysburg, Pennsylvania.

Perhaps best known for his leadership of the gallant band who reached the "High Water Mark of the Confederacy" at Gettysburg, Armistead was born at New Bern, son of a soldier and nephew of the defender of Fort McHenry in 1814. Appointed to West Point in 1834, he was a cadet for two years before being dismissed. In 1839 he was commissioned in the regular army, won two brevets for gallantry during the Mexican War, and was post commander at San Diego, California, when he resigned his commission as Captain in the 6th Infantry in May 1861. He was first made Major in the C.S. Army and then Colonel of the 57th Virginia. He served in western Virginia and in North

Carolina before being promoted to Brigadier General CSA on 1 April 1862. His brigade command began with the Peninsula campaign, where he distinguished himself at Malvern Hill. He was Provost Marshal of the Army of Northern Virginia during the Maryland campaign but returned to his brigade in time for Fredericksburg. As part of Pickett's division, Armistead's brigade was in the second line for the attack on Cemetery Ridge at Gettysburg on 3 July 1863. With his hat on the point of his sword, Armistead led about 150 of his men over a stone wall and into the batteries of Winfield S. Hancock's II Corps, where he was mortally wounded. In his dying hours he was attended by his old comrade, Hancock, whom he had last seen in San Diego. Armistead died a prisoner on 5 July. He was buried in Baltimore, his family's ancestral home.

   DAB; Boatner, *Civil War*; Warner, *Generals in Gray*; D.S. Freeman, *Lee's Lieutenants*, Vols. 1–3; Catton, *Glory Road*; Coddington; *B&L*, Vol. 3; *CMH*, Vol. III.

ASHBY, Turner, 1828–1862, Virginia, C.S. Army, killed in action 6 June 1862 at Harrisonburg, Virginia.

   Already a legend at the time of his death, Turner Ashby was the personification of the ideal of the Southern cavalry leader: dashing in action, beloved by his men, jealously independent of higher authority. A native of Fauquier County, Ashby was educated at home and private schools and became a grain dealer and a planter. He raised a volunteer cavalry company in 1859 to help put down John Brown's raid. At the beginning of the Civil War he helped to plan the takeover of the arsenal at Harper's Ferry from federal authorities. His mounted troops formed part of an independent regiment raised by Colonel Angus McDonald, and on 25 June 1861 Ashby became Lieutenant Colonel. He helped to mask the link-up of Johnston's and Beauregard's armies before Bull Run and served on picket duty along the upper Potomac. After McDonald retired, Ashby became Colonel of the regiment, now known as the 7th Virginia Cavalry, and in October 1861 he was made chief of cavalry for Stonewall Jackson's troops in the Valley of Virginia. On 23 May 1862 he was promoted Brigadier General. On 6 June 1862, near Harrisonburg, during Jackson's retreat up the Valley, Ashby was fighting a rearguard action. He was at the head of a regiment of supporting infantry when his horse was killed. Ashby pressed forward on foot and was killed in the next volley by a shot through the body.

   DAB; Boatner, *Civil War*; Warner, *Generals in Gray*; D.S. Freeman, *Lee's Lieutenants*, Vol. 1; *B&L*, Vols. 1&2; *CMH*, Vol. III.

B

BABCOCK, Willoughby, c. 1832–1864, New York, U.S. Volunteers, died 6 October 1864 of wounds received 19 September 1864 at Winchester, Virginia.

Babcock is one of those officers about whom little is known outside the details of his military career. So obscure is he that Boatner listed him as "Willoughby, Babcock." A native of Albany, he was Lieutenant in the 3rd New York, a three-months regiment, from April to August 1861. He accepted a commission as Captain in the 64th New York in November and was promoted Major in the 75th New York in December. The regiment served briefly in Florida before going to Louisiana, where Babcock became Lieutenant Colonel in July 1862. The 75th served in the siege of Port Hudson in May–July 1863 and Babcock was wounded there on 14 June. In August 1863 Nathaniel Banks, the department commander, relieved Babcock from duty for a letter critical of Banks which Babcock had written to a New York newspaper. Babcock was court-martialed and dismissed from the service, but he was reinstated in January 1864 on the recommendation of his superiors. About the same time the 75th New York was converted to mounted infantry and assigned to the Cavalry Division, XIX Corps. In February Babcock became chief of staff to the division commander, in March, aide to the Chief of Cavalry of the Military Division of West Mississippi, and later, Inspector General of Cavalry. He returned to the 75th when XIX Corps moved to Virginia in July 1864. That summer Babcock received permission to go home to recruit the regiment up to strength but Phil Sheriden delayed his departure owing to the imminent battles in the Shenandoah Valley. On 19 September 1864, at Winchester, Babcock was wounded badly enough to lose his leg. He died of the effects of the wound on 6 October. He was posthumously breveted Brigadier General USV to rank from 19 September.

Boatner, *Civil War*; Babcock; *OR*, Ser. I, Vols. 15&43, pt. 1.

BAKER, Edward Dickinson, 1811–1861, England–Illinois, U.S. Volunteers, killed in action 21 October 1861 at Ball's Bluff, Virginia.

Edward Baker, a longtime personal friend of Abraham Lincoln, was one of those "War Democrats" given a military commission at the beginning of the Civil War in an attempt to enlist the aid of his party in support of the Republican administration's war effort. Active in Whig politics as a young man, Baker resigned a seat in Congress in 1846 to command an Illinois volunteer regiment in the Mexican War. He was wounded while quelling a disturbance in a Georgia regiment but recovered to lead a brigade in the Mexico City campaign. Later he went to California, established a law practice in San Francisco, and then became U.S. senator from Oregon when that state was admitted to the Union. In May 1861 he declined an appointment as Brigadier General USV but at Lincoln's personal behest, he agreed to become Colonel of the 71st Pennsylvania in June. He joined the Army of the Potomac after Bull Run. Baker took command of a brigade on the Potomac in September and on 21 September he was offered a commission as Major General USV. On 21 October 1861, during a reconnaissance across the Potomac into Virginia, Baker moved his brigade to Ball's Bluff, where they were cornered by Confederate forces. Baker's handling of the situation was particularly inept. His folly reached its height when he advanced in front of his own skirmishers and was killed by a Southern sharpshooter. The battle was a disaster for the Union with 900 casualties of 1,700 engaged. Of these, 700 were captured. Baker, the real culprit, was never accused of wrongdoing. Instead, Charles Stone, his division commander, was arrested, imprisoned, and never again given a responsible command. At the time of his death Baker had not yet accepted the Major General's commission.

DAB; Boatner, *Civil War*; Warner, *Generals in Blue*; Catton, *Mr. Lincoln's Army* and *Glory Road*; *B&L*, Vol. 2.

BARKSDALE, William, 1821–1863, Tennessee–Mississippi, C.S. Army, died 3 July 1863 of wounds received 2 July 1863 at Gettysburg, Pennsylvania.

A pro-slavery, pro-states rights advocate who served in the U.S. Congress for eight years, Barksdale was born in Rutherford County. He graduated from the University of Nashville. Later he studied law in Mississippi, edited a pro-slavery newspaper, and served in the Mexican War. Elected to Congress in 1852, he remained a spokesman for states rights until his resignation in 1861. In March 1861 he was named Quartermaster General of Mississippi and then became Colonel of the 13th Mississippi. He led his regiment at Bull Run and in the Peninsula campaign until the death of Richard Griffith, when he succeeded to command of the Mississippi brigade. Of him at Malvern Hill R.E. Lee said, "He displayed the highest qualities of a soldier." Promoted Brigadier General CSA from 12 August 1862, he commanded the brigade at Antietam, at Fredericksburg, where his mission was to keep the Union army from bridging the Rappahannock, and at Chancellorsville. At Gettysburg, on 2 July 1863, Barksdale's brigade was one of those of McLaw's division which made the disjointed attacks on the Round Tops. At the forward limit of their advance, his men were counterattacked and broke under fire. The general, "almost frantic with rage," was mortally wounded as he tried to hold fast. He was captured and died the next day in Union hands.

BDAC; *DAB*; Boatner, *Civil War*; Warner, *Generals in Gray*; D.S. Freeman, *Lee's Lieutenants*, Vols. 2&3; Coddington; *B&L*, Vol. 3; *CMH*, Vol. VII (Mississippi).

BAYARD, George Dashiell, 1835–1862, New York, U.S. Volunteers, died 14 December 1862 of wounds received 13 December 1862 at Fredericksburg, Virginia.

Regarded by some as the premier Union cavalry leader in the East in the early days of the Civil War, Bayard was born in Seneca Falls, New York, but reared in Iowa. He graduated from West Point in 1856 and served on the frontier. He was at one time shot in the face with an arrow, a wound thought to be mortal. On another occasion, his killing of an Indian chief provoked a tribal uprising. In 1861 he was given leave of absence as an instructor at West Point to become Colonel of the 1st Pennsylvania Cavalry. Bayard was assigned to outpost duty on the Potomac with the Pennsylvania Reserve Division. Later he served in the Valley campaign of 1862. Promoted Brigadier General USV on 28 April 1862, he commanded the cavalry brigade of III Corps. During much of the fighting that spring he commanded a mixed brigade and it was one of his regiments which fired the volley that killed Turner Ashby at Harrisonburg on 6 June. During the Second Manassas campaign, Bayard's brigade performed outpost duty on the Rapidan. At Cedar Mountain, Bayard committed the tactical mistake of making a cavalry charge on massed infantry with the disastrous results expected. By this time much of the Union cavalry was so broken down by inept utilization as to be useless. Bayard's exhausted brigade was left behind in Virginia to recuperate during the Maryland campaign in September 1862. At Fredericksburg, on 13 December 1862, he was assigned to William Franklin's Grand Division but there was no employment for cavalry. Bayard was in attendance at Franklin's headquarters during the day. About noon he and his supporting battery commander were walking to lunch when Bayard was struck in the thigh by a stray cannon ball. He was carried into the headquarters house where he died the next day.

Cullum; Boatner, *Civil War*; Warner, *Generals in Blue*; Starr, Vol I; D.S. Freeman, *Lee's Lieutenants*, Vol. 2; *B&L*, Vols. 2&3.

BEE, Barnard Elliott, 1824–1861, South Carolina, C.S. Army, died 22 July 1861 of wounds received 21 July 1861 at Bull Run, Virginia.

Best known to history as the officer who bestowed the sobriquet "Stonewall" on General T. J. Jackson, Bee was a career U.S. Army officer before entering Southern service in 1861. Son of the man who later became Secretary of State of the Republic of Texas, Bee was born in Charleston, graduated from West

Point in 1845, and served briefly on the frontier before fighting in Mexico. He was wounded, twice breveted for gallantry, and presented a sword by the State of South Carolina for "patriotic and meritorious conduct." He continued in the regular army, became Captain in the 10th Infantry, raised and commanded a battalion of volunteers during the Utah expedition of 1858, and ultimately resigned his commission in March 1861. Bee was first commissioned Lieutenant Colonel, 1st South Carolina, an artillery regiment in Charleston. On 17 June he was appointed Brigadier General CSA and took over a brigade at Manassas Junction, Virginia. At Bull Run, on 21 July, his brigade was nearly destroyed before Bee rallied them by calling their attention to the steadiness of the Virginia brigade of Stonewall Jackson. Bee was mortally wounded before the Confederates turned the tide against the Union forces. He died 22 July in a log cabin on the battlefield.

DAB; Cullum; Boatner, *Civil War*; Warner, *Generals in Gray*; D.S. Freeman, *Lee's Lieutenants*, Vol. 1; *B&L*, Vol. 1; *CMH*, Vol. V.

BENEDICT, Lewis, 1817–1864, New York, U.S. Volunteers, killed in action 9 April 1864, Pleasant Hill, Louisiana.

Lewis Benedict was already a gentleman of early middle age and some local renown when he volunteered for military service at the outbreak of the Civil War. Born in Albany, he graduated from Williams College in 1837 and was admitted to the New York bar in 1841. He occupied a number of political positions, including state judge advocate, and in 1860 was elected to the state assembly. He entered military service in 1861 as Lieutenant Colonel of the 73rd New York (1st Fire Zouaves) and went to the Peninsula of Virginia in Joseph Hooker's division. He was captured at Williamsburg after he sprained his ankle and was confined in Libby Prison in Richmond and at Salisbury, North Carolina. Benedict was exchanged in September 1862 and was made Colonel of the 162nd New York (1st Metropolitan Guard) to rank from 12 September. In November the regiment went to New Orleans, where it became part of XIX Corps under Nathaniel Banks. Benedict took part in the Port Hudson campaign and was prominent in the assault of 14 June 1863. In the Red River campaign of 1864 he commanded a brigade of Emory's division, which was used to bolster Banks's faltering advance at Sabine Crossroads on 8 April. The next day, at Pleasant Hill, Louisiana, Benedict's brigade formed the left of the Union line and bore the brunt of the Confederate attack. Benedict was wounded early in the engagement and then again near the close. The second wound proved fatal and he died on the field. He was posthumously breveted Brigadier General USV to rank from 14 June 1863.

Appleton's; Boatner, *Civil War*; *OR*, Ser. I, Vols. 11, pt. 1; 26, pt. 1; 34, pt. 1; *B&L*, Vol. 4.

BENTON, Samuel, 1820–1864, Tennessee-Mississippi, C.S. Army, died 28 July 1864 of wounds received 22 July 1864 at Atlanta, Georgia.

A nephew of Senator Thomas Hart Benton of Missouri and cousin to Mrs. John Charles Fremont, Samuel Benton was born in Williamson County and taught school as a young man. After settling in Mississippi, he took up the law and was a state legislator. Benton was a delegate to the Mississippi state secession convention in 1861 and then served for a year as Captain in the 9th Mississippi. In early 1862 he was elected Colonel of the 37th (later the 34th) Mississippi, which served in northern Mississippi and central Tennessee. Transferred to the Army of Tennessee, Benton led his regiment in the north Georgia and Atlanta campaign until July 1864, when he took over Walthall's brigade. At the battle of Atlanta, on 22 July, Benton was struck in the chest by a shell fragment and wounded in the foot, which required amputation. He died on 28 July before being notified of his promotion to Brigadier General CSA to rank from 26 July.

Boatner, *Civil War*; Warner, *Generals in Gray*; *CMH*, Vol. VII (Mississippi).

BERRY, Hiram Gregory, 1824–1863, Maine, U.S. Volunteers, killed in action 3 May 1863 at Chancellorsville, Virginia.

Hiram Berry was one of those civilian soldiers who, coming into the army at the outbreak of the Civil War, rapidly rose to high rank through a combination of political influence and real tactical talent. Born in Rockland, before the war he was a carpenter, contractor, bank president, captain of militia, and mayor of Rockland. In June 1861, he raised and became Colonel of the 15th Maine. At Bull Run, the 15th took Henry House Hill late in the afternoon of 21 July but was driven off by Kirby Smith's attack. Berry was promoted Brigadier General USV on 17 March 1862 and commanded a brigade in the division of Phil Kearny on the Virginia Peninsula. At Williamsburg, Seven Pines, and Seven Days his brigade was distinguished by its conduct, but Berry exhausted himself and was on sick leave during the Second Manassas and Maryland campaigns. He returned in time for Fredericksburg and was again cited for his sterling service. A personal friend of Vice President Hannibal Hamlin, Berry corresponded with him frequently and used his influence to gain promotion to Major General USV in the winter of 1863 to rank from 29 November 1862. He commanded a division in III Corps at Chancellorsville and helped to hold the line against Jackson's surprise attack of 2 May 1863. In the confused fighting on 3 May Berry was riding from brigade to brigade to steady his troops when he was shot from his horse by a Confederate sharpshooter in a tree. He died soon after.

Boatner, *Civil War*; Warner, *Generals in Blue*; Catton, *Mr. Lincoln's Army* and *Glory Road*; *B&L*, Vols. 2&3.

BIDWELL, Daniel Davidson, 1819–1864, New York, U.S. Volunteers, killed in action 19 October 1864 at Cedar Creek, Virginia.

A prominent citizen of Buffalo, Bidwell belonged to a variety of militia organizations and was a local magistrate before the Civil War. He enlisted as a private in 1861, became a brigade inspector, and was appointed Colonel of the 49th New York in October 1861. He was with his regiment in VI Corps on the Peninsula of Virginia in 1862. The 49th also participated in the Maryland campaign but Bidwell was not with them. He returned for the Fredericksburg and Chancellorsville campaigns, but without special distinction, and temporarily commanded a brigade on the march to Pennsylvania in June 1863. At Gettysburg, with Bidwell back in command of the 49th, the entire brigade was barely engaged and suffered only fifteen casualties. Bidwell took permanent command of the brigade in the Wilderness campaign in 1864. He led it at Spotsylvania, Cold Harbor, and Petersburg and was commissioned Brigadier General USV on 11 August 1864. He went with VI Corps to the Shenandoah Valley that August and continued command of his brigade until he was killed by a shell at Cedar Creek on 19 October.

Boatner, *Civil War*; Warner, *Generals in Blue*; Coddington.

BLAISDELL, William, c. 1817–1864, New Hampshire–Massachusetts, U.S. Volunteers, killed in action 23 June 1864 at Petersburg, Virginia.

An old regular army enlisted man who owed his Civil War success to his personal acquaintance with General Winfield Scott, Blaisdell was born in Alexandria and entered service about 1833. He was on the staff of General Scott in Mexico and was wounded. He retired after twenty years' service and was appointed inspector in the Boston Customs House. At the outbreak of the Civil War, Scott offered him a commission in the regular army but Blaisdell preferred volunteer service. Commissioned Lieutenant Colonel of the 11th Massachusetts in June 1861, he was advanced to Colonel of the regiment in October. In the Virginia peninsula campaign of 1862, he was twice commended for meritorious conduct at Fair Oaks. Blaisdell commanded a provisional brigade in III Corps in the fall of 1862, guarding railroads in northern Virginia. He was absent on leave during the Fredericksburg campaign but returned to the army in the spring of 1863 and at Chancellorsville succeeded to command of a brigade. He was absent again from June to October 1863, sick and on recruiting duty. In November he returned and once more took command of a brigade in III Corps. In the reorganization of the Army of the Potomac in March 1864 his unit was transferred to II Corps and Blaisdell reverted to command of the 11th Massachusetts. During the Wilderness and Cold Harbor campaigns, Blaisdell, who was now one of the senior Colonels in the army, alternated between regimental and brigade command. His last command was the former Corcoran Legion, now a brigade in II Corps. On 23 June he was mortally wounded on his brigade picket line in front of the Confederate entrenchments at Petersburg. Carried off the field, he died the same day. He was posthumously breveted Brigadier General USV to rank from 23 June.

Boatner, *Civil War*; Bowen; *OR*, Ser. I, Vols. 11, pts. 1 & 2; 25, pt. 1; 40, pt.1; 51, pt. 1; Military Service Record.

BOHLEN, Henry, 1810–1862, Germany–Pennsylvania, U.S. Volunteers, killed in action 22 August 1862 at Freeman's Ford, Virginia.

One of a number of prominent German immigrants who owed their rank to their ability to raise recruits for the Union cause, Henry Bohlen was born in Bremen, emigrated to Philadelphia as a youth, and acquired a considerable fortune as a liquor dealer. At the beginning of the Civil War he raised the 75th Pennsylvania from among the German population of the city. They joined the Army of the Potomac and were assigned to Blenker's division. Bohlen, ranking as a Colonel from September 1861, assumed command of a brigade in December. In March 1862 he participated in the tragicomedy of the march of Blenker's division from Alexandria, Virginia, to the Shenandoah Valley. Without proper equipment, with no supplies and inadequate maps, they blundered around the countryside of northern Virginia for a month, laying waste along their route and outraging the inhabitants. The Valley campaign of 1862 was a story of continuous ineptitude on the part of Union commanders. Nevertheless, Bohlen did receive credit for the capable handling of his brigade at Cross Keys on 8 June. After Cedar Mountain in August, Bohlen's brigade was part of the covering force for Pope's withdrawal behind the Rappahannock. As Pope attempted to collect information on Lee's intentions he conducted numerous raids and forays. On 22 August Bohlen was sent across the river at Freeman's Ford and ran into Jackson's entire corps maneuvering into position. Bohlen, who had been promoted Brigadier General USV on 28 April 1862, was killed while supervising the withdrawal of his troops across the ford. His body was captured by Confederate forces but, still dressed in a colonel's uniform, was not immediately identified. Only later were his remains returned to Union hands for burial.

Boatner, *Civil War*; Warner, *Generals in Blue*; D.S. Freeman, *Lee's Lieutenants*, Vol. 2.

BOND, William Ross, 1918–1970, Maine–Maryland, U.S. Army, killed in action 1 April 1970 in War Zone D, Vietnam.

Eulogized as the "complete soldier" and as a leader of the army in future decades, William R. Bond was the only American general killed by ground fire in Vietnam while in the presence of his troops. Bond was born in Portland, graduated from the University of Maryland, where he was a star athlete, in 1940, and enlisted in the army in 1941. He rose to the rank of Staff Sergeant and received a direct commission in 1942. He participated in the invasion of Sicily, volunteered for duty with Darby's Rangers, and fought with them in Italy until he was captured at Anzio in 1944. Bond escaped from a German prison camp in Poland, joined the Soviet army, and fought with the Russians in their advance into Germany in 1945. After World War II he remained in the regular army and became an expert in political–military affairs. Promoted Major in 1945 and Lieutenant Colonel in 1952, he attended both Command and General Staff College and the Army War College. Bond saw service on the White House staff and as a member of a United Nations truce supervisory team in Jerusalem. Promoted Colonel in 1960, he was a member of the fledgling U.S. advisory command in Saigon in 1959–1960 and chief of staff of the U.S. assistance command in Thailand in 1965–1967. He was director of international and civil affairs for the army staff when he was promoted Brigadier General on 1 August 1969. Bond was assigned to command the 199th Light Infantry Brigade in Vietnam in November 1969. On 1 April 1970, while visiting a patrol which was in contact with the enemy in War Zone D, Bond was shot in the chest by a sniper a few minutes after getting out of his helicopter. He died shortly after being taken to a field hospital.

Army Register, 1970; *New York Times*, April 2 & 19, 1970; *Portland Press-Herald*, May 31, 1970; Military Service Record.

BRANCH, Lawrence O'Brien, 1820–1862, North Carolina, C.S. Army, killed in action 17 September 1862 at Antietam, Maryland.

A man of wealth, intellect, prominent connections, and great versatility, L. O'Brien (or O'Bryan) Branch, the name by which he was commonly known, was born at Enfield, Halifax County. He was reared by his uncle, the governor of the state, after his mother died and his father moved to Tennessee. As a youth he was tutored by Salmon P. Chase, attended the University of North Carolina, and eventually graduated from Princeton. Later he was a newspaper editor in Tennessee, practiced law in Florida, served in the Seminole War, was a railroad president, a congressman from North Carolina, and a renowned orator. He refused offers to be Postmaster General and Secretary of the Treasury in the Buchanan administration. In 1861 he became Quartermaster and Paymaster General for North Carolina. Subsequently he became Colonel of the 33rd North Carolina and, on 16 November 1861, Brigadier General, CSA. Branch commanded the defense of New Bern against the Burnside expedition. In the spring of 1862 he took his brigade to Virginia for the Peninsula campaign, Second Manassas, and the Maryland campaign. His brigade was part of A.P. Hill's Light Division and for a short time, while Hill was under arrest, Branch was division commander. His was one of the brigades which made the forced march from Harper's Ferry to Sharpsburg to support Lee at Antietam on 17 September 1862, arriving on the field barely in time to halt the Union advance. Soon after that day's fighting ended Branch was killed by a sniper firing into a group of officers conferring with General Hill.

BDAC; *DAB*; Boatner, *Civil War*; Warner, *Generals in Gray*; D.S. Freeman, *Lee's Lieutenants*, Vol. 2; *B&L*, Vol. 1; *CMH*, Vol. IV.

BRAUN, Gustav Joseph, 1895–1945, New York–Indiana, U.S. Army, missing in action, declared dead 17 March 1945 near Bologna, Italy.

A combat veteran of two world wars, Braun was born in Buffalo and enlisted in the National Guard after two years at the University of Indiana. He served on the Mexican border in 1916–1917 and was commissioned in the regular army in August 1917. He went to France with the 47th Infantry, 4th Division, was wounded twice in action, and won a Distinguished Service Cross for his actions. After the war he was promoted Captain in July 1920, had troop duty at various posts, and was an instructor at the Infantry School at Fort Benning. Braun had been a physical education major in college and was frequently assigned as recreation officer or participated in officially sponsored sports contests. From 1930 to 1933 he was in China and attended the Command and General Staff College in 1935. He was promoted Major the same year and in 1938 was an ROTC instructor at the University of California at Los Angeles. From 1939 to 1942 he held staff positions on the West Coast, first with IX Corps Area and then, after 1941, in VII Corps. Braun had been Lieutenant Colonel since 1940 and in February 1942 he was promoted Colonel. In February 1943 he was assigned as chief of staff of the 69th Division in Mississippi. In July 1944 he went to North Africa to be chief of staff of the 34th Division and in September became commander of the 133rd Infantry Regiment. In November the division reentered combat in Italy and the same month Braun became assistant division commander. He was promoted Brigadier General on 8 January 1945. On 17 March he was flying over enemy lines in front of his own position in a light observation plane when the aircraft was shot down. He was listed as missing in action from that date. He was declared dead after advancing American forces discovered his marked grave near Bologna on 20 April 1945.

Army Register, 1942 and 1946; *CMH, DSC, DSM*; Schnapper; *34th Division*; *New York Times*, March 30, April 24, 1945.

BRODHEAD, Thornton Fleming, 1822–1862, New Hampshire–Michigan, U.S. Volunteers, died 2 September 1862 of wounds received 30 August 1862 at Manassas, Virginia.

The first officer posthumously breveted Brigadier General during the Civil War, Brodhead was the son of a clergyman and studied law at Harvard. Later he moved to the Michigan Territory and opened a law practice in Detroit. He served in the 15th Infantry in Mexico, was breveted once for gallantry, and left the army as a Captain in 1848. He resumed his law practice, served in the Michigan senate, and was appointed Postmaster of Detroit by President Franklin Pierce, a family friend. In 1861 he raised the 1st Michigan Cavalry and became its Colonel on 22 August. Going to Virginia, he commanded his regiment and other Union cavalry in the Valley campaign of 1862 with notoriously poor results. For the Second Manassas campaign Brodhead's regiment was in Buford's brigade. This "broken down" force, mostly dismounted because of inadequate care for their horses, was the Union element separating the two wings of Lee's army. In the fighting on 29 and 30 August 1862 Buford's brigade formed the extension of Pope's left, which Lee turned, and it was there on 30 August that Brodhead was mortally wounded. He died on 2 September and was posthumously breveted Brigadier General USV to rank from 30 August.

Boatner, *Civil War*; Robertson; *OR*, Ser. I, Vol. 12, pt. 2; Ser. II, Vol. 2; National Archives, Records of the Post Office Department (RG 28).

BUCKNER, Simon Bolivar, Jr., 1886–1945, Kentucky, U.S. Army, killed in action 18 June 1945 on Okinawa.

Son of the Confederate general and governor of Kentucky of the same name, the younger Buckner was born and reared near Munfordville, attended Virginia Military Institute for two years, and graduated from West Point in 1908. He served with troop units, including two years in the Philippines, until 1917, when he transferred to the Aviation Section of the Signal Corps and trained units for overseas duty. He was promoted Captain in May and Major in August 1917. From 1920 to 1940 he spent almost seventeen years in the army's education system as either student or instructor. He was a student at, or on the faculty of, the Infantry School, the Command and General Staff College, and the Army War College. He was twice at West Point, including a tour as Commandant of Cadets in 1933–1936. Buckner was promoted Lieutenant Colonel in 1932 and Colonel in 1937. In the latter year he assumed command of a tank regiment, followed by an infantry regiment in 1938. He became chief of staff of the newly organized 6th Division in 1939. In July 1940 Buckner took over the Alaska Defense Command and was made Brigadier General on 1 September. He remained there four years, wresting a military command out of the wilderness, arbitrating interservice rivalries in his joint command, and recovering the Aleutians from the Japanese in the spring of 1943. He was promoted Major General on 4 August 1941 and Lieutenant General on 4 May 1943. In June 1944 he was transferred to Hawaii and began training the Tenth Army for the invasion of Okinawa, which occurred on Easter Sunday, 1 April 1945. With the largest fleet ever assembled and a formidable army of seven divisions, Buckner slowly drove the Japanese across the island for more than two months. Near the end of the battle, on 18 June, he was sitting on a rock in a forward observation post of the 8th Marine Regiment when it was hit by five Japanese shells. Despite immediate medical attention Buckner died within ten minutes. He was posthumously promoted General by special act of Congress on 19 July 1954.

Army Register, 1942–1946; Cullum, Vols. 7–9; Belote; Garfield; Johnston; Morison, Vols. 7 & 14; Schnapper; *Assembly*, July 1946; *New York Times*, April 2, June 19 & 20, 1945; *Time*, April 16, 1945.

BURDETT, Edward Burke, 1921–1967, Tennessee–Georgia, U.S. Air Force, died 18 November 1967 at Bac Mai, North Vietnam, of wounds received the same day.

One of two Air Force generals killed in action in Vietnam and the only one promoted posthumously to general officer rank, Burdett was the son of a career Foreign Service officer. He was born in Knoxville and traveled extensively with his family as a child. After attending a preparatory school he entered West Point in 1940 and graduated (accelerated) with the Class of June 1943. Burdett was commissioned into the Army Air Force, completed pilot training, and was posted to China with a photo-reconnaissance squadron. After World War II Burdett, who had been promoted Captain in 1945, volunteered for jet fighter training and became qualified in the F-80 Shooting Star. In 1946, while piloting one such aircraft, he survived a crash landing with only a fractured vertebra and soon returned to flying. Promoted Major in 1948 and Lieutenant Colonel in 1952, he served at the headquarters of Continental Air Command, attended the Air Command and Staff School, and was assigned variously in Panama, Italy, and Germany. Burdett was promoted Colonel in 1960 and completed tours of duty with the Office of the Joint Chiefs of Staff and headquarters of the Tactical Air Command. From 1965 to 1967 he commanded the 48th Tactical Fighter Wing at Lakenheath, England. In August 1967 Burdett took over the 388th Tactical Fighter Wing at Korat, Thailand, which was engaged in the bombing campaign over North Vietnam. On 18 November 1967, while piloting an F-105 over Bac Mai Airfield, Burdett was shot down. He was captured upon landing but died of his wounds the same day. On 21 November his name was included in a list of U.S. prisoners with no particulars on his condition. He was presumed to be a prisoner of war and in 1968 was selected for promotion to Brigadier General. He was neither nominated nor confirmed for promotion because of his supposed status. It was not until December of 1970 that his death was revealed. His remains were released to U.S. authorities in Hanoi on 6 March 1974 and positively identified on 3 April. In view of his previous selection for promotion he was posthumously confirmed as Brigadier General on 22 March 1974 to rank from the same day.

Air Force Register, 1972; *Congressional Record*, 92nd Congress, 2nd Session; *Air War, Vietnam*; *Assembly*, March 1975; *New York Times*, November 21, 1967; March 8 & 22, 1974; *Macon Telegraph*, December 23, 1970; April 3, 1974; Office of Air Force History.

BURNHAM, Hiram, c. 1814–1864, Maine, U.S. Volunteers, killed in action 29 September 1864 at Fort Harrison, Virginia.

Hiram Burnham was another of those civilian appointments who showed aptitude for military service during the Civil War. Known locally as a leader of men, Burnham was born in Narraguagus, where he engaged in politics and the lumber business. He was mustered into service in June 1861 as Lieutenant Colonel of the 6th Maine, a regiment he had helped to recruit. Burnham served in IV and VI Corps in the Peninsula campaign and in VI Corps at Antietam and Fredericksburg. At Chancellorsville he was given command of a separate light division for Sedgwick's assault on Marye's Heights. Burnham's regiment was in the brigade of David Russell at Gettysburg and was hardly engaged, but at Rappahannock Station in November 1863 they participated in the attack on the Confederate brigdehead, capturing over 1,600 prisoners with four guns and eight stands of colors. Burnham was promoted to Brigadier General on 27 April 1864 and transferred to brigade and, briefly, division command in XVIII Corps at Petersburg. On 29 September 1864, in an attack on Confederate Fort Harrison near Chafin's Farm, Burnham led his brigade across 1,400 yards of open, fire-swept ground and was killed during the successful attack. He was buried at his home in Maine.

Boatner, *Civil War*; Warner, *Generals in Blue*; *B&L*, Vols. 3 & 4.

BUTLER, Richard, 1743–1791, Ireland–Pennsylvania, U.S. Levies, died 4 November 1791 of wounds received the same day at St. Mary's, Ohio.

Richard Butler has the distinction of being the first of only four American generals killed in the Indian wars and the only officer ever commissioned "General of U.S. Levies." Brought to Pennsylvania by an older brother when he was a young boy, Butler served in the provincials on Bouquet's expedition in the Pontiac War of 1764. Later he was an Indian trader and led a militia company in Lord Dunsmore's War (1774). In 1776 he became an officer of the Pennsylvania Continentals and from 1777 to 1783 he commanded a series of Pennsylvania regiments. He led a battalion under Anthony Wayne at the storming of Stony Point in 1779 and was a negotiator during the mutiny of the Pennsylvania Line in 1781. Freeman calls him one of the best colonels in the Continental service, although Boatner says he had "meager qualifications." He was breveted Brigadier General on 30 September 1783 and retired. Later he was an Indian Commissioner in the Northwest Territories. When a new army was authorized in 1791 to handle continued Indian depredations, Butler was commissioned Major General of U.S. Levies, probably on 4 March. Two regiments of levies were raised for six months' service. Butler trained his troops that summer and in September embarked with Arthur St. Clair, commanding general of the army, on a punitive expedition from Cincinnati. By November the army had reached the headwaters of the Wabash near St. Mary's. St. Clair split his force, with Butler's levies on the east bank of the river. Butler seems to have known an Indian attack was imminent but never told St. Clair. On the morning of 4 November the Indians attacked Butler's camp, routing his troops and throwing them back on the regulars. Butler was wounded in the leg and took shelter in a tent. When the rout became general he refused evacuation. He almost certainly died of his wound, although a story was extant that he was tomahawked and his heart cut out of his body. St. Mary's was the worst defeat ever suffered in the Indian Wars with more than 600 killed and 300 wounded in a force of 1,400. George Washington attributed Butler's poor performance to illness.

DAB; Boatner, *American Revolution*; Heitman, *Continental Army*; D.S. Freeman, *Washington*, Vols. 5 & 6; Kohn; Guthman.

C

CALLAGHAN, Daniel Judson, 1890–1942, California, U.S. Navy, killed in action 12 November 1942 off Guadalcanal, Solomon Islands.

One of five admirals killed in action in World War II, and one of three who were posthumously awarded the Medal of Honor, Callaghan was born in San Francisco, graduated from Annapolis in 1911, and served his first tour of sea duty in the battleship *California*. He was commissioned Ensign in 1912, as was the custom of the time, and during that year was a member of a landing force in the first Nicaraguan intervention. From 1914 to 1916 he was aboard USS *Truxtun* off the coast of Mexico and commanded her briefly as Lieutenant (Junior Grade). During World War I he served in USS *New Orleans* as executive officer. He was promoted Lieutenant in March 1918. From 1920 to 1930 Callaghan alternated sea and shore duty, serving mainly in battleships and on the West Coast. He had been promoted Lieutenant Commander in 1921 and became Commander in 1931. He spent three years in the Battle Fleet on gunnery duty after which he was an ROTC instructor at the University of California at Berkeley. Callaghan was with the Pacific cruiser force from 1936 to 1938. In 1938 he was promoted Captain and became Naval Aide to President Franklin Roosevelt. He traveled extensively with the President and was one of his principal staff advisers until 1941, when Callaghan took command of USS *San Francisco*, a light cruiser. Callaghan was at Pearl Harbor in his ship on 7 December 1941. He was promoted Rear Admiral on 26 April 1942 and became chief of staff of the South Pacific Area in June. In support of the Guadalcanal campaign he assumed command of a task force of five light cruisers and several destroyers with his flag in *San Francisco*. He was joined by another task force under Rear Admiral Norman Scott. On the night of 12–13 November 1942 Callaghan and Scott led their combined force to meet the

Japanese fleet in Ironbottom Sound off Guadalcanal. In the engagement that followed eighteen Japanese ships were sunk at a cost of six American. At one juncture, as *San Francisco* slowed and ceased fire, she was hit by shells from the Japanese ships, killing Callaghan and almost every other man on the bridge. *San Francisco* survived and Callaghan was posthumously awarded the Medal of Honor for "faithfully directing close-range operations in the face of…superior enemy fire power."

Morison, Vol. 5; *MOH*; *New York Times*, November 17, 1942; U.S. Navy Office of Information.

CAMPBELL, Cleveland John, 1836–1865, New York, U.S. Volunteers, died 13 June 1865 of wounds received 30 July 1864 at Petersburg, Virginia.

Cleveland Campbell was another of the young intellectuals who forsook civilian pursuits for military service at the outbreak of the Civil War. Son of a congressman and state supreme court justice, he was born in New York City, graduated from Union College, and studied law at the University of Goettingen in Germany. When the war started he was practicing law in New York. He enlisted as a private in the 44th New York but in October 1861 he was commissioned Lieutenant in the 1st New York Cavalry. He also served as aide to General Innis Palmer. In October 1862 Campbell became 1st Lieutenant in the 102nd New York, and in April 1863, Captain in the 121st New York under Colonel Emory Upton. He fought in all the battles of the Army of the Potomac and became Lieutenant Colonel of the 23rd U.S. Colored Troops in March 1864. He participated in the spring campaign of 1864 in Virginia, notably at Bermuda Hundred, and succeeded to the colonelcy of his regiment on 15 July. On 30 July, at the battle of the Crater at Petersburg, Campbell was seriously wounded by a shell fragment in the lung while leading the 23rd forward. He never returned to active duty in the field. From August 1864 to June 1865 he commanded a recruiting rendezvous in New York harbor. On 13 June 1865 he died at his uncle's home in Castleton, New York, of consumption and chronic diarrhea brought on by the effects of his wound. He was posthumously breveted Brigadier General USV to rank from 13 March 1865. Campbell's first name is sometimes spelled Cleaveland.

Boatner, *Civil War*; *Harper's*; Phisterer, *New York in the War*; *Albany Evening Journal*, June 14, 1865; Cherry Valley (N.Y.) Historical Association; Military Service Record.

CANBY, Edward Richard Sprigg, 1817–1873, Kentucky–Indiana, U.S. Army, murdered by Indians, 11 April 1873 at the California Lava Beds.

The only full-rank regular army general officer killed in the course of the Indian Wars, Edward Canby was born in Kentucky, attended local schools there and then Wabash College in Indiana. He graduated from West Point in 1839, fought in the Seminole and Cherokee campaigns, and participated in the Mexican War, where he was twice breveted for gallantry. After a career on the frontier, in May 1861 he was made Colonel of the newly raised 19th U.S. Infantry and commander of the Department of New Mexico. At Val Verde, in February 1862, as he attempted to turn back the Confederate advance into the New Mexico Territory, he suffered a tactical defeat but a strategic victory when the victorious but starving Confederate army disintegrated for lack of supplies. He was breveted Brigadier General USA for this battle. Canby was promoted Brigadier General USV on 31 March 1862 and appointed Assistant Adjutant General of the Army in Washington. He commanded the federal troops called to New York City in July 1863 to suppress the draft riots. On 7 May 1864 he was appointed Major General USV and sent to command the Military Division of West Mississippi, one of the principal geographical divisions of the army, directly subordinate to Commanding General U.S. Grant. Canby was responsible for all military operations along the Mississippi River from St. Louis to New Orleans, and along the Gulf Coast from Texas to Florida. He was seriously wounded by a guerrilla sniper in Arkansas in November 1864, but effected the capture of Mobile Bay in September 1864 and Mobile in April 1865. He accepted the surrender of the Confederate armies of Dick Taylor and Kirby Smith in May 1865. Canby received the thanks of President Lincoln for his services and was breveted Major General USA for war services on 13 March 1865. After the demobilization of the volunteer army, Canby was promoted to Brigadier General USA on 28 July 1866. He served on occupation duty in the South until 1870, commanded the Department of Columbia (Pacific Northwest), and in 1873 took over the Military Division of the Pacific. On 11 April 1873, while negotiating with Modoc Indian representatives for their removal from the California Lava Beds, Canby and the other peace commissioners were attacked by the Indian chief, Captain Jack, and his associates. Canby was shot in the face and killed, his body stabbed and stripped. Jack was eventually captured, tried for murder, and hanged.

DAB; Boatner, *Civil War*; Warner, *Generals in Blue*; Utley; *B&L*, Vols. 2 & 4.

CARTER, John Carpenter, 1837–1864, Georgia–Tennessee, C.S. Army, died 10 December 1864 of wounds received 30 November 1864 at Franklin, Tennessee.

John C. Carter was another of the six Confederate generals killed or mortally wounded at Franklin during John Bell Hood's disastrous invasion of Tennessee in the autumn of 1864. Born in Waynesboro in Burke County, Carter attended the University of Virginia, studied law at Cumberland University in Tennessee, and settled in Lebanon as a teacher. Later he opened a law practice in Memphis. In 1861 he was commissioned Captain in the 38th Tennessee. After fighting at Shiloh he was rapidly promoted Major, Lieutenant Colonel, and Colonel, so that by October 1862 he was in command of the 38th at Perryville. He also led it at Stone's River and in the Chickamauga campaign of 1863, but was on detached duty during the battle for Chattanooga that November. For the Atlanta campaign of 1864 Carter was advanced to the command of his brigade and was promoted Brigadier General CSA on 7 July 1864. He commanded a division at Jonesboro, Georgia, in September 1864. For Hood's invasion of Tennessee, Carter's brigade was assigned to Brown's division. On 30 November, at Franklin, Carter was mortally wounded while leading the advance of his brigade in the second line of Brown's twilight attack on the Union defenses. Of the five general officers in Brown's division, two were killed, one mortally wounded, one seriously wounded, and one taken prisoner. Carter was carried to the Harrison House, where General John H. Kelly had died the previous September, and died there himself on 10 December.

Boatner, *Civil War*; Warner, *Generals in Gray*; McDonough and Connelly; *CMH*, Vol. VIII.

CASTLE, Frederick Walker, 1908–1944, Philippines–New Jersey, U.S. Army Air Force, missing in action, declared dead, 24 December 1944 over Liege, Belgium.

Freddy Castle was one of those young professional officers who formed the fledgling Army Air Corps at the beginning of World War II, giving it its character and its traditions. Son of an army officer, Castle was born in Manila, educated in New Jersey, and graduated from West Point in 1930. He served in the Air Corps only four years and then resigned to enter private industry. In January 1942 he was recalled to active duty as 1st Lieutenant and went immediately to England with General Ira Eaker to form the nucleus of the future Eighth Air Force. Castle was promoted Captain in February, Major in March, and Lieutenant Colonel in September 1942 as the Air Force staff grew. As chief supply officer he was responsible for organizing the entire network of bases and depots for logistical support of the Eighth. He was made Colonel in January 1943 and in June he returned to flying duty with the 94th Bomb Group. In April 1944 he became commander of the 4th Bomb Wing. Castle flew thirty missions over Germany, including the noted Regensburg raid, and was promoted Brigadier General on 11 November 1944. During the Battle of the Bulge in December 1944, Allied air was unable to support ground troops owing to poor weather conditions. On December 24 the weather finally cleared, and Castle led an air division of 2,000 B-17s to attack German airfields. Over Liege, Belgium, one of his engines failed. When his plane dropped out of formation it was attacked by seven German fighters. Castle refused to jettison his bombs to lighten his load because he knew he was over friendly troop positions. After two engines caught fire, he ordered the crew to bail out and he piloted the plane himself until it exploded. In 1946 Castle was posthumously awarded the Medal of Honor for "intrepidity and willing sacrifice of his own life to save members of his crew."

Cullum, Vol. 9; R. Freeman; *MOH*; *Assembly*, July 1946; *New York Times*, January 19, 1945; Military Service Record.

CHAMBLISS, John Randolph, Jr., 1833–1864, Virginia, C.S. Army, killed in action 16 August 1864 at Deep Bottom, Virginia.

Chambliss was one of those professionally trained officers who had left military service after a very short period and then came forward to bolster the ranks of the Confederacy. Born in the town which is now Emporia, he graduated from West Point in 1853 and resigned from the army the next year. For seven years he was a planter in Greenville County, an officer in the militia, and an aide to the governor. When the Virginia militia was absorbed into the C.S. Army in 1861, Chambliss became Colonel of the 41st Virginia and, in July 1861, Colonel of the 5th Virginia Cavalry. He served first in southern Virginia and then with the troops left to garrison northern Virginia when Lee undertook the Maryland campaign in 1862. In November 1862 his regiment joined Stuart's cavalry division in the brigade of W.H.F. "Rooney" Lee. Chambliss was at Fredericksburg and Chancellorsville and succeeded to the brigade command when Rooney Lee was wounded at Brandy Station in June 1863. Chambliss led the brigade at Gettysburg and Bristoe Station and in January 1864 was promoted Brigadier General CSA to rank from 19 December 1863. He continued in command of the brigade through the spring and summer of 1864. On 16 August 1864, while fighting Union Cavalry along the Charles City Road near Deep Bottom, Virginia, Chambliss was shot through the body and killed while standing in the road rallying his men. His father was a delegate to the Virginia secession convention and a member of the First Confederate Congress.

Cullum; Boatner, *Civil War*; Warner, *Generals in Gray*; D.S. Freeman, *Lee's Lieutenants*, Vol. 3; *B&L*, Vol. 3; *CMH*, Vol. III; *OR*, Ser. I, Vol. 42, pt. 1.

CHAMPLIN, Stephen Gardner, 1827–1864, New York–Michigan, U.S. Volunteers, died 24 January 1864 of wounds received 31 May 1862 at Fair Oaks, Virginia.

Another of the multitude of lawyers who became officers in the Union Army, Champlin was born in Kingston, attended Rhinebeck Academy, and opened a law practice in Albany in 1850. He moved to Grand Rapids in 1853, where he became a judge and then a county prosecutor. In June 1861 he was commissioned Major in the 3rd Michigan, which joined the Army of the Potomac in Virginia. That October Champlin was commended by General McClellan for the disposition of his troops in a minor affair and became Colonel of the regiment as a result. The next spring he took the 3rd to the Virginia Peninsula as part of III Corps. At Fair Oaks (Seven Pines), Virginia, on 31 May 1862, Champlin was wounded in the hip seriously enough to be invalided for over two months. For his part in the action he was again commended, this time by his brigade and division commanders. He returned to duty for the Second Manassas campaign. He was not yet ready for active duty and his wound broke open, completely incapacitating him. He was commended once again but was described as "disabled." Champlin returned to Michigan as commander of the recruiting district at Grand Rapids and was made Brigadier General USV on 29 November 1862.

He remained on duty in Grand Rapids until his death from the effects of his wound on 24 January 1864.

Boatner, *Civil War*; Warner, *Generals in Blue*; *Appleton's*.

CHANDLER, Theodore Edson, 1894–1945, Maryland–New Hampshire, U.S. Navy, died 7 January 1945 of wounds received 6 January 1945 off Luzon, Philippine Islands.

One of five flag officers killed in combat in the history of the U.S. Navy and scion of a distinguished naval family, Chandler was born in Annapolis, son of an admiral and grandson of a former Secretary of the Navy. He attended the Manlius School in New York, graduated from the Naval Academy in 1915, and served in battleships until World War I. In 1917, he went to the destroyer *Conner* and served in her until 1919, including patrol duty at Brest, France. Later he had additional destroyer duty and obtained a master's degree from the University of Michigan. From 1923 to 1926 he was in battleships again and then spent two years at Yorktown, Virginia, at the mine depot. Chandler was in the Asiatic Fleet and later commanded the USS *Pope* on the Yangtze Patrol. He attended the Army Industrial College, was on the Battle Force staff, and commanded another destroyer, USS *Buchanan*. From 1935 to 1938 he was naval attache at Paris, Madrid, and Lisbon. He cruised in the *Nashville* from 1938 to 1940 and commanded another cruiser, USS *Omaha*, from 1941 to 1943. Chandler was officially commended in November 1941 for his seizure of a German motor vessel masquerading under U.S. colors. Chandler was promoted Rear Admiral on 23 October 1942 and commanded all Allied air and naval units at Curaçao in the Caribbean from April 1943 to July 1944. At that time he went to the Mediterranean to command a cruiser division for the invasion of southern France. Subsequently he went to the Pacific and commanded a battleship division during the battle at Surigao Strait in the Philippines on 25 October 1944. During the invasion of Luzon in January 1945, Chandler again commanded a cruiser division. Aboard his flagship, USS *Louisville*, on 6 January, he was on the bridge when the ship was hit by a *kamikaze* on the starboard side. Chandler was drenched with burning gasoline from the exploding plane but helped to man a fire hose before reporting to sick bay. His lungs had suffered irreparable scorching and he died the next day.

Morison, Vols. 1, 10, 11, 12, 13; U.S. Navy Office of Information; *New York Times*, January 17, 1945.

CHAPIN, Edward Payson, 1831–1863, New York, U.S. Volunteers, killed in action 27 May 1863 at Port Hudson, Louisiana.

Chapin was another lawyer and active militia officer who entered military service at the beginning of the Civil War. Son of a clergyman, he was born in Waterloo. Moving to Buffalo, he was admitted to the bar in 1852. He was also Captain of a militia company which was mustered into active service as part of the 44th New York in September 1861. Chapin became Major in January

1862. He was senior officer present with the regiment during the Virginia Peninsula campaign of 1862 and distinguished himself at Yorktown. Wounded during the Seven Days battles, he was promoted Lieutenant Colonel in July 1862. He resigned his commission the same month in order to become Colonel of the 116th New York at Baltimore in September 1862. The regiment went to New Orleans with Nathaniel Banks that November. When the troops in the Department of the Gulf were organized into XIX Corps, Chapin was appointed brigade commander in the 1st Division. On 27 May 1863, during Banks's general assault on Port Hudson, Chapin, at the head of his brigade, advanced to the foot of the Confederate parapet where he was shot and killed. In September 1863 he was posthumously promoted to Brigadier General to rank from the date of his death.

Boatner, *Civil War*; Warner, *Generals in Blue*; *B&L*, Vol. 3.

CHAPLIN, Daniel, 1820–1864, Maine, U.S. Volunteers, died 20 August 1864 of wounds received 17 August 1864 at Deep Bottom, Virginia.

A man of some sensitivity who appears to have been psychologically affected by the heavy losses of his regiment, Chaplin was raised on his uncle's farm, worked as a bookkeeper, and had an interest in military affairs. He enlisted in the 2nd Maine in April 1861 and was elected Captain of his company in May. He served with his regiment at Bull Run and became Major in September 1861. He participated in the Virginia Peninsula campaign and in May 1862, at Hanover Court House, refused an order to withdraw, even though his men were out of ammunition. Chaplin's service was so outstanding that he was commissioned Colonel of the newly raised 1st Maine Heavy Artillery (18th Maine) in August 1862. He was assigned to the defenses of Washington, where he remained until the spring of 1864 when the heavy artillery regiments were assigned as infantry to the Army of the Potomac. The 1st Maine was sent to II Corps. They lost heavily in the assaults at Spotsylvania and Cold Harbor, suffering more than 400 casualties in each engagement. Chaplin became very depressed by these losses and began to predict his own death. Nevertheless, he continued to perform his duties creditably. On 17 August 1864, at Deep Bottom, in front of Petersburg, Chaplin was on the brigade picket line when he was struck in the lung by a sniper's bullet. He died three days later. Chaplin was breveted Brigadier General USV to rank from 17 August.

Boatner, *Civil War*; Shaw; *OR*, Ser. I, Vols. 40, pt. 1; 42, pt. 1.

CLEBURNE, Patrick Ronayne, 1828–1864, Ireland–Arkansas, C.S. Army, killed in action 30 November 1864 at Franklin, Tennessee.

One of the best division commanders in the Confederate service, with a reputation as a superb combat leader, Patrick Cleburne was one of only two foreign-born officers to rise to Major General rank in the CSA. Son of a doctor, he was born in County Cork, enlisted in the British army after failing the entrance examination for medical school, and came to America with his family in 1849. Settling in Helena, he trained as an apothecary, opened a drugstore, and then took up the law. When Arkansas seceded in 1861 Cleburne organized the Yell Rifles, seized the Little Rock Arsenal, was commissioned Captain and then Colonel of the 1st Arkansas. This was followed by a transfer to the 15th Arkansas and on 4 March 1862, promotion to Brigadier General, CSA. Cleburne commanded a brigade at Shiloh and at Richmond, Kentucky, and a division at Perryville in October 1862. He was promoted to Major General CSA on 13 December 1862. He led his division through the Stone's River and Chickamauga campaigns, and was given the thanks of the Confederate Congress for saving the supply trains of Bragg's army after Chattanooga in November 1863. In the winter of 1864 Cleburne invited considerable controversy by his proposal, in a circular letter to his fellow officers in the Army of Tennessee, to conscript and arm slaves. Cleburne fought in all the battles of the Atlanta campaign of 1864 and went on Hood's Tennessee campaign that fall. On 30 November 1864, at Franklin, Tennessee, Cleburne was killed while galloping alone toward the Union lines. His body lay all that night on the battlefield and was discovered the next morning by searchers after it had been stripped of all articles of value by scavengers. Cleburne was one of six Confederate generals killed or mortally wounded at the tragic battle of Franklin.

DAB; Boatner, Civil War; Warner, Generals in Gray; Connelly, Autumn of Glory; McDonough and Connelly; B&L, Vol. 4; CMH, Vol. X (Arkansas).

COBB, Thomas Reade Rootes, 1823–1862, Georgia, C.S. Army, killed in action 13 December 1862 at Fredericksburg, Virginia.

One of the most brilliant legal scholars of his time, and brother of Howell Cobb, former U.S. senator, cabinet officer, and governor of Georgia, Thomas Cobb was born in Jefferson County. He attended the University of Georgia and entered legal practice. His codification of Georgia's statute law and criminal law and his editing of Georgia supreme court decisions won him renown statewide and nationally. Cobb was an ardent secessionist and, with his brother, played a leading role in taking Georgia out of the Union. He was delegate to the convention which established the Confederacy and was briefly a Confederate congressman. In August 1861 he raised and became Colonel of Cobb's Georgia Legion, a mixed force of infantry and cavalry, which he took to Virginia in September. Despite his dislike for professional military officers, he learned their trade well enough to win a reputation for gallant leadership in the Seven Days battles, at Second Manassas, and in Maryland. R.E. Lee urged him to expand his legion to brigade size, which Cobb did not do, but he was nonetheless promoted Brigadier General CSA on 1 November 1862. In his first battle at the head of his brigade at Fredericksburg on 13 December 1862, Cobb was wounded in the leg by a sniper's bullet after the repulse of the first Union assault. He was taken to a house on the field, but the surgeon could not stop the flow of blood from the severed arteries. Cobb died within a few minutes. He was buried near his alma mater in Athens, Georgia. At his funeral, his body was wrapped in the red general's sash of the deceased David Twiggs, a fellow Georgian, who had surrendered U.S. forces in Texas to state authorities in 1861.

DAB; Boatner, *Civil War*; Warner, *Generals in Gray*; D.S. Freeman, *Lee's Lieutenants*, Vol. 2; *B&L*, Vols. 1 & 3; *CMH*, Vol. VI; *Handbook of Augusta*.

COBHAM, George Ashworth, Jr., 1825–1864, England–Pennsylvania, U.S Volunteers, killed in action 20 July 1864 at Atlanta, Georgia.

George Cobham was a regimental officer who frequently served at brigade level and was posthumously breveted to general officer for gallantry in action. Son of a barrister in Liverpool, he was brought to Warren, Pennsylvania, by his mother and her second husband after his father died. He was educated at Allegheny College and became a contractor and bridge builder. The 111th Pennsylvania was raised in Erie in December 1861 and Cobham became its Lieutenant Colonel in January 1862. The regiment went to Baltimore, on to West Virginia, joined Pope's Army of Virginia in the summer of 1862, and eventually became part of XII Corps in the Army of the Potomac. In the meantime, Cobham became Colonel in November 1862. At Fredericksburg and Chancellorsville he commanded his brigade, and at Gettysburg he was commended for his action. He accompanied XII Corps to Tennessee in the fall of 1863 and was again in command of the brigade at Lookout Mountain in November 1863. In the Atlanta campaign of 1864 Cobham commanded a brigade in XX Corps and at Resaca captured a four-gun battery for which he was again commended. At Peach Tree Creek, on 20 July 1864, Cobham was killed while repelling a Confederate attack on his lines. He was posthumously breveted Brigadier General USV to rank from 19 July 1864.

Boatner, *Civil War*; Coddington; Boyle; *OR*, Ser. I, Vols. 31, pts. 1 & 2; 38, pts. 1 & 2.

COVINGTON, Leonard, 1768–1813, Maryland, U.S. Army, died 14 November 1813 of wounds received 13 November 1813 at Chrysler's Farm, near Morrisburg, Ontario, Canada.

One of two American generals killed in the War of 1812, Leonard Covington was born in Aquasco, received a liberal education, and was reared to be a planter. He married in 1789 but his wife died within three years. He entered the army as Coronet of dragoons in March 1792, and in March 1793 was promoted Lieutenant to rank from October 1792. As a member of Anthony Wayne's Legion of the United States, Covington participated in the relief of Fort Recovery and had a prominent part in the battle at Fallen Timbers in August 1794. Succeeding to the command of the Legion cavalry at the latter engagement, he led them through the three lines of the Indian defenses and personally killed two of the enemy. After the peace treaty he left the army and took up farming in Maryland. Later he served in the state senate and the U.S. House of Representatives. In January 1809 he returned to the service as Lieutenant Colonel of the regiment of light dragoons and served on the southwestern frontier for three years. In June 1810 he became Colonel of dragoons and was commander of U.S. troops which occupied Mobile and New Orleans. In July 1813 Covington transferred to Sackets Harbor, New York, for the invasion of Canada and was promoted Brigadier General USA to rank from 1 July 1813. He commanded a brigade in the campaign of October–November 1813. At Chrysler's Farm on 13 November his brigade was on the left of the American line. The battle was fought in a storm of mixed sleet and snow and Covington was prominent on a white horse. During the battle he was misled by the gray greatcoats of the opposing force into thinking they were Canadian militia rather than British regulars. As he led his men forward to seize the British cannon, he was felled by a shot from the farmhouse. His second in command was killed and their brigade was thrown into confusion. Covington was evacuated back across the St. Lawrence with a wound in the lower abdomen and died the next day.

BDAC; Heitman, *U.S. Army*; *Twentieth Century*; Boyd; Wailes; Berton.

CUSTER, George Armstrong, 1839–1876, Ohio, U.S. Army, killed in action 25 June 1876 at Little Big Horn, Montana.

Perhaps the most notorious American general ever killed in action, both for the manner of his death and the flamboyance of his character, George Armstrong Custer was born in Harrison County, Ohio, but spent most of his formative years with his half-sister and her husband in Monroe, Michigan. He taught school briefly before graduating from West Point last in the class of June 1861 (accelerated). Immediately joining the Army of the Potomac, Custer served as a staff officer for various commanders, including George McClellan, until 29 June 1863, when he was promoted directly from Captain of volunteers to Brigadier General USV. He was given command of the Michigan cavalry brigade. Under his command it fought in every battle of the Army of the Potomac and suffered the highest casualty rate of any Union cavalry unit in the war. In October 1864 he took command of the 3rd Division of the Cavalry Corps, which he led in the final stages of the Shenandoah Valley and Petersburg campaigns. Wounded once during the war, he was breveted five times for his conduct in action. He was breveted Major General USA on 13 March 1865 and promoted Major General USV on 15 April 1865. Mustered out of volunteer service in February 1866, Custer was appointed Lieutenant Colonel, 7th Cavalry in July the same year. He participated in the Sioux campaign of 1867, was court-martialed and suspended from duty for disobedience of orders, but restored by General Sheriden in 1868. He took a leading role in the Plains campaign of 1868–1869, highlighted by his attack on the friendly Cheyenne village of Black Kettle in November 1868. Custer took part in the Stanley expedition to protect railroad surveyors in 1873 and led his own Black Hills mapping expedition in 1874. In the Sioux War of 1876, Custer's regiment formed part of Terry's column moving to the Yellowstone from Fort Abraham Lincoln. On 22 June he was sent to find and fix the Sioux position. On 25 June Custer divided his regiment in the

face of a vastly superior enemy, allowed himself with five troops to be surrounded, and lost his own life along with those of every man under his personal
command. It was the worst disaster suffered during the Indian Wars of the
nineteenth century.

   DAB; Boatner, *Civil War*; Warner, *Generals in Blue*; *B&L*, Vol. 4; Cullum;
Graham; Godfrey; Utley.

D

DALTON, James Leo, 2nd, 1910–1945, Connecticut, U.S. Army, killed in action 16 May 1945 at Balete Pass, Luzon, Philippine Islands.

One of the youngest ground forces general officers of World War II, James L. Dalton was termed by his division commander as "the greatest soldier I ever knew." Dalton was born in New Britain, attended local schools and graduated from West Point in 1933. He served with the 3rd Cavalry in Vermont but transferred to the infantry after a riding accident in 1934. He became company commander in the 35th Infantry Regiment, Hawaiian Division, in 1940. In 1941 the Hawaiian Division became the 25th Infantry Division and Dalton served successively as company commander, battalion commander, regimental operations officer, and regimental executive officer in the 35th Infantry. He fought on Guadalcanal, at Munda on New Georgia, and in the Philippines. Rising through the ranks, he was promoted Colonel in March 1943 and led the 161st Infantry Regiment in the same division thereafter, earning commendations from his corps commander and from General Douglas MacArthur. On 21 March 1945 he became assistant commander of the 25th Division, and on 27 March he was promoted Brigadier General. Leading the division in the Luzon campaign, Dalton was killed by a sniper's bullet to the head while reconnoitering Balete Pass on 16 May 1945. The Philippine government renamed Balete Pass in his honor. As well as being a superlative soldier, Dalton had a life-long interest in the arts. His wife was the poet Katherine Starbird.

Army Register, 1942–1946; Cullum, Vols. 8 & 9; *Assembly*, June 1975; Rutherford; *New York Times*, May 17, 1945; *Burlington Free Press*, May 17, 1945.

DANIEL, Junius, 1828–1864, North Carolina, C.S. Army, died 13 May 1864 of wounds received 12 May 1864 at Spotsylvania, Virginia.

Junius Daniel was another professionally trained soldier who returned from civilian life to join the Confederate cause. Son of a U.S. congressman, he was born in Halifax County and graduated from West Point in 1851. He served on the frontier for seven years before resigning in 1858 to manage his father's plantation in Louisiana. In June 1861, Daniel entered Confederate service as Colonel of the 14th North Carolina. He spent the first year of the war organizing and training North Carolina troops. In 1862 the 14th North Carolina was transferred to Virginia and Daniel fought in the Peninsula campaign. He was promoted to Brigadier General CSA on 1 September 1862. Going to southern Virginia and North Carolina at that time, he did not return to the Army of Northern Virginia until June 1863. He distinguished himself at Gettysburg, where his brigade suffered severe losses, and in the Wilderness. At Spotsylvania, on 12 May 1864, Daniel was mortally wounded while leading his brigade in an attempt to retake the works at the Mule Shoe or Bloody Angle. He died the next day.

Boatner, *Civil War*; Warner, *Generals in Gray*; Cullum; D.S. Freeman, *Lee's Lieutenants*, Vol. 3; *B&L*, Vol. 4; *CMH*, Vol. IV.

DARBY, William Orlando, 1911–1945, Arkansas, U.S. Army, killed in action 30 April 1945 at Lake Garda, Italy.

Famed in American military history as the organizer and leader of "Darby's Rangers," William O. Darby was born in Fort Smith, graduated from West Point in 1933, and served with artillery units until 1942. Promoted Captain in 1940 and Major in 1942, he was sent to Northern Ireland to organize, train, and command the 1st Ranger Battalion to be recruited from among U.S. troops already in the British Isles. He was made Lieutenant Colonel in August 1942 and took his new battalion to North Africa for the Torch invasion of November 1942. There, his Rangers established a reputation for unparalleled combat effectiveness which they sustained for the next two years. Darby led by example and was at the forefront of every action in Tunis, Sicily, and Italy. He three times refused promotion to higher rank so that he could remain with the Rangers, and was three times wounded. The height of his feats came at Salerno in September 1943 when he commanded a division-sized organization of American and British troops for twenty-one days in protecting the flank of Fifth Army's bridgehead. After the Anzio landing only 200 of the 1,500 original Rangers were left, and Darby, who had been a Colonel since December 1943, took over the 179th Infantry Regiment of the 45th Division. In September 1944 he went to Washington to the Operations Division of the War Department General Staff. There he remained until April 1945 when he availed himself of an opportunity to accompany Chief of Army Air Forces, General "Hap" Arnold, on a world tour. Arriving in Europe, Darby learned that the assistant commander of the 10th Mountain Division had been wounded. He hurried to

Italy to offer himself as a replacement. Accepted on 22 April, within three days he was spearheading a drive across the Po River. On 30 April, while at Torbole on Lake Garda, Darby and six others were killed by a German 88mm shell which landed on the breakwater where they were standing. On 14 May 1945 Darby was confirmed as Brigadier General USA to rank from 30 April.

Army Register, 1942–1946; Cullum, Vols. 8 & 9; Templeton; Schnapper; *Assembly*, July 1946; *Time*, May 14, 1945; *New York Times*, July 16, 1943 and May 2, 1945.

DAVIDSON, William Lee, 1746–1781, Pennsylvania–North Carolina, North Carolina State Troops, killed in action 1 February 1781 at Cowan's Ford, North Carolina.

A leader in the local Committee of Public Safety before the American Revolution, William L. Davidson was born in Lancaster, Pennsylvania. When he was four his family joined in the migration southward along the Appalachian chain and finally settled in Rowan County on the North Carolina frontier. In April 1776 Davidson joined the 4th North Carolina Continentals as Major. He marched to Pennsylvania with his regiment in 1777 and was cited for gallantry at Germantown that October. Becoming Lieutenant Colonel of the 5th North Carolina, he commanded that regiment at Valley Forge and until it was consolidated with the 3rd North Carolina in June 1778. He fought at Monmouth and remained in the northern theater until the North Carolina brigade marched to Charleston in the winter of 1780. Davidson took advantage of the march to stop off to visit his family en route. Before he could rejoin his regiment Charleston was encircled by the British, so he stayed home. In June 1780 Davidson was given command of a force of 300 militia by Governor Rutherford. He arrived at the Ramseur's Mills battle site too late to participate, but was shot through the body during an engagement at the Yadkin River later that summer. As a result, he missed the American disaster at Camden in August. He returned to duty in the fall and became Brigadier General of state troops. His troops were with Daniel Morgan at Cowpens in January 1781, but Davidson was away on recruiting duty, a mission entrusted him by Nathaniel Greene. After Davidson raised 800 men, he was given the task of guarding the fords of the Catawba River while Greene withdrew his army to the northeast. Davidson's force was unequal to the protection of a forty-mile front. On 1 February 1781, with about 300 men, he attempted to prevent a crossing at Cowan's Ford by Cornwallis's whole army. His attempt was unsuccessful and he was killed while trying to rally his fleeing militiamen. Davidson College is named in his honor.

DAB; *Appleton's*; Boatner's *American Revolution*; Davidson; Lumpkin.

DEARING, James, 1840–1865, Virginia, C.S. Army, died 23 April 1865 of wounds received 6 April 1865 at High Bridge, Virginia.

James Dearing was a cadet at the United States Military Academy who resigned when Virginia seceded from the Union in April 1861. Born in Campbell County, he had attended Hanover Academy before entering West Point in 1858. He was appointed Lieutenant in the Confederate artillery after his resignation and served at Bull Run and on the Virginia Peninsula. He distinguished himself at Seven Pines as Captain commanding a battery. After Fredericksburg, in December 1862, he was promoted Major and commanded the artillery battalion supporting Pickett's division. When Longstreet's corps was sent to southside Virginia and North Carolina in the spring of 1863, Dearing supervised all of the corps artillery. He led his battalion at Gettysburg, where he supported Pickett's charge on 3 July. When Pickett's division was sent to the Department of Virginia and North Carolina in the fall of 1863, Dearing was promoted to temporary Colonel in command of the Department cavalry. In April 1864 he was promoted Lieutenant Colonel of artillery and given command of the horse artillery of the Army of Northern Virginia. Three weeks later, on 29 April, he was promoted to Brigadier General CSA and given command of a cavalry brigade at Petersburg. He participated in the actions against the Union advance toward Petersburg, at Drewry's Bluff, and on the Petersburg lines that summer. In early 1865 Dearing took over a brigade in the Cavalry Corps of the Army of Northern Virginia. At High Bridge, on 6 April, while countering the attempt of Union troops to cut off the retreat of Lee's army, Dearing was mortally wounded in a pistol duel with Union general Theodore Read, who was also killed. Taken to Lynchburg, Dearing died there on 23 April, two weeks after Lee's surrender.

Boatner, *Civil War*; Warner, *Generals in Gray*; D.S. Freeman, *Lee's Lieutenants*, Vols. 1 & 3; *B&L*, Vol. 4; *CMH*, Vol. III.

DESHLER, James, 1833–1863, Alabama, C.S. Army, killed in action 20 September 1863 at Chickamauga, Georgia.

James Deshler, a graduate of West Point in 1854, never resigned his commission in the U.S. Army when he joined the Confederacy, but instead was dropped from the rolls in July 1861. Son of an engineer who had emigrated from Pennsylvania to Alabama, Deshler was born in Tuscumbia. While in the U.S. Army he had served on the Plains and in the Utah expedition. In the Confederate service he was appointed Captain of artillery and was brigade adjutant during the Cheat Mountain campaign in West Virginia in 1861. He was wounded in both legs at Allegheny Summit in December 1861, but recovered in time to become Colonel and chief of artillery to the corps of General T.H. Holmes in the Peninsula campaign. Deshler accompanied Holmes to the Trans-Mississippi Department in July 1862 as chief of staff. Subsequently, he took command of a brigade under Thomas Churchill at Arkansas Post. When Churchill surrendered on 11 January 1863, Deshler became a prisoner and was not exchanged until June. He was promoted Brigadier General CSA on 28 July 1863 and assigned to command a brigade in the Army of Tennessee. At Chickamauga, on 20 September 1863, he was killed by a shell while inspecting his troops before resuming the Confederate assault.

Cullum; Boatner, *Civil War*; Warner, *Generals in Gray*; Connelly, *Autumn of Glory*; *B&L*, Vol. 3; *CMH*, Vol. VII (Alabama).

DILLARD, John Albert Broadus, Jr., 1919–1970, Illinois, U.S. Army, killed in action 12 May 1970 near Pleiku, Vietnam.

John A.B. Dillard was the highest-ranking general of combat support branches killed in action in the history of the U.S. Army. Born in East St. Louis, he graduated from Virginia Military Institute in 1942 and immediately entered on active duty in the army. He was a platoon leader and company commander in Europe in World War II and was wounded in 1945. Promoted Major in 1950, Dillard was a battalion operations officer in Korea, attended the Command and General Staff College, and obtained a master's degree from New York University in 1955. Dillard was promoted Lieutenant Colonel the same year and later commanded an engineer battalion in Hawaii. He attended the Air War College, directed military construction projects, and served on the Joint Staff at the Pentagon. Dillard was promoted Colonel in 1962 and spent five years, from 1963 to 1968, as district engineer at Los Angeles and Pacific Division engineer at San Francisco. He became Brigadier General on 27 October 1966. In June 1968 he went to Korea as chief engineer of U.S. forces and he went directly from there to Vietnam in November 1969 as commander of engineer troops. Dillard was promoted Major General on 1 April 1970. On 12 May 1970, while flying in a helicopter near Pleiku with Carroll "Hap" Adams, Dillard's ship was hit by enemy ground fire, crashed, and burned. Both Dillard and Adams perished in the crash.

Army Register, 1970; The Army Library; *New York Times*, May 14, 1970; *San Francisco Examiner*, November 28, 1966; March 1, 1967; May 14, 16, 17, 18, 1970; Military Service Record.

DOLES, George Pierce, 1830–1864, Georgia, C.S. Army, killed in action 2 June 1864 at Bethesda Church, Virginia.

Considered to be one of the best non-professional generals of the Army of Northern Virginia, George Doles was born at Milledgeville, then the capital of the state. He was educated locally and embarked on a commercial career. He also served as Captain of a militia company which he brought into the 4th Georgia in 1861. The regiment was stationed at Norfolk, Virginia, in the early part of the war. Doles was elected Colonel in May 1862, and took the 4th to the Army of Northern Virginia that summer. He fought at South Mountain, where he narrowly escaped the capture of most of his regiment, and at Antietam. He was promoted Brigadier General CSA on 1 November 1862 and led a Georgia brigade at Fredericksburg and Chancellorsville, where he was cited for extreme gallantry. At Gettysburg, Doles was again almost captured when his horse bolted for the Union lines, but he was saved by falling off. Doles commanded his brigade in the Wilderness and bore the brunt of the 10 May 1864 Union attack on the Mule Shoe or Bloody Angle at

Spotsylvania. On 2 June 1864, at Bethesda Church, he was killed by a sniper while supervising the entrenchment of his lines.

Boatner, *Civil War*; Warner, *Generals in Gray*; D.S. Freeman, *Lee's Lieutenants*, Vols. 2 & 3; *B&L*, Vol 4; *CMH*, Vol. VI.

DUNOVANT, John, 1825–1864, South Carolina, C.S. Army, killed in action 1 October 1864 near Petersburg, Virginia.

John Dunovant's was one of the most peculiar general officer appointments in the Confederate States Army. A native of Chester, he was a Sergeant in the Palmetto Regiment during the Mexican War. He was commissioned Captain in the newly formed 10th U.S. Infantry Regiment in 1855. In December 1860 Dunovant resigned his U.S. commission when South Carolina seceded from the Union. He was made Major of South Carolina militia and then Colonel of the 1st South Carolina Regulars. In garrison near Charleston for over a year, Dunovant was cashiered for drunkenness in June 1862 and dismissed from the service with the endorsement of President Jefferson Davis. Before the end of the year he was appointed Colonel of the 5th South Carolina Cavalry by the governor. In May 1864 his regiment went to Virginia with Matthew Butler's South Carolina cavalry brigade. When Butler was promoted to division command, on the recommendation of President Davis, Dunovant was given the brigade and promoted to Brigadier General CSA on 22 August 1864. After the Confederate loss of Fort Harrison in September, Dunovant was killed in action along the Vaughn Road south of the James River on 1 October 1864.

Boatner, *Civil War*; Warner, *Generals in Gray*; *CMH*, Vol. V.

DUTTON, Arthur Henry, 1838–1864, Connecticut, U.S. Volunteers, died 5 June 1864 of wounds received 26 May 1864 at Bermuda Hundred, Virginia.

A young, professional officer who rose from 2nd Lieutenant to brigade commander in only two years, Arthur Dutton graduated from West Point in the Class of June 1861 (accelerated). He was commissioned in the Corps of Engineers and joined the staff of the commander of the Department of Washington. In September 1862 he was appointed Colonel of the 21st Connecticut, which joined the Army of the Potomac in IX Corps. Later he went to North Carolina, where he commanded a brigade in IX Corps, was chief of staff of the District of North Carolina, and was on the staff of the Department commander. In May 1864 Dutton commanded a brigade in XVIII Corps in the advance of Ben Butler's army from Fort Monroe to Petersburg. At Bermuda Hundred, on 26 May 1864, he led his brigade on a reconnaissance when they came upon a well-hidden Confederate entrenchment. Dutton, who was in the skirmish line, was mortally wounded. He was carried to Baltimore, where he died on 5 June. He was posthumously breveted Brigadier General USV to rank from 16 May 1864 for action at Drewry's Bluff ten days before Bermuda Hundred.

Cullum; Boatner, *Civil War*; *Twentieth Century*; *OR*, Ser. I, Vols. 18; 36, pt. 1; 51, pt. 1.

E

EASLEY, Claudius Miller, 1891–1945, Texas, U.S. Army, killed in action 19 June 1945 on Okinawa.

Noted in the pre-World War II army as a rifle and pistol shooting champion, Claudius M. Easley was born at Thorpe Springs and graduated from Texas Agricultural & Mechanical College in 1912. He served on the Mexican border with the Texas National Guard in 1916–1917, and then entered the regular army as 1st Lieutenant in August 1917. He remained on the border with the 37th Infantry Regiment for the duration of World War I. Promoted Captain in 1920, Easley devoted much of his time over the next twenty years to improving rifle and pistol shooting in the army. In 1938 he was captain of the Infantry pistol and rifle teams, both of which were national champions that year. On normal troop duty, he served principally with the 37th and 4th Infantry in the United States. He also spent three years in the Philippines with the 31st Infantry. Easley was promoted Major in 1930 and Lieutenant Colonel in 1939. He commanded the Civilian Conservation Corps district at Los Angeles for two years and was a graduate of both the Command and General Staff course and the Army War College. From 1940 to 1942 he was assigned to the Supply Division of the War Department General Staff. He became Colonel in December 1941 and was sent to Louisiana in February 1942 to command the 325th Infantry Regiment of the 82nd Division. On 27 July 1942, Easley was promoted Brigadier General USA and in August was assigned as assistant commander of the 96th Division. It was his leadership in marksmanship training which won for the division its nickname, the "Deadeyes." He went to the Pacific with the 96th, participated in the Leyte invasion in October 1944, where he was wounded, and went with his division to Okinawa in the spring of 1945. On 19 June 1945, while supervising operations in the closing phases of the battle, Easley crawled to the summit of a small hill to direct fire on a Japanese machine gun. As he peered over the crest, he was killed instantly by a shot through the head.

Army Register, 1942–1946; Belote; O. Davidson; Schnapper; *New York Times*, June 21, 1945.

EGBERT, Harry Clay, 1839–1899, Pennsylvania, U.S. Volunteers, killed in action 26 March 1899 at Malinta, Luzon, Philippine Islands.

Harry C. Egbert was one of two former volunteer general officers killed while commanding regiments in America's imperial wars in the Far East. Son of a Navy medical officer, he entered service as a 1st Lieutenant in the 12th Infantry Regiment in September 1861. He fought at Gaines's Mill and Malvern Hill on the Virginia Peninsula before being wounded and captured at Cedar Mountain in August 1862. After a brief stay at Libby Prison, he was exchanged. Egbert served in staff positions at Fredericksburg and throughout the campaigns of 1863. Returning to his regiment for the 1864 campaign, he was wounded again at Bethesda Church in June. In August 1864 he was breveted Captain for action at the North Anna River and Major for Bethesda Church. After recovering from his wound, he was assigned to provost marshal duties in Illinois from January to June 1865. He was promoted Captain in the 12th Infantry in April 1865. Egbert spent the next twenty-five years as a company officer in garrison and in Indian fighting, notably during the Nez Percé War of 1877 and the Wounded Knee campaign of 1890. In 1890 he became Major in the 17th Infantry and in 1893, Lieutenant Colonel of the 6th. He participated in the Santiago campaign in Cuba in 1898, and was wounded at El Caney on 1 July. He was retroactively promoted to be Colonel of the 22nd Infantry to date from 1 July. On 1 October 1898 Egbert was commissioned Brigadier General USV, but his appointment expired sixty days later. He was honorably discharged from the volunteer service on 1 December 1898. Assigned to the Philippines, he took his regiment there in March 1899. With barely time to disembark, the 22nd became involved in the chase of the Insurrectionists across Luzon. On 26 March 1899, as General Lloyd Wheaton's brigade engaged the entrenched rebels at Malinta, Egbert was shot in the abdomen. He was carried to the rear on a stretcher but died before he reached the aid station. His last words to Wheaton were, "I am too old; I must die."

Army Register, 1900; Heitman, *U.S. Army*; *Harper's*; *New York Times*, March 27, April 9 & 25, 1899; *OR*, Ser. I, Vols. 21; 27, pt. 1; Ser. III, Vol. 3.

ELLIOTT, Stephen, Jr., 1830–1866, South Carolina, C.S. Army, died 21 February 1866 of wounds received 30 July 1864 at Petersburg, Virginia, and 19 March 1865 at Bentonville, North Carolina.

Stephen Elliott was the last Confederate general officer combat fatality. Son of a clergyman, he was born in Beaufort, attended Harvard briefly, then graduated from South Carolina College in 1850. He was a successful planter and a noted yachtsman and fisherman, and served in the legislature. He was Captain of a militia artillery company and entered Confederate service at its head in 1861. Elliott remained in South Carolina until 1864, fighting at Port Royal in November 1861, Pocataligo in October 1862, and Fort Sumter in September 1863. Sent to Petersburg, Virginia, in May 1864 as Colonel of Holcomb's South Carolina Legion, he was promoted Brigadier General CSA on 24 May. In the trenches, he took command of a South Carolina brigade which was at the salient blown up by a Union mine at the battle of the Crater on 30 July. Elliott was shot through the body and his left arm paralyzed during the ensuing fighting. Invalided home, he recovered sufficiently to command coast defenses on James Island. Later he joined General Joseph Johnston's Army of Tennessee for the Carolinas campaign of 1865 and was wounded again at Bentonville, North Carolina, on 19 March. After the war, Elliott returned to Beaufort, where he eked out a living as a fisherman. He sat in the state legislature and ran unsuccessfully as a candidate for the U.S. Congress. He moved to Aiken and died there as a result of his wounds on 21 February 1866. His father was not the Episcopal bishop of Georgia, but another priest of the same name.

Boatner, *Civil War*; Warner, *Generals in Gray*; D.S. Freeman, *Lee's Lieutenants*, Vol. 3; *Twentieth Century Biographic Dictionary; B&L*, Vols. 1 & 4; *CMH*, Vol. V.

ELLIS, Augustus Van Horne, c. 1825–1863, New York, U.S. Volunteers, killed in action, 2 July 1863 at Gettysburg, Pennsylvania.

Noted for his ferocity in battle as well as for the crudeness of his language, A. Van Horne Ellis, as he was known, was the son of a doctor. He engaged in business in Orange County before the Civil War. With his five brothers, he enlisted in the 71st New York Militia in 1861 and fought at Bull Run, where he was cited for his actions. After the 71st was discharged, Ellis raised and became Colonel in September 1862 of the 124th New York. The first action of the 124th was at Fredericksburg, Virginia, where Ellis was once again singled out for mention of his coolness under fire. Serving in III Corps at Chancellorsville, the unit was involved in the desperate fighting of 3 May 1863 and won for themselves the nickname "Orange Blossoms" for their home county in New York. At Gettysburg the regiment went into action with only 238 men present for duty but withstood Confederate attacks all day on 2 July. So confident were they of their combat ability that the officers beseeched Ellis to allow them to counterattack. When he finally relented, the regiment advanced into a withering hail of musket fire and had to withdraw. Ellis moved forward on horseback, virtually alone, his figure obscured by smoke. He was seen to suddenly reel in the saddle and fall to the ground. His men made a desperate effort and managed to recover his body, which was found to be shot through the head. He was posthumously breveted Brigadier General USV to rank from the date of his death.

Boatner, *Civil War*; *New York at Gettysburg*; *OR*, Ser. I, Vols. 25, pt. 1; 27, pt. 1; Orange County (N.Y.) Historical Society.

ELSTNER, George Ruter, c. 1841–1864, Ohio, U.S. Volunteers, killed in action 8 August 1864 at Atlanta, Georgia.

George R. Elstner was another Union officer who never served above regimental level while alive, but who was recognized posthumously for his gallantry. A native of Cincinnati, he entered service as 1st Lieutenant and adjutant of the 50th Ohio in July 1862. The regiment joined the Army of the Ohio and Elstner was cited for his participation at Perryville, Kentucky, that October. He became Major in May 1863 and Lieutenant Colonel on 1 July 1863. With his regiment, he formed part of Ambrose Burnside's Army of the Ohio during the Chattanooga and Knoxville campaigns of late 1863. During the advance on Atlanta in the spring of 1864, Elstner led the regiment while its Colonel commanded the brigade. On 8 August 1864, in front of Atlanta, in a position south of Utoy Creek, the 50th Ohio repelled three Confederate cavalry charges and then advanced as skirmishers against the enemy rifle pits. Elstner was killed instantly by a bullet through the brain while at the head of his troops. He was posthumously breveted Brigadier General USV to rank from the date of his death.

Boatner, *Civil War*; *OR*, Ser. I, Vols. 16, pt. 1; 45, pts. 1 & 2; Military Service Record.

F

FARNSWORTH, Elon John, 1837–1863, Michigan–Illinois, U.S. Volunteers, killed in action 3 July 1863 at Gettysburg, Pennsylvania.

Elon J. Farnsworth was one of three young volunteer officers spot-promoted to Brigadier General rank on the eve of the battle of Gettysburg. The other two, George Custer and Wesley Merritt, went on to greater fame and glory. Farnsworth was killed four days later. Born in Michigan, Farnsworth accompanied his family to Illinois when he was seventeen but returned to the University of Michigan for his education. Expelled from school because of a student prank, he joined the Utah expedition of 1857 as a civilian foragemaster and remained in the West until 1861. When the Civil War began, he returned to join the 8th Illinois Cavalry being raised by his uncle and was commissioned Lieutenant in September 1861. Over the next twenty-two months he participated in forty-one separate engagements, never missing one of his regiment's actions. Promoted Captain in December 1861, he was also acting quartermaster of IV Corps on the Virginia Peninsula. When the Cavalry Corps of the Army of the Potomac was organized in the spring of 1863, Farnsworth was appointed aide to its commander, Alfred Pleasanton. That June, George Meade, the Army commander, asked Pleasanton to recommend some young officers for promotion. Pleasanton selected Custer, Farnsworth, and Merritt. Meade forwarded their names to the War Department for promotion, but also gave them battlefield promotions to Brigadier General USV to rank from 29 June 1863. Pleasanton divided up his own rank insignia for the three young men and Farnsworth received a single one-star shoulder strap to wear. During the first two days at Gettysburg, he led his brigade in skirmishes with the Confederate cavalry. On 3 July, he was foolishly ordered by his division commander, Judson Kilpatrick, to charge Confederate infantry over broken ground. Against his own better judgement, Farnsworth did so at the head of the 1st Vermont Cavalry. Only 15 of the 300 men who started the charge made it to their objective. Farnsworth was one of these but he fell with five mortal wounds in front of the lines of the 15th Alabama. He was posthumously confirmed in his final rank.

DAB; Boatner, *Civil War*; Warner, *Generals in Blue*; Starr, Vol. 1; Coddington; *B&L*, Vol. 3.

FORREST, Nathan Bedford, 1905–1943, Tennessee–Georgia, U.S. Army Air Force, missing in action, declared dead 13 June 1943 over Kiel, Germany.

Nathan Bedford Forrest was the great-grandson of the Confederate cavalry leader of the same name, and was the first American general killed in action in Europe in World War II. The younger Forrest was born in Memphis, son of a leader of the United Confederate Veterans and of the Ku Klux Klan. As a teenager he moved with his family to Atlanta. After high school he graduated from West Point in 1928. He was assigned to the cavalry but within two months transferred to the Air Corps, took flight training, and joined a pursuit squadron. Forrest served in Panama from 1931 to 1934, was assigned to the Civilian Conservation Corps in Los Angeles, and later was an air group staff officer. Made Captain in 1935 and Major in 1941, he commanded the 5th Bomb Wing (later 2nd Bomber Command), despite his junior rank, from February 1941 to February 1942. During this time he spent two months in London with the Royal Air Force and was there when the United States declared war on Germany. Forrest returned to the United States and was promoted Lieutenant Colonel in January and Colonel in March 1942. He was successively operations officer and chief of staff of the 2nd Air Force from February 1942. He was promoted Brigadier General on 1 November 1942. Returning to England as an observer in June 1943, in preparation for taking over a command there, Forrest began flying missions with the 402nd Provisional Bomb Wing. On 13 June 1943, flying in the lead B-17 of a daylight raid over Kiel, Forrest's plane was attacked by six German fighters and went down in flames. Because parachutes were seen descending from the burning aircraft some hope was held for his survival, and he was listed as missing in action. He was finally declared dead on 14 June 1944.

Army Register, 1943; Cullum, Vols. 7–9; R. Freeman; *New York Times*, March 13, 1931; June 26, September 16, 1943; *Newsweek*, July 5, 1943; Military Service Record.

FORT, Guy Osborne, 1879–1942, Michigan–New York, Philippine Army, executed by the Japanese 9 (or 13) November 1942 at Dansalan, Mindanao, Philippine Islands.

Guy O. Fort has the distinction of being the only American-born general officer executed by the enemy, although not the only one to die in enemy hands, nor the only one in U.S. service to have been executed. He was born in Keelersville and enlisted in the 4th U.S. Cavalry in 1899. He served for almost three years in the Philippines, took his discharge there in 1902, and in 1904 accepted a commission as 3rd Lieutenant in the Philippine Constabulary, the national police force. He had progressed through the grades to Major by 1917 when he resigned. Fort spent the next four years as a plantation manager on Mindanao, but was recommissioned a 3rd Lieutenant in 1921. Again he climbed the promotion ladder, reaching Colonel in 1929. He was noted for his study and observance of native rituals and customs, and was extremely successful in "talking in" outlaw bands. Fort continued in the Constabulary until November 1941, when he was sent to Bohol to activate and take command of the 81st Division, Philippine Army. On 17 November the division was inducted into the U.S. Armed Forces, Far East, and on 20 December 1941 Fort was appointed Brigadier General, Philippine Army. He took his division to Mindanao in January 1942 and recruited several native battalions to strengthen it. In April 1942 the division was redesignated Lanao Force. Fort commanded the division in action against better organized and better equipped Japanese forces from 29 April until he was ordered to surrender, under protest, on 27 May 1942. Taken to Manila as a prisoner, he was returned to Lanao by his captors in November to persuade the guerrillas to stop resisting the occupation. Fort refused to cooperate and was executed by firing squad in Dansalan, Lanao Province, Mindanao, on 9 or 13 November 1942. Despite rumors to that effect, his fate was not actually determined until 1945.

SMS, Guy O. Fort; Chynoweth; Kuder; Records of the Adjutant General's Office (RG 407).

FRANCINE, Louis Raymond, 1837–1863, Pennsylvania–New Jersey, U.S. Volunteers, died 16 July 1863 of wounds received at Gettysburg, Pennsylvania, 2 July 1863.

More Gallic than American in his upbringing, Louis R. Francine, nevertheless, was another of the young American intellectuals who rallied to the Union cause in 1861. Son of a French immigrant descended from a noble family, Francine was born in Philadelphia but reared in Camden, New Jersey. In 1851 he was sent to Paris for his education and did not return to America until the outbreak of war in 1861. He raised a company of infantry in Cape May County, which became Company A, 7th New Jersey in September 1861, with Francine as Captain. The regiment immediately joined the Army of the Potomac organizing near Washington. The 7th went to the Virginia Peninsula in the spring of 1862 and was engaged at Williamsburg and elsewhere. Francine became Lieutenant Colonel in July 1862 and Colonel in December. Meanwhile, the 7th had been to Antietam and Fredericksburg. At Chancellorsville a curious incident occurred, in which Francine, thinking the brigade commander had been wounded, led the regiment off the field and then back again several hours later. The brigade commander was later court-martialed and dismissed from the service for his part in the incident but Francine went uncensured. During the battle, the 7th captured five stands of colors and over 300 prisoners, including the 2nd North Carolina *in toto*. Francine lost his voice in the din and, on his surgeon's advice, again retired from the field. At Gettysburg, on 2 July, the 7th New Jersey was detached from its parent brigade in III Corps and sent to support another brigade. Cast adrift, as it were, the regiment found itself outflanked on the left. Francine pushed his right forward and led a charge to get clear. He was cut down in the attempt. Carried from the field, he lived until 16 July. He was posthumously breveted Brigadier General USV to rank from 2 July 1863.

Boatner, *Civil War*; Coddington; Francine; *OR*, Ser. I, Vols. 25, pt. 1; 27, pt. 1; New Jersey State Library.

G

GARDINER, Alexander, 1833–1864, New York–New Hampshire, U.S. Volunteers, died 7 or 8 October 1864 of wounds received 19 September 1864 at Opequan Creek, Virginia.

Alexander Gardiner was unfortunate enough to be killed in the only battle in which he ever participated. Born in Catskill, he attended school in New Hampshire and then returned to New York City to study law and take up its practice. He spent two years in Kansas during the border troubles there, but returned to New Hampshire in 1859 to resume his law practice. In September 1862 Gardiner became Lieutenant and adjutant of the 14th New Hampshire. The regiment went to the defenses of Washington in April 1863 and to New Orleans in April 1864. In the interim Gardiner had been promoted directly to Major in September 1863. He was *de facto* commander of the 14th during most of its stay in Louisiana. In July 1864 XIX Corps, including the 14th New Hampshire, was transferred to Virginia for the Shenandoah Valley campaign. In September the Colonel was discharged and Gardiner was promoted to replace him, over the head of the Lieutenant Colonel. At Opequan Creek, on 19 September, in the 14th's first combat engagement, while rallying fugitives from other regiments around his colors, Gardiner was wounded in the leg and captured. When the Union army recovered its lost ground, he was recaptured about five hours later. Gardiner's leg was amputated to save his life, but he died on 7 or 8 October 1864. He was posthumously breveted Brigadier General USV to rank from 19 September.

Boatner, *Civil War*; Waite; *OR*, Ser. I, Vol. 43, pt. 1.

GARLAND, Samuel Jr., 1830–1862, Virginia C.S. Army, killed in action 14 September 1862 at South Mountain, Maryland.

Highly thought of in the Army of Northern Virginia by Robert E. Lee and others, Samuel Garland was born in Lynchburg, a collateral descendant of President James Madison. He graduated from Virginia Military Institute in 1849 and the University of Virginia law school in 1851. Following his father's profession he opened his own law practice in Lynchburg. After John Brown's raid in 1859 Garland organized the Lynchburg Home Guard militia company and as its Captain led it into Confederate service as part of the 11th Virginia in April 1861. The same month he was commissioned Colonel and led the 11th to Bull Run. Garland was commended for his action at Dranesville, Virginia, in December 1861. At Williamsburg in May 1862 he was wounded and had to give up regimental command, but remained on the field as a staff officer. He was promoted Brigadier General CSA on 23 May 1862 and led a brigade for the rest of the Peninsula campaign and at Second Manassas. At South Mountain, Maryland, on 14 September 1862, Garland's brigade was posted at Fox's Gap to delay the advance of McClellan's army as it pursued Lee's forces into Maryland. Despite pleas from his subordinate commanders to go to a place of greater safety, Garland remained on the regimental lines. He was mortally wounded by the side of one of his colonels and died within a few hours.

Boatner, *Civil War*; Warner, *Generals in Gray*; D.S. Freeman, *Lee's Lieutenants*, Vols. 1 & 2; *CMH*, Vol III.

GARNETT, Richard Brooke, 1817–1863, Virginia, C.S. Army, killed in action 3 July 1863 at Gettysburg, Pennsylvania.

Richard B. Garnett, son of a Tidewater family, was born in Essex County and graduated from West Point in the same class with his first cousin, Robert S. Garnett, in 1841. He served in Florida and the West, and was at New Orleans during the Mexican War. He continued in frontier service until he resigned his Captain's commission in May 1861 to be appointed Major of Confederate artillery. On 14 November 1861 he was promoted Brigadier General CSA and given command of the famed Stonewall Brigade under the stern eye of its former commander, Thomas J. Jackson. At Kernstown, Virginia, on 23 March 1862, Garnett withdrew his brigade in the face of superior Union forces and incurred the wrath of Jackson by doing so. He was relieved of command and arrested, and charges were preferred against him. Jackson also banned Garnett from ever serving under him again. The ensuing court-martial, in August 1862, was interrupted for the battle of Cedar Mountain and never reconvened. Garnett was released from arrest and given George Pickett's old brigade in Longstreet's Corps. He fought at Antietam and Fredericksburg and went to southside Virginia in the spring of 1863 with Longstreet. At Gettysburg, on 3 July 1863, Garnett led his brigade in the front line of Pickett's charge. Too ill to walk, he was conspicuous on horseback. As his command approached the Union line he disappeared into the pall of powder smoke which hung over the line. A few minutes later his riderless horse came galloping back. Garnett's body was never identified from among the other dead. Several years after the war his sword was discovered in a Baltimore pawn shop.

Cullum; Boatner, *Civil War*; Warner, *Generals in Gray*; D.S. Freeman, *Lee's Lieutenants*, Vols. 1–3; Coddington; *B&L*, Vol. 3; *CMH*, Vol III.

GARNETT, Robert Selden, 1819–1861, Virginia, C.S. Army, killed in action 13 July 1861 at Carrick's Ford, Virginia.

Robert S. Garnett was the first general on either side killed in action in the Civil War. Like his first cousin, Richard S. Garnett, he was born in Essex County and graduated from West Point in 1841. Robert Garnett was an instructor at the Military Academy, aide to Generals Wool and Taylor in the Mexican War, and won two brevets for gallantry. He fought Indians in Texas and the Pacific Northwest and was Major, 9th U.S. Infantry when he resigned his commission in April 1861. His first appointment was Colonel and Adjutant General of the Virginia state troops under General R.E. Lee. On 13 June 1861 Garnett was promoted Brigadier General CSA, the highest rank in the Confederacy at that time, and assumed command on the northwest Virginia front. His mission was to repel the Union advance from Ohio under McClellan and Rosecrans. Forced by superior numbers to evacuate his positions, he withdrew through the mountains toward the Cheat River. The weather was bad but Garnett was determined to save his supply trains. At Carrick's Ford, on 13 July 1861, he personally commanded a small force holding the river crossing while awaiting the arrival of reinforcements. Garnett was shot in the back from across the river as he turned to see if the expected support troops were on the way. He fell from his horse and died as the Union forces crossed. His body was captured but was eventually returned to the Confederate side. Strangely enough, he was buried in Brooklyn, New York.

DAB; Cullum; Boatner, *Civil War*; Warner, *Generals in Gray*; D.S. Freeman, *Lee's Lieutenants*, Vol. 1; *B&L*, Vol. 1; *CMH*, Vol. III.

GARROTT, Isham Warren, 1816–1863, North Carolina–Alabama, C.S. Army, killed in action 17 June 1863 at Vicksburg, Mississippi.

One of the few Confederate generals to be promoted after his death, Isham Garrott was born in Wake or Anson County. He graduated from the University of North Carolina, studied law, and moved to Alabama. There he practiced law, served in the state legislature, and supported states rights. He was an elector for the Southern Democratic ticket in 1860 and was Alabama's commissioner to North Carolina to urge his native state's secession. Garrott raised and became Colonel of the 20th Alabama in 1861. He was on garrison duty at Mobile and then in eastern Tennessee until the spring of 1863. When reinforcements were collected from all over the South to go to Vicksburg, the 20th Alabama, as part of Edward Tracy's brigade, was among those sent. Tracy was killed at Port Gibson on 1 May 1863 and Garrott took over the brigade. He remained in command during the battle of Champion's Hill and the withdrawal of Pemberton's army into the city of Vicksburg. On 17 June 1863, while inspecting an outpost, Garrott borrowed a rifle from a soldier to fire at the opposing picket line. As he raised his head above the parapet he was killed by a Union sharpshooter. Garrott's commission as Brigadier General CSA to rank from 28 May 1863 was received at army headquarters after his death.

Boatner, *Civil War*; Warner, *Generals in Gray*; *CMH*, Vol. VII (Alabama).

GIBBONS, Lloyd Henry, 1895-1945, Illinois-Missouri, U.S. Army, killed in action 5 April 1945 at Kassel, Germany.

Lloyd H. Gibbons was another officer whose formal promotion to general was approved only after his death. Born in Jacksonville, he was living in Missouri when he enlisted as a private at Fort Riley in August 1917. He was subsequently Sergeant and Battalion Sergeant Major in the 353rd Infantry Regiment, 89th Division. He was commissioned in the regular army in June 1918 and assigned to the 9th Division, which saw no overseas service in World War I. After the war Gibbons spent four years on recruiting duty in New York and then five years with a troop unit in Hawaii. Promoted Captain in 1932, he was an ROTC instructor at Georgia Institute of Technology from 1930 to 1936. This was followed by two years in the Philippines, attendance at the Command and General Staff school, and promotion to Major in 1939. Gibbons was assigned to the 28th Infantry and served with the regiment in the 1st and 8th Divisions. Made Lieutenant Colonel in June 1941, he was an instructor at the Infantry and Artillery Schools until August 1943. Gibbons became Colonel in June 1942; he was assigned to an Army Ground Forces staff position from August 1943 to August 1944. This was followed by his posting as assistant commander of the 69th Division at Camp Shelby, Mississippi. Gibbons went to France with the division in October 1944 and went into action in December. By 5 April 1945, they had moved into Kassel, Germany. Gibbons was killed that day when his jeep hit a land mine while he was directing the Werra River crossing north of the city. On 11 April he was posthumously confirmed as Brigadier General USA to rank from 30 March 1945.

Army Register, 1942-1946; *69th Division*; Records of the Adjutant General's Office (RG 407); Colonel Gordon D. Ingraham (69th Division G-4) to the author, October 16, 1973.

GIESY, Henry H., c. 1836-1864, Ohio, U.S. Volunteers, killed in action 28 May 1864 at Dallas, Georgia.

Virtually nothing is known about the early life of Henry Giesy, not even his middle name. He was a native of Lancaster and a practicing attorney when the Civil War began. He was commissioned Captain in the 17th Ohio, a three-month regiment, in April 1861. He was mustered out in August and reentered service as a 2nd Lieutenant in the 46th Ohio in October. He was promoted Captain in December. The regiment was at Shiloh in Sherman's division and subsequently served in all of the battles of the Army of the Tennessee. Giesy was promoted Major in September 1862 and was with the regiment at Vicksburg and Jackson, Mississippi. From October 1863 to January 1864 he was provost marshal of the 4th Division, XV Corps. For the spring campaign of 1864 in Georgia he had command of the regiment while the colonel, C.C. Walcutt, was commanding the brigade. At Dallas, or New Hope Church, on 28 May 1864, a Confederate assault was made on the lines of XV Corps. Walcutt's brigade was attacked by Armstrong's dismounted cavalry along the Villa Rica road. The attack was beaten back with almost 300 casualties, but Giesy was killed at the head of his regiment. He was posthumously breveted Brigadier General USV to rank from the date of his death.

Boatner, *Civil War*; *OR*, Ser. I, Vol. 38, pt. 3; *B&L*, Vol. 4; Military Service Record.

GIRARDEY, Victor Jean Baptiste, 1837–1864, France–Georgia, C.S. Army, killed in action 16 August 1864 at Deep Bottom, Virginia.

Victor Girardey had the distinction of being the only officer in Confederate service advanced from company grade to general officer in a single promotion. He was born in the Department of Haut-Rhin and at the age of five was brought to Augusta, Georgia, with his family. Orphaned when he was sixteen he completed his education in New Orleans and married there. He entered the C.S. Army from Louisiana as 1st Lieutenant in October 1861, but was credited to Georgia. In June 1862 he became Captain and assistant adjutant general to General Ambrose R. "Rans" Wright of Georgia. Girardey remained with Wright through all of the battles of the Army of Northern Virginia for the next two years. On 21 May 1864 he was transferred to the divisional staff of General William Mahone in the same capacity he had served Wright so well. Rendering the same excellence of service, his arrangements for the Confederate counterattack at the battle of the Crater at Petersburg on 30 July 1864 were notable. When Wright became ill and a successor was needed for his brigade, Generals Lee and Mahone had no hesitation in recommending Girardey. On 3 August 1864 he was promoted Brigadier General CSA to rank from 30 July. Less than two weeks later, on 16 August, he was killed while resisting the advance of the Union II Corps at Deep Bottom.

Boatner, *Civil War*; Warner, *Generals in Gray*; D.S. Freeman, *Lee's Lieutenants*, Vol. 3; *CMH*, Vol. VI.

GIST, States Rights, 1831–1864, South Carolina, C.S. Army, killed in action 30 November 1864 at Franklin, Tennessee.

This peculiarly named officer was one of six Confederate generals killed or mortally wounded in the abortive battle at Franklin. He was born in the Union District during the nullification crisis, hence his name. He attended South Carolina College and Harvard law school before opening his own legal practice. Always active in militia affairs, he was made Brigadier General in 1859, and Adjutant and Inspector General after secession. He accompanied Barnard Bee to Bull Run as a volunteer aide in July 1861 and after the latter's death assumed command of the brigade, although still a state officer. He returned to his duties in South Carolina until appointed Brigadier General CSA on 20 March 1862. He commanded a brigade on coast defense duty around Charleston until May 1863. At that time his brigade and that of General W.H.T. Walker were sent to Mississippi to aid in the relief of Vicksburg. Gist fought under Walker's command at Jackson, Mississippi, in July 1863 and at Chickamauga in September. He led Walker's division at Chattanooga and served under him again for the Atlanta campaign in the spring of 1864. He was assigned to General John Brown's division for Hood's invasion of Tennessee. At Franklin, On 30 November, Gist was encouraging his men to advance against the Union defenses when his horse was shot from under him. Continuing on foot, he was shot in the chest and killed. Every one of the five generals in Brown's division was a casualty: three killed, one wounded, and one captured.

Boatner, *Civil War*; Warner, *Generals in Gray*; D.S. Freeman, *Lee's Lieutenants*, Vol. 1; McDonough and Connelly; *B&L*, Vols. 1, 3, 4; *CMH*, Vol. V.

GLADDEN, Adley Hogan, 1810–1862, South Carolina–Louisiana, C.S. Army, died 12 April 1862 of wounds received 6 April 1862 at Shiloh, Tennessee.

Relatively old compared with many of his Civil War colleagues, Adley H. Gladden was born in the Fairfield District and became a cotton broker early in life. He served as a volunteer in the Seminole War and was appointed postmaster of Columbia by President Tyler. He distinguished himself as Major and Lieutenant Colonel of the Palmetto Regiment in the Mexican War and was seriously wounded in the assault on Mexico City. After the war he settled in New Orleans. In 1861 he was offered the lieutenant colonelcy of the 1st South Carolina but chose to be a delegate to the Louisiana secession convention. Gladden became Colonel of the 1st Louisiana Regulars and joined Braxton Bragg in his siege of Pensacola. He was promoted Brigadier General CSA on 30 September 1861. In the spring of 1862 Gladden's brigade was part of the reinforcement Bragg took to Albert Sidney Johnston's army at Corinth, Mississippi. On the first day at Shiloh, 6 April 1862, Gladden was wounded by a shell fragment and his arm was amputated in a field hospital. He was evacuated to Corinth, where he died on 12 April.

Boatner, *Civil War*; Warner, *Generals in Gray*; Connelly, *Army of the Heartland*; *B&L*, Vol. 1; *CMH*, Vol. X (Louisiana).

GODWIN, Archibald Campbell, 1831–1864, Virginia–North Carolina, C.S. Army, killed in action 19 September 1864 at Winchester, Virginia.

Archibald Godwin was one of those people who is good at whatever he turns his hand to. A native of Nansemond County, he was reared by his grandmother and went to California when he was nineteen. A successful miner and rancher, he entered politics and was narrowly defeated for the Democratic nomination for governor in 1860. Returning to the East, he was engaged in business in

North Carolina in 1861. He was commissioned Major in the C.S. Army and was made assistant provost marshal for Libby Prison in Richmond. Later he organized the prison compound at Salisbury, North Carolina. In 1862 he became Colonel of the 57th North Carolina. Godwin's regiment was in garrison at Richmond and then fought at Fredericksburg and Chancellorsville. Godwin commanded Robert Hoke's brigade at Gettysburg and at Rappahannock Station in November 1863, where he was forcibly captured while organizing a last ditch resistance. When he was exchanged he was promoted Brigadier General CSA on 5 August 1864 and made permanent commander of Hoke's old brigade. Six weeks later, while with Ramseur's division at Winchester, Virginia, he was killed on 19 September by a shell fragment.

Boatner, *Civil War*; Warner, *Generals in Gray*; D.S. Freeman, *Lee's Lieutenants*, Vol. 3; *B&L*, Vol. 4; *CMH*, Vol. IV.

GORDON, James Byron, 1822–1864, North Carolina, C.S. Army, died 18 May 1864 of wounds received 12 May 1864 at Meadow Bridge, Virginia.

A cavalry officer who was engaged in all the battles of the Army of Northern Virginia until his death, James B. Gordon was born in Wilkesboro. He was educated at Emory and Henry College in Virginia and became a farmer, businessman, and state legislator. In 1861 he enlisted in a state guard company and was soon elected Captain. In May 1861 he was appointed Major of the 1st North Carolina Cavalry. His regiment had their first encounter with Union troops in Virginia in November 1861. In the spring of 1862 Gordon was promoted Lieutenant Colonel of Hampton's South Carolina Legion and became Colonel of the 1st North Carolina Cavalry in the spring of 1863. He became Brigadier General CSA on 28 September 1863. Leading the North Carolina Cavalry Brigade through the fall of 1863 and spring of 1864, Gordon participated in many engagements and was wounded in October 1863. At the opening of the spring campaign of 1864 his brigade was the first force to meet the Union advance into the Wilderness. Gordon was mortally wounded at Meadow Bridge, Virginia, on 12 May 1864, one day after the fight at Yellow Tavern. He was carried to Richmond, where he died on 18 May.

Boatner, *Civil War*; Warner, *Generals in Gray*; D.S. Freeman, *Lee's Lieutenants*, Vol. 3; *B&L*, Vol. 4; *CMH*, Vol. IV.

GOWEN, George Washington, c. 1840–1865, Pennsylvania, U.S. Volunteers, killed in action 2 April 1865 at Petersburg, Virginia.

George W. Gowen's contribution to the Civil War came as much through his engineering skills as through his leadership. A civil engineer before the war, he entered service as 1st Lieutenant of the 48th Pennsylvania, a regiment of coal miners which later dug the tunnel for the Petersburg mine. The 48th was sent to Fort Monroe, Virginia, went on to Burnside's North Carolina expedition in 1861, where Gowen was commended, and then returned to the Army of the Potomac as part of IX Corps. Gowen was present at Antietam and Fredericksburg, having been promoted Captain in September 1862. He went west with IX Corps in the spring of 1863 and fought at Vicksburg, Mississippi, and Knoxville, Tennessee. Gowen was cited for his work on repairing and upgrading the railroads of East Tennessee and became assistant engineer officer for IX Corps in September 1863. He was made aide to the IX Corps commander in August 1864, and in December became Lieutenant Colonel of the 48th. Gowen was promoted Colonel and returned to command of the regiment on 1 March 1865. At Petersburg, on 2 April 1865, while leading an assault on Fort Mahone, Gowen was struck in the face by a shell and killed instantly. He was posthumously breveted Brigadier General USV to rank from 2 April 1865. Gowen is indexed in *Official Records* as "Gowan."

Boatner, *Civil War*; Gould; *OR*, Ser. I, Vols. 9; 42, pt. 2; 46; pts. 1 & 3; 51, pt. 1; Pennsylvania Historical and Museum Commission.

GRACIE, Archibald, Jr., 1832–1864, New York–Alabama, C.S. Army, killed in action 2 December 1864 at Petersburg, Virginia.

Archibald Gracie was a Northerner whose southern residence and commercial interests led him to join the Confederacy in the Civil War. He was born in New York City to a prominent family and was educated in Germany. Later he entered West Point and graduated in 1854. He served on the frontier for two years before resigning his commission to go into business with his father in Mobile. He was also active in the militia and in 1861 was Captain of the company which seized the U.S. Arsenal at Mount Vernon, Alabama. In July 1861 Gracie became Major of the 11th Alabama, and in the spring of 1862, Colonel of the 43rd Alabama. Gracie served in eastern Tennessee and in Kentucky under General Edmund Kirby Smith and was promoted to Brigadier General on 4 November 1862. He commanded a brigade at Chickamauga in September 1863 and was wounded at Bean's Station, Tennessee, in December 1863, after the siege of Knoxville. Moving to the eastern theater, Gracie's brigade garrisoned Richmond at the beginning of the campaign of 1864. Gracie was at Drewry's Bluff during Ben Butler's advance on Petersburg in May 1864, and then in the Petersburg defenses. He was killed in the trenches by an exploding shell while observing the Union forces through a telescope on 2 December 1864. It was the day after his thirty-second birthday. Despite his southern sympathies Gracie remained on good terms with his father throughout the war. The family home in New York is now the official residence of the city's mayor.

DAB; Cullum; Boatner, *Civil War*; Warner, *Generals in Gray*; *B&L*, Vols. 3 & 4; *CMH*, Vol. VII (Alabama).

GRANBURY, Hiram Bronson, 1831–1864, Mississippi–Texas, C.S. Army, killed in action 30 November 1864 at Franklin, Tennessee.

Hiram Granbury was one of six Confederate generals killed or mortally wounded at the disastrous battle of Franklin, Tennessee. He was a native of Copiah County and attended Oakland College. Later he went to Waco, where he practiced law and engaged in county politics. In 1861 he raised a company of infantry in Waco and was its Captain when it became part of the 7th Texas. In October 1861 he became Major of the regiment under Colonel John Gregg. Granbury was captured at Fort Donelson, Tennessee, in February 1862, was exchanged, and then succeeded Gregg as Colonel. Throughout 1863 he commanded the 7th at Raymond and Jackson, Mississippi, at Chickamauga, and at Chattanooga, where he succeeded to a brigade command. He was commended by General Patrick Cleburne for his role in the retreat from Tennessee and was promoted Brigadier General CSA on 29 February 1864. Granbury commanded the Texas brigade of the Army of Tennessee during the Atlanta campaign of 1864 and during John Bell Hood's abortive invasion of Tennessee that fall. In the attack on the Union positions at Franklin on 30 November, several Confederate brigades were trapped in a crossfire in a ditch in front of the Northern lines. Granbury was killed in the hand-to-hand fighting which took place there.

Boatner, *Civil War*; Warner, *Generals in Gray*; McDonough and Connelly; *B&L*, Vol. 4; *CMH*, Vol. XI.

GRAVES, Davis Dunbar 1903–1944, New York, U.S. Army Air Force, missing in action, declared dead 8 February 1944 at San Stefano, Italy.

Davis D. Graves was the only Army Air Force general killed in World War II who was not associated with strategic bombing. Born in Buffalo, he graduated from Stanford University in 1927 and became a Flight Cadet in the Air Corps Reserve. He entered active duty as a 2nd Lieutenant in 1929 and remained in the 95th Pursuit Squadron until 1933. Promoted 1st Lieutenant in 1934 and Captain in 1935, Graves spent two years in Panama, followed by three years at Bolling Field in Washington, D.C., on the base staff. From 1939 to 1941 he was operations and intelligence officer of an air group. In March 1941 Graves was promoted to Major, and in January 1942 he was made Lieutenant Colonel and commander of the 56th Pursuit Group. In June 1942 he took over the New York Air Defense Wing of the First Air Force, charged with the air defenses of the Greater New York area. He was promoted Colonel in August 1942, and in December given command of the 2nd Air Defense Wing. Graves went with his wing to North Africa in January 1943 to provide air base defense for the Twelfth Air Force during the Tunisian and Mediterranean campaigns. In August 1943 his unit was redesignated the 63rd Fighter Wing and he was concurrently named Air Commander, Corsica. Graves was promoted Brigadier General USA on 21 January 1944. On 8 February 1944 Graves piloted one of a flight of eight B-25s of the 310th Bomb Group on a raid on enemy shipping at San Stefano. His plane was hit by enemy ground fire, went into the sea, and sank. No survivors were located despite frantic searches and Graves was listed as missing in action. He was declared dead on 9 February 1945.

Army Register, 1944–1945; *New York Times*, March 10 & 12, 1944; Records of the Adjutant General's Office (RG 407); Military Service Record.

GREEN, Martin Edwin, 1815–1863, Virginia–Missouri, C.S. Army, killed in action 25 June 1863 at Vicksburg, Mississippi.

Martin E. Green was one of several secession leaders in Missouri who fought to take their state out of the Union and later became generals in the Confederate States Army. He was born in Fauquier County, Virginia, but emigrated to Missouri as a young man and opened a sawmill in the northeastern part of the state. At the opening of the Civil War he raised a cavalry command from among Southern sympathizers and brought it into the Missouri State Guard as "Green's Missouri Cavalry Regiment." He joined Sterling Price's army right after the battle at Wilson's Creek and participated in the capture of Lexington in September 1861. He was appointed Brigadier General in the State Guard by Governor Jackson and led a nominal division at Pea Ridge, Arkansas, in March 1862. When the State Guard was dissolved in April 1862 Green accepted a commission as Colonel CSA and accompanied Price's Army of the West into Mississippi. He commanded a brigade under General Lewis Little at Iuka and succeeded that officer as division commander after Little was killed. Green had been promoted Brigadier General CSA on 21 July 1862 and commanded his division at the battle of Corinth in October 1862. During the Vicksburg campaign in 1862–1863 Green commanded a brigade in Bowen's division, fighting at Port Gibson and Vicksburg proper. He was slightly wounded on 25 June 1863 and was killed on 27 June when he was shot in the head while observing Union siege activities from his lines. His brother was a U.S. senator from Missouri.

Boatner, *Civil War*; Warner, *Generals in Gray*; Bevier; *B&L,* Vol. 1; *CMH*, Vol. IX (Missouri).

GREEN, Thomas, 1814–1864, Virginia–Texas, C.S. Army, killed in action 12 April 1864 at Blair's Landing, Louisiana.

Thomas Green suffered the curious fate of being killed in a duel between horse artillery and river gunboats. He was born in Amelia County, Virginia, and removed to Tennessee with his family when he was a child. His father became justice of the Tennessee Supreme Court. The younger Green graduated from the University of Nashville and took up law. He went to Texas in 1836 and fought under Sam Houston at San Jacinto. Green became clerk of the Texas Supreme Court and later was a Captain of Texas volunteers in the Mexican War. In August 1861 he became Colonel of the 5th Texas Cavalry and fought at Valverde, New Mexico, in February 1862 and at Galveston in January 1863. Green went to Louisiana and became Brigadier General CSA on 20 May 1863. He led a cavalry brigade at Lafourche, Fordoche, and Bayou Bourbeau. In the Red River campaign of 1864 Green's cavalry division was actively engaged at Mansfield and Pleasant Hill, Louisiana, with two of his brigades fighting as infantry. After Richard Taylor's Confederate army withdrew toward Arkansas, Green was left to watch the Union forces. On 12 April 1864, at Blair's Landing, Louisiana, Green's horse artillery batteries fired on Union gunboats and transports as they descended the Red River. He was killed by a shell of the return fire. Green had been recommended for Major General but was never promoted.

Boatner, *Civil War*; Warner, *Generals in Gray*; *B&L*, Vols. 3 & 4; *CMH*, Vol. XI.

GREEN, William N., Jr., 1843–1864, Massachusetts, U.S. Volunteers, died 14 May 1864 of wounds received 9 April 1864 at Pleasant Hill, Louisiana.

William N. Green was the youngest American general ever killed in combat. His pre-Civil War antecedents are vague. He was a student in Worcester when he enlisted in the 25th Massachusetts in September 1861. He accompanied the Burnside expedition to the North Carolina coast and was discharged at Roanoke in February 1862. He went to New York, where he was commissioned 2nd Lieutenant in the 102nd New York in March. He served in the Shenandoah Valley campaign of 1862 and was briefly Franz Siegel's aide. Green returned to his regiment in time to be captured at Cedar Mountain, Virginia, in August 1862, but not before he had personally captured a Confederate flag in that battle. He was paroled in September and returned to the 102nd as a Captain in December 1862. In May 1863 Green resigned from the 102nd and in August was commissioned Lieutenant Colonel in the 173rd New York at Port Hudson. He remained with this regiment in the Department of the Gulf for the rest of his life. At the battle at Pleasant Hill, Louisiana, on 9 April 1864, during Nathaniel Banks's Red River campaign, the 173rd New York was part of Lewis Benedict's brigade. During the fighting the regimental commander retired from the field without orders, leaving Green in charge. Green was soon after wounded in the elbow and was evacuated to New Orleans. The arm was amputated and Green applied for convalescent leave. Before he could depart he died in the hospital on 14 May 1864. He was posthumously breveted Brigadier General USV to rank from the day of the battle.

Boatner, *Civil War*; Phisterer, *New York in the War*; *OR*, Ser. I, Vol. 34, pt. 1; Military Service Record.

GREGG, John, 1828–1864, Alabama–Texas, C.S. Army, killed in action 7 October 1864 near Richmond, Virginia.

John Gregg was a latecomer to the Army of Northern Virginia but firmly established his reputation as a fierce fighter in his first battle under Robert E. Lee in May 1864. Gregg was born in Lawrenceville, Alabama, graduated from LaGrange College, studied law, and emigrated to Texas in 1852. There he was a district judge, a member of the secession convention in 1861, and a representative to the First Provisional Confederate Congress. He resigned from Congress after Bull Run and went home to Texas to recruit a regiment, the 7th Texas, of which he became Colonel. Gregg and his regiment were captured at Fort Donelson, Tennessee, in February 1862. After he was exchanged he was promoted Brigadier General CSA on 29 August 1862. He commanded troops in the Gulf states and served under General Joseph Johnston in the Vicksburg campaign of 1863. Later his brigade went to Tennessee and was in the division of Bushrod Johnson at Chickamauga in September 1863, where Gregg was badly wounded. When Longstreet's corps returned to Virginia from Tennessee in 1864, Gregg came with them in command of Hood's old Texas brigade. In the Wilderness, on 6 May 1864, Gregg had his finest moment when the charge of his brigade under the personal eye of General Lee saved the shaken Confederate line. Thereafter Gregg served at Spotsylvania and in the long siege of Petersburg until he was killed on 7 October 1864 in a clash along the New Market road below Richmond.

DAB; Boatner, *Civil War*; Warner, *Generals in Gray*; D.S. Freeman, *Lee's Lieutenants*, Vol. 3; *B&L*, Vols. 3 & 4; *CMH*, Vol. XI.

GREGG, Maxcy, 1814–1862, South Carolina, C.S. Army, died 14 or 15 December 1862 of wounds received 13 December 1862 at Fredericksburg, Virginia.

Maxcy Gregg was one of the most cultured men of the antebellum South, an amateur astronomer and botanist, and a student of classical languages. He was born in Columbia, a descendant of two prominent families. He graduated from South Carolina College, passed the bar, and practiced law. He was a lifelong bachelor. Gregg was a leading secessionist and advocated resumption of the slave trade to replenish the South's labor pool. He served as a Major in the Mexican War but saw no action. In January 1861 he raised and became Colonel of the 1st South Carolina, a six-month regiment, for the defense of Charleston. In April 1861 he took his regiment to Virginia, but their enlistment expired in July and he had to return to South Carolina for new recruits. He returned to northern Virginia in August 1861, and on 12 December was appointed Brigadier General CSA. Gregg commanded his brigade with distinction on the Virginia Peninsula, at Second Manassas, where he was wounded, and at Antietam. On 13 December 1862, at Fredericksburg, in a tragic mistake, Gregg had his brigade stack arms in the belief that they were in a support position. When they were rushed by Union troops he was shot from his horse while trying to keep his men from firing on what he thought were other Confederate units falling back. Seriously wounded in the spine, he was carried into a nearby house where he dictated a victory dispatch to the governor of South Carolina. In a dramatic deathbed reconciliation, Gregg and Stonewall Jackson repaired an old misunderstanding. Gregg died around midnight of 14/15 December.

DAB; Boatner, *Civil War*; Warner, *Generals in Gray*; D.S. Freeman, *Lee's Lieutenants*, Vols. 1 & 2; *B&L*, Vol. 3; *CMH*, Vol. V.

GRIFFITH, Richard, 1814–1862, Pennsylvania–Mississippi, C.S. Army, died 29 or 30 June 1862 of wounds received 29 June 1862 at Savage's Station, Virginia.

Richard Griffith owed his rank and his position in the Confederate Army to his long-term personal friendship with Jefferson Davis. Griffith was born near

Philadelphia, graduated from Ohio University in Athens, and was a school-teacher in Vicksburg at the start of the Mexican War. He enlisted in the Mississippi Rifles, was made 1st Lieutenant and regimental adjutant, and formed an enduring relationship with his colonel, Davis. After the war Griffith returned to Jackson and was, in turn, a banker, U.S. Marshal, and State Treasurer. In 1861 he was elected Colonel of the 12th Mississippi and went with his regiment to northern Virginia. On 12 November 1861 Griffith became Brigadier General CSA and, by the personal intervention of President Davis, was given a brigade of four Mississippi regiments. Griffith's brigade was in reserve at Seven Pines in the Virginia Peninsula campaign. During the Seven Days battles they were heavily engaged throughout. At Savage's Station, on 29 June, Griffith was mortally wounded. He was carried to Richmond, where he died either the same day or the next.

Boatner, *Civil War*; Warner, *Generals in Gray*; D.S. Freeman, *Lee's Lieutenants*, Vol. 1; *CMH*, Vol. VII (Mississippi).

H

HACKLEMAN, Pleasant Adam, 1814–1862, Indiana, U.S. Volunteers, killed in action 3 October 1862 at Corinth, Mississippi.

Pleasant A. Hackleman was a lawyer by profession, a Republican by conviction, and an advocate of peaceful settlement of sectional differences. He was born in Franklin County, the son of an officer in the War of 1812. Admitted to the bar when he was twenty-five, he was successively clerk of the county court, clerk of the state legislature, candidate for Congress, delegate to the Republican national convention in 1860, and delegate to the Washington Peace Conference of 1861. In May 1861 Hackleman was appointed Colonel of the 16th Indiana and brought his regiment to Washington by way of Baltimore shortly after mobs in the streets had attacked another regiment en route to the capital. The 16th Indiana was posted on guard duty along the upper Potomac during Hackleman's tenure in the East. On 28 April 1862 he was appointed Brigadier General USV and ordered to join U.S. Grant's army in northern Mississippi. He was given command of a brigade occupying the city of Corinth that summer. When Earl Van Dorn and Sterling Price, with their Confederate Army of the West, attacked Corinth on 3 October, Hackleman's brigade was heavily involved in the defense. As the Union troops slowly gave ground in the face of the Southern onslaught, Hackleman was killed attempting to rally them. The Northern forces eventually won the victory but Hackleman died in a hotel room in Corinth that night.

Boatner, *Civil War*; Warner, *Generals in Blue*; *B&L*, Vol. 2.

HANSON, Roger Weightman, 1827–1863, Kentucky, C.S. Army, died 4 January 1863 of wounds received 2 January 1863 at Stone's River, Tennessee.

Roger W. Hanson was born in Clark County. He served as a Lieutenant in the Kentucky volunteers during the Mexican War, studied law, and went to California as a Forty-niner. He later returned to Kentucky, where he practiced law and served in the state legislature. He was a conservative Democrat who was a Fillmore elector in 1856, an unsuccessful candidate for Congress in 1858, and a supporter of the Union Party in 1860. After war became inevitable in 1861, Hanson joined the Confederate forces forming in his state. He was commissioned Colonel of the 2nd Kentucky (Confederate) in September 1861 but was captured at Fort Donelson in February 1862. He was exchanged in October 1862, accompanied Nathan Bedford Forrest to Nashville that November, and went with John Hunt Morgan on the latter's third raid into Kentucky in December. Hanson was promoted Brigadier General CSA on 13 December 1862 and assigned to command a brigade in John C. Breckenridge's division. At Stone's River, or Murfreesboro, Tennessee, Hanson's brigade was not heavily engaged the first two days. On 2 January 1863, he led his troops in an assault which cost them over 400 casualties and in which Breckenridge's division lost over 1,700. Hanson himself was mortally wounded. He died in a house near the battlefield on 4 January.

DAB; Boatner, *Civil War*; Warner, *Generals in Gray*; *B&L*, Vol. 3; *CMH*, Vol. IX (Kentucky).

HARKER, Charles Garrison, 1835–1864, New Jersey, U.S. Volunteers, killed in action 27 June 1864 at Kenesaw Mountain, Georgia.

Charles G. Harker was a professional officer of proven combat experience who was denied the reward of promotion until it was almost too late to enjoy it. Orphaned as a child, he clerked in a store for a man who later was elected to Congress and gave Harker an appointment to West Point. Harker graduated in 1858 and served in the far Northwest until the Civil War. Promoted Captain in the regular army in May 1861, he was assigned to drill volunteer troops in Ohio. In November 1861 Harker was commissioned Colonel of the 65th Ohio. He fought under James A. Garfield at Shiloh and participated in the siege of Corinth. By October 1862 he was commanding a brigade, which he led at Perryville, Kentucky, and at Stone's River with such distinction that he was recommended for promotion. He continued with his brigade in the Army of the Tennessee and was once again recognized for leadership at Chickamauga in September 1863. For the siege of Chattanooga and the advance on Atlanta, Harker's brigade was transferred to IV Corps from XIV Corps, but he rendered his same sterling service. In April 1864 he was finally made Brigadier General USV to rank from 20 September 1863, the date of Chickamauga. During the advance to Atlanta, Harker was wounded at Resaca in May 1864. At Kenesaw Mountain, Georgia, on 27 June 1864, Harker led his brigade in a charge against an entrenched enemy line. He was shot from his horse and died within a few hours.

Cullum; Boatner, *Civil War*; Warner, *Generals in Blue*; *B&L*, Vol. 4.

HATTON, Robert Hopkins, 1826–1862, Ohio–Tennessee, C.S. Army, killed in action 31 May 1862 at Fair Oaks, Virginia.

Northern born and bred but Southern educated, Robert H. Hatton was one of a few free staters who threw in their lot with the Confederacy. He was born in eastern Ohio but graduated from Cumberland University at Lebanon, Tennessee. He was first a school teacher. Later he took up the law and pursued an erratic career in politics as state legislator, unsuccessful candidate for governor, and then, Know-Nothing congressman. Hatton was commissioned Colonel of the 7th Tennessee in May 1861 and served in West Virginia until the spring of 1862. He was involved in the Cheat Mountain campaign and served under Stonewall Jackson in the early phases of the Valley campaign. Hatton was appointed Brigadier General CSA on 23 May 1862, largely because of his political connections, and was given command of a Tennessee brigade in the defenses of Richmond. Eight days later, on 31 May, he was killed at the head of his brigade in the tangled woods around Fair Oaks Station.

BDAC; Boatner, *Civil War*; Warner, *Generals in Gray*; D.S. Freeman, *Lee's Lieutenants*, Vol. 1; *B&L*, Vol. 2; *CMH*, Vol. VIII.

HAYS, Alexander, 1819–1864, Pennsylvania, U.S. Volunteers, killed in action 5 May 1864 in the Wilderness, Virginia.

Alexander Hays was another professionally trained officer who had eschewed military service for civilian pursuits but returned when civil war threatened. He was educated locally in Pennsylvania and attended Allegheny College for three years before entering West Point. He graduated from the Military Academy in 1844, served on the frontier and then in Mexico. Hays resigned his commission in 1848 to go into the iron business in Pennsylvania. For a time he tried his hand at gold mining in California and then came back to Pittsburgh to build bridges. In May 1861 he was recommissioned in the regular army as Captain and also became Major in the 12th Pennsylvania, a three-month regiment. In October he became Colonel of the 63rd Pennsylvania and fought through the Peninsula and Second Manassas campaigns, being wounded in the latter. He was successively breveted Major, Lieutenant Colonel, and Colonel in the regular army for his actions. Hays was promoted Brigadier General USV on 29 September 1862 and took command of a brigade in the defenses of Washington. In June 1863 he took over a division in II Corps, Army of the Potomac, on the eve of Gettysburg. Hays was central in the action of repelling Pickett's charge on 3 July despite his misgivings about Meade's ability to lead the army. In March 1864, with the consolidation of units in the army, Hays was reduced to command of a brigade in his old division. He was killed at the head of his troops in the Wilderness on 5 May 1864 at the opening of the campaign to capture Richmond. He was posthumously breveted Major General USV to rank from the day of his death. Hays had been a personal friend of U.S. Grant from West Point and Mexico. On the news of his death in the front line of action, Grant's only comment was, "It was just like him."

DAB; Cullum; Boatner, *Civil War*; Catton, *Stillness at Appomattox*; Coddington; *B&L*, Vol. 3.

HELM, Benjamin Hardin, 1831–1863, Kentucky, C.S. Army, killed in action 20 September 1863 at Chickamauga, Georgia.

No better example exists of the divisions caused by the American Civil War than the division between Ben Hardin Helm and his wife's brother-in-law, Abraham Lincoln. Hardin was born at Bardstown and graduated from West Point in 1851. He served in Texas one year before resigning from the army to practice law in Louisville. He was later a state legislator and commonwealth attorney. Helm married Mary Todd Lincoln's half-sister and, despite their political differences, he and his lawyer brother-in-law were on good terms. In April 1861 Lincoln offered Helm a commission as paymaster in the U.S. Army but the latter chose to raise and become Colonel of the 1st Kentucky Cavalry (Confederate). He was promoted Brigadier General CSA on 14 March 1862 and led a brigade under John C. Breckenridge in Mississippi and Louisiana. Helm was injured in a fall when his horse was shot from under him at Baton Rouge in August 1862. In January 1863 he joined Braxton Bragg's army in Tennessee to take over the brigade of Roger W. Hanson, killed at Stone's River. Helm led the brigade through the Tullahoma campaign and at Chickamauga. There, on 20 September 1863, in the assault on the Union left, Helm's brigade was repulsed in front of the breastworks and he was mortally wounded. He died on the battlefield the same day.

Cullum; Boatner, *Civil War*; Warner, *Generals in Gray*; Connelly, *Autumn of Glory*; *B&L*, Vol. 3; *CMH*, Vol. IX (Kentucky).

HERKIMER, Nicholas, 1728–1777, New York, New York Militia, died 16 August 1777 of wounds received 6 August 1777 at Oriskany, New York.

Nicholas Herkimer, or Herchheimer, was the son of a farmer, Indian trader, and militia officer who had come to New York's Mohawk Valley from the German Palatine. The younger Herkimer inherited from his father a moderate landholding and the leadership of the local German community. He was also an outspoken separatist in an area in which the dominant social force was the strongly Tory family of Sir William Johnson. On the outbreak of war in 1775 Herkimer became chairman of the county committee of safety and was promoted from Colonel to Brigadier General in the New York militia. In July 1777 Herkimer began raising the militia to go to the relief of Fort Schuyler (Stanwix), which was under siege by St. Leger's column, part of Burgoyne's two-pronged invasion from Canada. On 4 August he started out with a force of 800 men and 400 ox carts. When Herkimer's force arrived within ten miles of the fort he tried to arrange a concerted attack on St. Leger's troops by his column and the defenders. Instead, the militia regimental commanders insisted on pushing forward. Herkimer allowed himself to be persuaded and set off without either flank or advanced guard. The British and their Indian companions set up an ambush at a creek crossing at a place called Oriskany. Herkimer and three regiments made the crossing safely but while the ox carts were on the causeway the British sprang their trap. Herkimer was wounded in the leg in the first volley and many of his officers were felled. The regiment behind the ox carts took to their heels but those in front could neither advance nor retreat. Nevertheless, they performed remarkably well. Herkimer kept his head and controlled the fighting from the center of his defensive position. Hand-to-hand fighting ensued. The militia worked in pairs to protect one another and after six hours the Indians tired of the fighting and left the field. Herkimer was carried to his home and his leg was amputated about ten days later. The surgeon could not control the bleeding and he died about 16 August.

DAB; *Appleton's*; Boatner, *American Revolution*.

HILL, Ambrose Powell, 1825–1865, Virginia, C.S. Army, killed in action 2 April 1865 at Petersburg, Virginia.

Named by Robert E. Lee as the best Major General in the Confederate Army, Ambrose Powell Hill suffered an incapacitating disorder which rendered erratic his behavior later in the war. He was born in Culpepper, graduated from West Point in 1847, and served in the closing operations of the Mexican War. Later he participated in the final removal of the Seminoles and was assigned to the U.S. Coast Survey. He resigned in March 1861 and after Virginia seceded he became Colonel of the 13th Virginia. Hill served in western Virginia and at Bull Run. On 28 February 1862 he became Brigadier General CSA. He distinguished himself at Williamsburg on the Virginia Peninsula and on 26 May 1862 was promoted to Major General CSA. Taking command of what later became the "Light Division" he fought through the Seven Days and Second Manassas. At Antietam he made the famous march from Harper's Ferry which saved Lee's left flank. At Chancellorsville, in May 1863, Hill briefly commanded Jackson's corps after the latter was wounded until he also became a casualty. After Jackson's death Hill was promoted Lieutenant General CSA on 23 May 1863 and took command of the newly created III Corps. It was during the Gettysburg campaign and afterward that his abnormal behavior first became evident. He was sick in an ambulance on the first day at Gettysburg, carried out an assault without a reconnaissance at Bristoe Station in November in 1863, and was absent sick for much of the Wilderness and Spotsylvania campaigns of 1864. Hill did perform creditably in the defenses of Richmond and Petersburg. On 2 April 1865, with the opening of the final campaign of the war, Hill was killed while riding from Lee's headquarters to his own. With a single companion he was riding near a wooded area when he was shot through the heart by a Union straggler. His wife's two sisters were married to Confederate Generals John Hunt Morgan and Basil Duke.

DAB; Cullum; Boatner, *Civil War*; Warner, *Generals in Gray*; D.S. Freeman, *Lee's Lieutenants*, Vols. 1–3; J.I. Robertson; *B&L*, Vols. 2 & 3; *CMH*, Vol. I.

HILL, Henry Root, 1876–1918, Illinois, U.S. Army, killed in action 16 October 1918 near Montfaucon, France.

Henry Root Hill remains the only general in U.S. history who voluntarily accepted a demotion to a lower grade and then was killed in combat. He was a native of Quincy and a furniture dealer by profession. In 1894 he enlisted in the Illinois National Guard. He was mustered into federal service as Sergeant of the 5th U.S. Volunteers in April 1898 but saw no combat duty and was mustered out in October. Hill was commissioned 2nd Lieutenant in May 1899 and rose to be Brigadier General in the Guard on 2 December 1914. In June 1916 he was called for duty on the Mexican border and commanded the 2nd Brigade, 12th Provisional Division, until January 1917. Hill was recalled to active duty in July 1917 as commander of the 65th Brigade, 33rd Division (Illinois National Guard), at Camp Logan, Texas. In May 1918 the division went to France. Hill remained in command of his brigade until 28 July, when he was relieved from duty, placed under arrest, and sent to the rear for reclassification, allegedly for violation of the division commander's policy on wearing steel helmets during training. Given a choice between a general's command in the supply system or a reduced rank in the infantry, Hill supposedly said, "I came to France to fight." He was discharged as Brigadier General on 31 August 1918 and mustered in as Major of infantry, battalion commander in the 128th Regiment, 32nd Division. On 16 October, while leading his battalion against a German position near Montfaucon in the Meuse-Argonne offensive, Hill was killed by small arms fire. He was posthumously awarded the Distinguished Service Cross. Hill's body was returned to Quincy in 1921 and buried with the honors due a Brigadier General.

ROS, Henry R. Hill; Adjutant General of Illinois, *Hill*; *32nd Division*; Moore; Coffman; *New York Times*, October 25, 1918; *Chicago Tribune*, September 24, 1921.

HILL, Sylvester Gardner, 1820–1864, Rhode Island–Iowa, U.S. Volunteers, killed in action 15 December 1864 at Nashville, Tennessee.

Sylvester G. Hill was born in North Kingstown, Rhode Island. A cabinet maker by trade and an abolitionist by inclination, he moved to Ohio as a young man, went to California with the Forty-niners, and engaged in the lumber business in Muscatine, Iowa, before the Civil War. Hill raised a company for active duty in July 1862 and was mustered into service as Colonel of the 35th Iowa in September. The regiment went to Arkansas that November and then to Mississippi for the Vicksburg and Jackson campaigns. Hill took command of a brigade in XVI Corps in 1864 and led it on the Red River expedition. He was wounded at Pleasant Hill on 9 April and again, in the ankle, at Yellow Bayou on 18 April. In the latter fight his second son, who was a member of his staff, was killed. Hill took part in A.J. Smith's expedition to Tupelo, Mississippi, in July 1864. He remained at Memphis with his brigade for the rest of 1864, except for the intervention into the Missouri raid of Sterling Price in September. In December, when Hood's army threatened Nashville, the detachment of XVI Corps at Memphis was sent there. On 15 December, while assaulting a Confederate fortification at the head of his brigade, Hill entered the work and was struck in the forehead by a musket ball. He died instantly. He was recommended for posthumous promotion to Brigadier General USV by his division commander but instead was breveted to that rank effective from the date of his death. Hill left his widow with nine children. His son Rowland G. Hill graduated from West Point in 1881 but took his own life while on active duty during the Spanish American War.

Boatner, *Civil War*; *Muscatine County*; *Iowa Soldiers*; Heitman, *U.S. Army*; *B&L*, Vol. 4; *OR*, Ser. I, Vols. 34, pt. 1; 39, pt. 1; 45, pts. 1 & 2; Military Service and Pension Records; Musser Public Library, Muscatine.

HOCHMUTH, Bruno Arthur, 1911–1967, Texas, U.S. Marine Corps, killed in action 14 November 1967 near Hue, Vietnam.

Bruno Hochmuth is the only general killed in combat in the history of the U.S. Marine Corps and was the first American general killed in Vietnam. He was born in Houston, graduated from Texas Agricultural and Mechanical College in 1935, and was commissioned in the Marine Corps. He served at San Diego and in China with the 6th and 4th Marines and then returned to the United States in 1940 to join the 7th Marine Defense Battalion. From 1941 to 1943 he was in Samoa and was promoted Major in 1942. Later he was on the staff of III Amphibious Corps at Saipan and commanded a battalion of the 4th Marines on Okinawa. After two years of occupation duty in Japan, Hochmuth attended the Industrial College of the Armed Forces. As a Lieutenant Colonel he commanded the 2nd Marines at Camp Lejeune. In January 1951 he was promoted Colonel and in 1952–1953 he was on the staff of 2nd Marine Division. Later he taught at the Canadian Staff College and was with the 3rd Marine Division on Okinawa. From 1957 to 1960 Hochmuth was with the Recruiting Command and was promoted Brigadier General in November 1959. As a staff officer at Headquarters, Marine Corps, he was promoted Major General in August 1963. He returned to Recruiting Command as its commander until 1967. In March 1967 Hochmuth took over the 3rd Marine Division in northern Vietnam and commanded it through some of the bitterest fighting of the war. On 14 November 1967, while he was flying over his division's positions north of Hue, his helicopter was hit by enemy ground fire, exploded in mid-air, and fell into a lake. There was some speculation that an explosive charge had been secretly placed aboard the helicopter before it took off but whatever the cause, General Hochmuth was killed in the blast. His body was recovered and buried in San Diego.

New York Times, November 15 & 17, 1967; *Newsweek*, November 27, 1967; USMC Historical Division.

HOGUN, James, died 1781, Ireland–North Carolina, Continental Army, died 4 January 1781 while a prisoner of war at Haddrell's Point, South Carolina.

James Hogun was one of four American generals who died while prisoners of the British during the Revolutionary War. Nothing is known about his life before his arrival in Halifax County, North Carolina, in 1751 and his marriage there the same year. In the pre-Revolutionary period he served on the county Committee of Safety and in the provincial congress. He became Major of the Halifax County militia in 1776 and Colonel of the 7th North Carolina on 26 November that year. He accompanied Nash's North Carolina brigade to Pennsylvania in 1777 and was present, but not actively engaged, at Brandywine. At Germantown, Hogun performed creditably enough to be noted by Congress. When new North Carolina regiments were called for in 1778, Hogun went home on recruiting duty. In August he returned to the main army with one of these regiments and served in garrison at White Plains and West Point. Hogun was promoted Brigadier General on 9 January 1779 and took command of the North Carolina brigade. He succeeded Benedict Arnold in command in Philadelphia from March to November 1779, and then returned to his brigade. Hogun's was one of two brigades selected to go to the defense of Charleston, South Carolina, in the winter of 1780. Leaving very early in the winter, they did not complete the journey for three months. Hogun was able to bring only 700 effectives to the defense of the doomed city, and they were all captured when Benjamin Lincoln surrendered to Sir Henry Clinton on 12 May 1780. Hogun was offered parole but refused. He remained with his men at Haddrell's Point and helped them resist the efforts of British recruiters for an expedition to the West Indies. He died a prisoner on 4 January 1781.

DAB; Boatner, *American Revolution*; D.S. Freeman, *Washington*; Vol. 5; Clark.

HUMPHREY, Thomas William, 1835–1864, Ohio–Illinois, U.S. Volunteers, killed in action 10 June 1864 at Brice's Crossroads, Mississippi.

Thomas W. Humphrey was probably born in Danville, Ohio, and was brought to Belvidere, Illinois, by his family when he was about five years old. His father was a farmer and the younger Humphrey followed that career until he entered service for the Civil War in September 1862 as Lieutenant Colonel of the 95th Illinois. The regiment went to Jackson, Tennessee, in November and was assigned to XVII Corps in January 1863. Humphrey was wounded twice at Vicksburg, being reported dead after the second wound when he received a concussion and remained unconscious for an extended period. In May 1863 he was promoted Colonel and regimental commander. He briefly commanded a brigade in October and November 1863. Humphrey's regiment took part in the Red River campaign in the spring of 1864 but they were back in Memphis by

May. The regiment was in the column which General Samuel Sturgis led into
Mississippi in June 1864 to prevent Forrest's cavalry from interfering with
Sherman's lines of communications. Many of the veterans had gone home on
leave and the regiment was much reduced in numbers. At Brice's Crossroads
(Guntown), on 10 June, Forrest turned on his pursuers and destroyed Sturgis's
column, sending the remnants streaming back toward Tennessee. Humphrey
was severely wounded in the leg while trying to rally his men and died of
arterial bleeding before he could be carried off the field. He was subsequently
buried on the family farm in a ceremony attended by General Sturgis. Humphrey was posthumously breveted Brigadier General USV to rank from 10 June
1864.

Boatner, *Civil War*; *Boone County*; *OR*, Ser. I, Vols. 24, pt. 2; 34, pt. 1; 39, pt.
1 (under "Brice's Crossroads"); *B&L*, Vol. 4; *Belvidere Standard*, June 28, 1864;
Military Service and Pension Records; Mrs. Helen Maxwell Williams, Belvidere, Ill., to the author, October 29, 1985.

J

JACKSON, Conrad Feger, 1813–1862, Pennsylvania, U.S. Volunteers, killed in action 13 December 1862 at Fredericksburg, Virginia.

Conrad F. Jackson was a member of the famous Pennsylvania Reserves which established such a fine reputation in the early years of the Civil War. He was born in Berks County, worked for the U.S. Revenue Service, and was involved in railroading around Pittsburgh. Jackson was a longtime militia enthusiast and in 1861 his company became part of the 9th Pennsylvania Reserves, later the 38th Pennsylvania, with Jackson as Colonel. The regiment's first active assignment was on outpost duty on the Potomac. During the Peninsula campaign of 1862 Jackson succeeded to brigade command for the Seven Days battles. He was promoted Brigadier General USV on 17 July 1862. The Pennsylvania Reserve Division returned to northern Virginia for the Second Manassas campaign but Jackson was absent sick until after the Maryland campaign that fall. He returned to his brigade in time to fight at Fredericksburg. There, on 13 December 1862, he was killed by a bullet through the head while he sat on the railroad track at Hamilton's Crossing conversing with an aide.

Boatner, *Civil War*; Warner, *Generals in Blue*; *B&L*, Vol. 3.

JACKSON, James Streshly, 1823–1862, Kentucky, U.S. Volunteers, killed in action 8 October 1862 at Perryville, Kentucky.

An officer who was killed before he had an opportunity to realize his potential, James S. Jackson was the son of a farmer. He received a fine education culminating in law school at Transylvania University, from which he graduated in 1845. Jackson enlisted in the 1st Kentucky Cavalry, the "Hunters of Kentucky," for the Mexican War. In 1860 he won a seat in Congress as a Unionist but resigned in December 1861 to become Colonel of the 3rd Kentucky Cavalry (Union), which he had raised the previous summer. Jackson was assigned to Crittenden's division in the Army of the Ohio and marched to Grant's support at Shiloh, but was not actively engaged there. He was promoted Brigadier General USV on 16 July 1862 and given command of the cavalry of the Army of Kentucky. Jackson's troops were not present at the defeat of that Army at Richmond in August 1862 because they had been sent off to scout Confederate Kirby Smith's advance. Jackson was next assigned to command an infantry division in the Army of the Ohio. He had two brigades of green troops. At Perryville, Kentucky, on 8 October 1862, the full force of the Confederate attack fell on Jackson's line, which was on the left of the Union position. Jackson was standing by his supporting battery attempting to encourage his troops and hurry his reserve brigade into line when he was shot dead on the spot.

   BDAC; Boatner, *Civil War*; Warner, *Generals in Blue*; *B&L*, Vol. 3.

JACKSON, Thomas Jonathan, 1824–1863, Virginia, C.S. Army, died 10 May 1863 of wounds received 2 May 1863 at Chancellorsville, Virginia.

   "Stonewall" Jackson, considered by many historians to be the premier tactician of American arms, was reared in the mountains of western Virginia by his father's brother, a miller and farmer. Jackson was indifferently educated before arriving at West Point. He graduated there in 1846, went immediately to Mexico with an artillery battery, and was twice breveted for gallantry. He also joined the church while in Mexico and remained a fervent Christian for the rest of his life. Jackson resigned from the army in 1851 and taught at Virginia Military Institute for ten years. In 1859 he commanded a company of cadets at John Brown's hanging and in 1861 he took a battalion of cadets to Richmond to be drillmasters. He was commissioned Colonel of Virginia militia in 1861 and sent to Harper's Ferry to organize and command state troops, the genesis of the Stonewall Brigade. Jackson was made Brigadier General CSA on 17 June 1861. His distinguished performance at Bull Run in July earned him his sobriquet and a promotion to Major General on 7 October. He was sent to the Shenandoah Valley in November 1861, and his campaign there in the spring of 1862 is a classic still studied in military schools. In the Seven Days battles around Richmond he acted as a *de facto* corps commander, but his performance was strangely out of character. His subsequent leadership at Second Manassas, Antietam, Fredericksburg, and Chancellorsville was unquestionably outstanding. On 10 October 1862 he was promoted Lieutenant General and formally given a corps command. On 2 May 1863, at the end of the first day's fighting at Chancellorsville, Jackson and his staff rode forward of his own lines for a reconnaissance. Mistaken for a Union patrol, they were cut down by fire from their own men. Jackson's left arm had to be amputated but it was thought that he would survive. However, pneumonia set in and he died on 10 May. Of him R.E. Lee wrote, "He has lost his left arm but I have lost my right."

   DAB; Cullum; Boatner, *Civil War*; Warner, *Generals in Gray*; Henderson; D.S. Freeman, *Lee's Lieutenants*, Vols. 1 & 2; *B&L*, Vol. 1–3; *CMH*, Vol. 1.

JENKINS, Albert Gallatin, 1830–1864, Virginia, C.S. Army, died 21 May 1864 of wounds received 9 May 1864 at Cloyd's Mountain, Virginia.

Albert Gallatin Jenkins, except for the Gettysburg campaign of 1863, spent all of the Civil War years until his death in the backwaters of western Virginia. A Harvard-educated lawyer who never practiced at the bar, Jenkins was born in Cabell County, attended Virginia Military Institute, and graduated from Jefferson College in Pennsylvania. After law school he returned to his farm in Virginia, from where he launched a political career which saw him through two terms in Congress. He resigned in April 1861 to raise a cavalry company in his home county and then became Colonel of the 8th Virginia Cavalry. He engaged in a number of raids against Union lines, but in February 1862 he left the field to enter the Confederate Congress. While still a Congressman, on 5 August 1862, he was promoted Brigadier General CSA and returned to the army. In June 1863, when the government was collecting troops to support Lee's invasion of Pennsylvania, Jenkins's brigade was attached to Jeb Stuart's cavalry division. Jenkins was in the army's advance and scouted as far as Harrisburg. Slightly wounded during the battle at Gettysburg, he was back to duty in a few days. When the campaign ended he returned to his old haunts. In the spring of 1864, as federal raiders from east Tennessee and West Virginia began to make incursions into southwestern Virginia, Jenkins's area heated up. On 9 May 1864 he attempted to interrupt George Crook's raid against the Virginia and Tennessee Railroad. In a clash at Cloyd's Mountain in Pulaski County Jenkins was wounded in the arm, captured, and paroled. While he was a prisoner his arm was amputated at the shoulder by a federal surgeon but he died on 21 May.

DAB; Boatner, *Civil War*; Warner, *Generals in Gray*; D.S. Freeman, *Lee's Lieutenants*, Vols. 2 & 3; Coddington; *B&L*, Vol. 4; *CMH*, Vol. II (West Virginia).

JENKINS, Micah, 1835–1864, South Carolina, C.S. Army, killed in action 6 May 1864 at the Wilderness, Virginia.

Micah Jenkins, like Stonewall Jackson, had the misfortune to be killed by the fire of his own troops under strangely similar circumstances. Jenkins was born on Edisto Island into an aristocratic family. He graduated from South Carolina Military College in 1854 and helped to organize Kings Mountain Military School, where he remained until 1861. When the Civil War started he was elected Colonel of the 5th South Carolina and led his regiment at Bull Run. Later he organized the famous Palmetto Sharpshooters, which he commanded in the Peninsula campaign, greatly distinguishing himself. Jenkins was promoted Brigadier General CSA on 22 July 1862 and took command of the brigade of Richard H. Anderson. Jenkins was severely wounded at Second Manassas in August and missed the Maryland campaign, but he returned to duty in time for Fredericksburg. He accompanied Longstreet's corps to south-side Virginia in the spring of 1863 and remained there until the fall, missing

Chancellorsville and Gettysburg. When Longstreet was sent to Chickamauga to support Braxton Bragg's army in September 1863, Jenkins went as commander of Hood's division. Their stay in Georgia and Tennessee was an unhappy one, full of acrimony and bad feeling over seniority and promotions. Jenkins came back to Virginia at the head of his brigade for the 1864 campaign and was engaged in the Wilderness. On the night of 6 May 1864 Jenkins and Longstreet, while riding near their own lines, were shot by men of Mahone's brigade in a manner similar to how and near the same spot where Jackson had been shot the year before. Longstreet was hit in the throat but survived; Jenkins took a bullet in the brain and died in delirium several hours later.

DAB; Boatner, *Civil War*; Warner, *Generals in Gray*; D.S. Freeman, *Lee's Lieutenants*, Vols. 1–3; *B&L*, Vol. 4; *CMH*, Vol. V.

JOHNSTON, Albert Sidney, 1803–1862, Kentucky–Texas, C.S. Army, killed in action 6 April 1862 at Shiloh, Tennessee.

Albert Sidney Johnston was considered at the time of the Civil War to be the finest soldier in America. The Confederate government felt itself especially blessed to win his services. He was, by brevet, one of three Union generals to join the Confederacy, and the one with the highest reputation as a commander in the field. He was born in Washington, Kentucky, the son of the village physician, attended Transylvania College, and graduated from West Point in 1826. Johnston served in the 6th Infantry for eight years, taking an active part in the Black Hawk War. In 1834 he resigned from the army because of his wife's poor health but she died the next year and he went to Texas. There he enlisted in the Republican Army in 1836 and became Brigadier General in 1837 and Secretary of War from 1838 to 1840. He resigned from government that year but returned in 1846 as Colonel of Texas volunteers. In 1849 President Zachary Taylor appointed Johnston paymaster in the regular army. When the 2nd Cavalry Regiment was formed in 1855 Johnston was made Colonel by an old academy acquaintance, Jefferson Davis. He commanded various departments, led the expedition against the Mormons in 1857, for which he was breveted Brigadier General USA, and on the outbreak of the Civil War was commander of the Department of the Pacific. When Texas seceded Johnston resigned his commission effective 3 May 1861 despite being offered a major generalcy in the U.S. Army. His first appointment was as Brigadier General CSA, but on 31 August 1861 he was commissioned General CSA to rank from 30 May 1861, one of only six such appointments made during the war. In September he was placed in command of the Western Department, all of the Confederacy west of the Alleghenies except for the Gulf Coast. His tenure was not a successful one. Maneuvered out of Kentucky, his forces were defeated at Logan Cross Roads and Forts Henry and Donelson. In March 1862 Johnston concentrated his forces from all over the South at Corinth, Mississippi. On 6 April he attacked the unsuspecting army of U.S. Grant at Pittsburg Landing (Shiloh Church) on the Tennessee River. While personally leading a charge

Johnston was shot in the leg and died of arterial bleeding before the seriousness of the wound was realized. Albert Sidney Johnston is the only man in this collection to have held general officer rank in three armies.

DAB; Cullum; Boatner, *Civil War*; Warner, *Generals in Gray*; Connelly, *Army of the Heartland*; *B&L*, Vol. 1; *CMH*, Vol. I.

JONES, John Marshall, 1820–1864, Virginia, C.S. Army, killed in action 5 May 1864 in the Wilderness, Virginia.

John M. Jones was the first Confederate general killed in the terrible battles which raged across Virginia in the campaign of 1864. He was born in Charlottesville and graduated from West Point in 1841. He was an instructor at the Military Academy during the Mexican War, served on the frontier and in the Utah expedition, and resigned his commission in May 1861. He was appointed Captain in the Confederate service and was staff officer to various generals for the next two years, winning numerous commendations for bravery. He was promoted Lieutenant Colonel of artillery in 1862 and was adjutant and inspector general to Jubal Early. On 15 May 1863 Jones was promoted directly to Brigadier General and given the brigade of the cashiered John R. Jones (no relation). Jones was wounded in the attack on Culp's Hill at Gettysburg on 2 July 1863 and wounded again at Payne's Farm in November. At the opening of the spring campaign of 1864 Jones's brigade was the first to engage the union troops crossing the Rappahannock. In the face of a furious Union assault Jones's men broke and ran. He is variously described as having been killed while trying to rally them or while sitting on his horse gazing at the enemy.

Cullum; Boatner, *Civil War*; Warner, *Generals in Gray*; D.S. Freeman, *Lee's Lieutenants*, Vols. 2 & 3; *B&L*, Vol. 4; *CMH*, Vol. III.

JONES, William Edmondson, 1824–1864, Virginia, C.S. Army, killed in action 5 June 1864 at Piedmont, Virginia.

Noted for his irascibility both in the Old Army and in the Confederacy, "Grumble" Jones was born in Washington County, attended Emory and Henry College, and graduated from West Point in 1848. He served nine years in the Mounted Rifle Regiment before resigning in 1857 to take up farming in Virginia. In 1861 he raised his own cavalry company, whose members included John S. Mosby, and joined Jeb Stuart's 1st Virginia Cavalry for Bull Run. He succeeded Stuart as Colonel in September 1861 but was voted out in the armywide election of regimental officers in 1862. Jones went back to the Valley of Virginia, where he became Colonel of the 7th Virginia Cavalry and fought with Stonewall Jackson at Cedar Mountain and Second Manassas in August 1862. On 19 September 1862 Jones was promoted Brigadier General CSA and led an irregular cavalry brigade in the Valley and with Stuart on the Gettysburg campaign of 1863. In September 1863 he was sent to southwestern Virginia to organize the cavalry there. In November he took a brigade to East Tennessee to support Longstreet's siege of Knoxville. In the spring of 1864, while countering David Hunter's foray down the Valley, Jones collected an *ad hoc* force of 5,000 men. At Piedmont, on 5 June, he was killed while in the front line of his command. His body was captured by the advancing Union forces but was later returned to his friends. Jones's nickname of "Grumble" dated from the personality change he underwent after the drowning of his bride in 1852 while en route to his station in Oregon.

Cullum; Boatner, *Civil War*; Warner, *Generals in Gray*; D.S. Freeman, *Lee's Lieutenants*, Vols. 2 & 3; *B&L*, Vols. 3 & 4; *CMH*, Vol. III.

K

KALB, Johann (Baron DeKalb), 1721–1780, Germany, Continental Army, died 19 August 1780 of wounds received 16 August 1780 at Camden, South Carolina.

"Baron" DeKalb was one of the best of the European officers who came to America to join the cause for independence during the Revolutionary War. He was born in Bavaria, the son of a peasant, and left home when he was sixteen. Six years later he was a Lieutenant in a French infantry regiment. He fought in the War of the Austrian Succession and the Seven Years' War, married well, and retired in 1765. He visited America as a French government agent and reported on British-American relations. Kalb reentered military service in 1774 and became Brigadier General. In 1777 he joined with Lafayette in travelling to America, and on 15 September 1777 he was commissioned Major General in the Continental Army. He joined the army at Valley Forge and in the spring of 1778 was named second in command to Lafayette for the abortive invasion of Canada. He returned to the main army as a division commander and was present but not engaged at Monmouth in June 1778. He continued with the army but without active campaigning until April 1780. Kalb was then ordered to take the Maryland and Delaware Continentals south to aid in the defense of Charleston. He got as far as North Carolina before hearing of the fall of the city, and he decided to press on to rally local militia. In July he turned his troops over to Horatio Gates, new commander of the Southern Department. Gates retained Kalb as commander of his Continental infantry and moved forward toward Lord Cornwallis's base at Camden. Cornwallis came out to meet Gates, and the two forces collided on 16 August 1780. The American troops were much fatigued by their long march and poor rations. As usual the American militia fled. Kalb was left alone on the field with a single brigade of Continentals. He was wounded several times, including a saber cut on the head, but he refused to surrender. Finally, after receiving a total of eleven wounds, he fell and the remnants of his force disintegrated. Kalb was captured, carried into Camden, and died on 19 August.

DAB; *Appleton's*; Boatner, *American Revolution*; D.S. Freeman, *Washington*, Vol. 4; Wright.

KEARNY, Philip, 1814–1862, New York–New Jersey, U.S. Volunteers, killed in action 1 September 1862 at Chantilly, Virginia.

Philip Kearny was one of the most cosmopolitan officers in the Union army in the American Civil War. He was born into a wealthy family in New York City and was the nephew of General Stephen Watts Kearny, conqueror of New Mexico and California during the Mexican War. Phil Kearny graduated from Columbia University in 1833, traveled extensively, and studied law. Commissioned in the 1st Dragoons in 1837, he attended the French cavalry school at Saumur, was an observer in Algeria during the French occupation, and was aide to Commanding Generals Macomb and Scott of the U.S. Army. Kearny resigned his commission in April 1846 but reentered service within five weeks and commanded General Scott's personal escort in Mexico. He lost an arm in the Mexico City campaign and was breveted Major. He resigned from the U.S. Army again in 1851, traveled around the world, retired briefly to New Jersey, and then joined the army of Napolean III for the campaign of 1859 in northern Italy. Kearny participated in every cavalry charge at the battles of Magenta and Solferino and was awarded the Legion of Honor. He returned to the United States and in August 1861 he was appointed Brigadier General USV to rank from 17 May 1861 with command of the New Jersey brigade. He commanded a division of III Corps during the Virginia Peninsula campaign of 1862 and distinguished himself at Williamsburg and Seven Pines and during the Seven Days battles. On 4 July 1862 he was promoted Major General USV. By August his division was with John Pope's army at Second Manassas, where Kearny, with Joseph Hooker and Jesse Reno, managed to turn Stonewall Jackson's left before R.E. Lee overwhelmed Pope. Withdrawing toward Centerville, Virginia, Kearny's division was struck on 1 September by Jackson's corps. In a fight that lasted until dark in a driving rain, Kearny was killed when he rode right into the Confederate lines, as was Isaac I. Stevens at the same time. Kearny's body was identified by one of his pre-war associates, A.P. Hill, and was returned to the Union forces the next day. He was the inventor of the "Kearny patch," the forerunner of unit shoulder insignia in the U.S. Army.

DAB; Boatner, *Civil War*; Warner, *Generals in Blue*; Catton, *Mr. Lincoln's Army*; D.S. Freeman, *Lee's Lieutenants*, Vol. 2; *B&L*, Vol. 2.

KEERANS, Charles Leslie, Jr., 1899–1943, North Carolina, U.S. Army, missing in action, declared dead, 11 July 1943 over Sicily.

Charles L. Keerans was the first American general killed in the European theater in World War II and the first U.S. airborne general ever killed, although, paradoxically, he was not parachute-qualified himself. Keerans was born in Charlotte and entered West Point in 1917. His class was given accelerated graduation in November 1918, recalled as officer students, and regraduated in June 1919. Keerans resigned in February 1920 but was recommissioned in July 1920. In the slow years between the world wars he served with the 22nd Infantry Regiment in New York, the 65th in Puerto Rico, and the 5th in Massachusetts. He attended signal and field artillery training, was a staff officer in the 14th Brigade, and attended the Command and General Staff School. Promoted Captain in 1935 and Major in 1940, Keerans was also an instructor at the Infantry School. With formation of the airborne forces in 1941 he became executive officer of the 88th Airborne Battalion as Lieutenant Colonel ranking from that September. This was followed in 1942 by an assignment of the Airborne Command staff and promotion to Colonel in July. In August he was made chief of staff of the recently created 101st Airborne Division. Although not well thought of by his fellow officers, who included Matthew Ridgeway, Maxwell Taylor, James Gavin, and Anthony McAuliffe, Keerans was next appointed assistant commander of the 82nd Airborne Division and was promoted Brigadier General on 7 February 1943. He went to North Africa with the 82nd in May 1943 and began training for the invasion of Sicily, scheduled for July. On 10 July four battalions of the 82nd jumped into Sicily as part of the initial invasion force. On 11 July a force of 2,000 men was flown to Sicily for a second jump. Keerans, who was not parachute-qualified, had been ordered by Ridgeway to remain in North Africa with the base force, but he accompanied the second group as an observer. Jittery gunners in the invasion fleet anchored off Sicily and on the beaches opened fire on the unidentified planes as they approached the drop zones. Pilots took evasive action and scattered their jumpers all over Sicily and into the sea. Twenty-three planes failed to return to Tunisia and 20 percent of the jump force were casualties. Keerans was reported missing in action and was declared dead on 12 July 1944.

Army Register, 1943–44; Cullum, Vols. 7–9; Morison, Vol. 9; Bradley; Ridgeway; Devlin; Blair; Breuer; *New York Times*, August 10, 1943; *Charlotte Observer*, August 10, 1943; *Omaha World-Herald*, August 10, 1943.

KELLY, John Herbert, 1840–1864, Alabama, C.S. Army, died 4 September 1864 of wounds received 2 September 1864 at Franklin, Tennessee.

John H. Kelly, the youngest general in the Confederate Army at the time of his appointment, was born in Pickens County. He was orphaned as a child and was reared by his maternal grandmother. He entered West Point in 1857 but resigned in December 1860 upon the secession of South Carolina from the Union. He became 2nd Lieutenant in the C.S. Army and rose rapidly in rank thereafter. Going to Missouri with General William J. Hardee, Kelly received two promotions in October 1861: first to Captain and assistant adjutant general and then to Major of the 14th Arkansas, to rank from the previous September. He commanded the 9th Arkansas Battalion at Shiloh in April 1862 and was promoted Colonel of the 8th Arkansas a month later. For the next eighteen months Kelly led his regiment, at Perryville, Kentucky, in October 1862, Stone's River, Tennessee, in January 1863, and through the Tullahoma campaign of the summer of 1863. At Chickamauga, Georgia, in September 1863, he commanded an infantry brigade. On 16 November 1863 Kelly became Brigadier General CSA, the youngest man ever appointed to that grade in the C.S. Army. He commanded a cavalry brigade and then a division under Joseph Wheeler in the Atlanta campaign of 1864. While operating against Sherman's lines of communications Kelly was mortally wounded near Franklin, Tennessee, on 2 September 1864. He was carried to a house south of town, where he died, probably on 4 September. It was the same house in which General John C. Carter, victim of the battle at Franklin in November, died three months later.

Boatner, *Civil War*; Warner, *Generals in Gray*; *CMH*, Vol. VII (Alabama).

KIDD, Isaac Campbell, 1884–1941, Ohio, U.S. Navy, killed in action 7 December 1941 at Pearl Harbor, Hawaii.

Isaac Campbell Kidd was the first U.S. Navy flag officer ever killed in combat and the first U.S. general or flag officer combat fatality of World War II. He was born in Cleveland, graduated from Annapolis in 1906, and went immediately to Panama in the USS *Columbia*. Later he went on a cruise around the world. In a time when midshipmen were not commissioned until they had spent two years at sea, Kidd was not appointed Ensign until 1908. He served in the *New Jersey*, the *North Dakota*, and the *Pittsburgh*, was flag secretary to the commander of the Pacific Fleet, and by World War I was an instructor at Annapolis. During the war he was at sea in the USS *New Mexico* and thereafter was flag lieutenant to the commander, Atlantic Fleet. Later he was on the staff at Annapolis again and finally commanded his own vessel, USS *Vega*, 1927. In 1935 Kidd was promoted Captain and became commander of a destroyer squadron. He attended the Naval War College and was on the staff there until 1938. In September 1938 he returned to the Pacific Fleet as Captain of the battleship *Arizona*, a fateful assignment. In February 1940 he became commander of Battleship Division One and on 1 July 1940 he was promoted Rear Admiral. On 7 December 1941 Kidd was aboard *Arizona*, his flagship, with her captain when the news of the Japanese attack on Pearl Harbor was flashed to the fleet. Within one minute of the notification to get under way *Arizona* was hit by a torpedo and eight bombs. One bomb, which exploded in the magazine, set off a detonation which killed Kidd and the captain and sank the ship. Over 1,100 men of a complement of 1,500 were killed or missing. Kidd was posthumously awarded the Medal of Honor for his efforts to get his battleship division out of the anchorage under fire.

Morison, Vol. 3; *MOH*; *New York Times*, December 11, 1941; U.S. Navy Office of Information.

KIRBY, Edmund, 1840–1863, New York, U.S. Volunteers, died 28 May 1863 of wounds received 3 May 1863 at Chancellorsville, Virginia.

Edmund Kirby was a twenty-three-year-old Lieutenant when he was promoted to Brigadier General on his deathbed by President Abraham Lincoln. Kirby was the third generation of his family to serve in the U.S. Army. He was the grandson of General Jacob Jennings Brown, the Commanding General of the Army, his father was an officer, and his cousin was Edmund Kirby Smith, the Confederate commander in the Trans-Mississippi Department. Young Kirby was graduated from West Point in May 1861, entered the artillery, and commanded a battery at Bull Run two months after leaving the Academy. Later he was assigned to the defenses along the upper Potomac and commanded a battery in the Virginia Peninsula campaign of 1862. Kirby did not return to northern Virginia in time for Second Manassas, but at Antietam he commanded an artillery section of two guns. His battery was only lightly engaged at Fredericksburg in December. At Chancellorsville, on 3 May 1863, Kirby's regular battery became entangled in the evacuation of Union forces to United States Ford on the Rappahannock and he could not get to the field of action. Going ahead personally, he was given command of the 5th Maine, a volunteer battery whose own commander had been wounded. Under heavy fire from the Confederate II Corps artillery the 5th Maine lost five men killed, nineteen wounded, and forty-three horses killed. The guns had to be hauled off the field by hand during which time Kirby was struck in the thigh by a canister round. As the men attempted to aid him, he ordered them to remove the guns first. After he was taken to a base hospital in Washington, his leg was amputated and he lingered near death for several weeks. When he was visited by President Lincoln, Kirby expressed a concern for his widowed mother and Lincoln promoted him to Brigadier General USV on the spot, 23 May 1863, thus insuring an adequate pension. Kirby died on 28 May. Cullum does not show Kirby's promotion to Brigadier General.

Cullum; Boatner, *Civil War*; Warner, *Generals in Blue*; *B&L*, Vols. 2 & 3.

KIRK, Edward Needles, 1828–1863, Ohio–Illinois, U.S. Volunteers, died 21 or 29 July 1863 of wounds received 31 December 1862 at Stone's River, Tennessee.

Edward N. Kirk was reared and educated as a Quaker but did not allow his religion to interfere with his perceived duty to his country. Born in Jefferson County, he was educated in a Friends Academy, taught school, and was admitted to the bar in 1853. He practiced law for a year in Baltimore before moving to Illinois, where he continued his practice. In 1861 Kirk was instrumental in raising the 34th Illinois and became its Colonel. He commanded the brigade of which his regiment was a part in the Army of the Ohio from January to April 1862. At Shiloh he was heavily engaged on the second day and was wounded. He returned to duty the next June and remained with the brigade until the end of the year, but was not engaged at Richmond or Perryville, Kentucky, in the summer or fall. On 29 November 1862 Kirk was promoted Brigadier General USV. At Stone's River, Tennessee, on 31 December 1862, Kirk's brigade was next to last on the extreme right of the Union line. In the meeting engagement that day the Confederate left overwhelmed the Union right. Kirk's brigade received the brunt of the attack, suffering 500 casualties in a few minutes. Kirk was severely wounded himself. He was permanently disabled and had to be transported to his home in Sterling, Illinois. He died there the next July. Published sources claim that the date was 29 July but Kirk's gravestone is marked 21 July. Phisterer writes that Kirk died of disease or other cause in Chicago on 29 July.

Boatner, *Civil War*; Warner, *Generals in Blue*; Phisterer, *Statistical Record*; *B&L*, Vol. 3.

KITCHING, John Howard, 1840–1865, New York, U.S. Volunteers, died 10 January 1865 of wounds received 19 October 1864 at Cedar Creek, Virginia.

J. Howard Kitching, as he was known, may have been as much a victim of his own weak constitution as he was of the wound to which his death is attributed. Kitching was a sickly child in a wealthy family in New York City. He was tutored at home and attended private schools before finishing his education in Switzerland. He refused an appointment to West Point and entered his father's business in 1860. In 1861 he entered service as a private in the Lincoln (New York) Cavalry, but in September he was commissioned Captain in the 2nd New York Artillery. Kitching was mustered out of service in July 1862 in order to accept a commission as Lieutenant Colonel in the new 135th New York, which he received in September. The next month the regiment was redesignated the 6th New York Heavy Artillery. Kitching became Colonel in April 1863 and the regiment moved to Maryland, where it became part of VIII Corps. He commanded a brigade in the defenses of Washington and provided ammunition guards for the trains of the reserve artillery of the Army of the Potomac. In May 1864 the regiment transferred to V Corps as infantry and fought at Spotsylvania and Cold Harbor with Kitching as brigade commander. He was commended for his leadership by General George Meade and continued with his unit in the rifle pits at Petersburg through July and August. Kitching was recommended for Brigadier General USV in July. In August, when Washington was threatened, the 6th New York went back to the defenses of the capital. Later it formed part of a provisional division, which Kitching commanded, sent out from Washington to join Phil Sheridan's Shenandoah campaign. At Cedar Creek, on 19 October 1864, when the Union left flank was turned by the first Confederate rush, Kitching was wounded, but it was thought not to be serious. He returned to Dobbs Ferry, New York, to recuperate and died there 10 January 1865. He might have survived had he been of stronger constitution. In April 1865 he was posthumously breveted Brigadier General USV to rank from 1 August 1864.

Boatner, *Civil War*; *Harper's*; Irving; *OR*, Ser. I, Vols. 36, pts. 1–3; 40, pt. 3; 42, pt. 2; 43, pts. 1 & 2.

L

LAWTON, Henry Ware, 1843–1899, Ohio–Indiana, U.S. Volunteers, killed in action 18 December 1899 at San Mateo, Luzon, Philippine Islands.

Henry Ware Lawton, hero of three wars and Medal of Honor winner, was the first serving American general killed outside the North American continent. He was born in Manhattan, Ohio, near Toledo, and moved with his family to Indiana when he was five years old. Orphaned a few years later, he was reared by an uncle, educated in a church college near Fort Wayne, and enlisted in the 9th Indiana at the outbreak of the Civil War. In August 1861 Lawton was commissioned 1st Lieutenant in the 30th Indiana. By war's end he was Lieutenant Colonel, Brevet Colonel, and commander of the 30th. In 1893 he was awarded a belated Medal of Honor for action at Atlanta, Georgia, on 3 August 1864 when he led a charge of skirmishers against enemy rifle pits and stubbornly and successfully resisted two determined counterattacks to retake the works. After the Civil War, Lawton briefly attended Harvard Law School, but he entered the regular army as 2nd Lieutenant in the 41st Infantry, a black regiment, in 1866. He became 1st Lieutenant in 1867 and his regiment was renumbered the 24th in 1869. He spent the next twenty years on frontier duty, highlighted by service with Ranald Mackenzie of the 4th Cavalry in Texas in 1874–1875 and as commander of the famous chase of Geronimo in northern Mexico in 1886. He had been promoted Captain in 1879 and was made Major in the Inspector General's Department in 1888, subsequently rising to Colonel in 1898. Lawton was appointed Brigadier General USV on 4 May 1898 at the start of the Spanish-American War. He commanded a brigade and a division in the Santiago campaign in Cuba and was rewarded with promotion to Major General USV on 8 July 1898. He served as military governor of the city and province of Santiago until his return to the United States, when he assumed command of

IV Corps at Mobile. Lawton went to the Philippines in March 1899 to command a division in the suppression of the native insurgency. He vigorously pursued the insurgents across Luzon all through 1899, concluding with the push against Emilio Aguinaldo's main force in October–December. On 19 December 1899, in the crossing of the Mariquina River opposite San Mateo, Lawton was conspicuous in a white helmet and yellow slicker worn to ward off the typhoon weather. As he stood on the river bank he was shot in the lungs and probably choked on his own blood when his aides laid him down in the mud.

DAB; Heitman, *U.S. Army*; *Twentieth Century*; Utley; *MOH*; *New York Times*, December 20, 22, 24, 1899.

LIM, Vicente, 1888–1945, Philippines, Philippine Army, executed by the Japanese probably on 6 January 1945 at Manila.

Vicente Lim was one of two non-Caucasian generals of American forces who was a World War II fatality. Of Chinese extraction, he was born on Luzon and graduated from West Point in 1914, the first Filipino cadet and graduate. He was commissioned in the Philippine Scouts of the U.S. Army and was promoted through the ranks to Major in 1920. In 1926 he returned to the United States to attend courses at the Infantry School, the Command and General Staff School, and the Army War College. Lim went back to Manila in 1929 and served with the 45th Infantry (PS) until 1936. Promoted Lieutenant Colonel in 1935, he retired on a physical disability in 1936. He was appointed Brigadier General Philippine Army on 1 July 1936 and became assistant chief of staff in charge of war plans under General Douglas MacArthur. In 1939 he became deputy chief of staff. When war broke out in December 1941 Lim became commander of the just-activated 41st Division of the Philippine Army and fought on Bataan, notably at Abucay in January 1942. He was captured on 9 April 1942 and imprisoned. Later he was released because of his poor health. In 1943 he took over coordination between U.S. forces in Australia and guerrilla groups on Luzon. Lim was en route to a rendezvous with a U.S. submarine on Mindoro Island when he was recaptured by the Japanese in February 1944. He continued his personal resistance even in captivity and was eventually executed in Manila, probably on 6 January 1945. He was officially declared dead on 11 November 1945.

Army Register, 1942; Cullum, Vols. 7–9; Morton; *Intelligence Activities*; *Assembly*, January 1949.

LISCUM, Emerson Hamilton, 1841–1900, Vermont, U.S. Volunteers, killed in action 13 July 1900 at Tientsin, China.

Emerson H. Liscum was another of the Civil War officers who remained in service after 1865 and participated in America's expansionism at the end of the nineteenth century. A native of Huntington, he volunteered for service in May 1861 and was a Corporal in the 1st Vermont for three months before being mustered out. In February 1862, he enlisted in the 12th U.S. Infantry, was commended for gallantry at Cedar Mountain, Virginia, in August 1862, where he was wounded, and was commissioned 2nd Lieutenant in March 1863. Liscum was wounded again at Gettysburg and breveted for gallantry at Petersburg. He left the army in November 1864 but returned as Captain in the 25th Infantry in 1866 and spent the next thirty years fighting Indians and in garrison duty. In 1870 he transferred to the 19th Infantry and in 1892 he was promoted Major in the 22nd Infantry. Liscum was made Lieutenant Colonel of the 24th Infantry, a black regiment, in 1896 and commanded the regiment in the Santiago campaign in Cuba in 1898. At San Juan Hill, while temporarily in command of his brigade, he was wounded in the shoulder and evacuated to the United States. He was promoted Brigadier General USV on 12 July 1898 but never held an active command at that rank. He remained on sick leave for the rest of 1898, and his commission expired on 31 December. Liscum was sent to the Philippines in April 1899 and became Colonel of the 9th Infantry there. He was temporarily a brigade commander during operations against the insurgents in 1899–1900. In July 1900 Liscum and his regiment were sent to China to assist in the relief of Peking from the besieging Boxers. At the assault on Tientsin on 13 July the 9th Infantry was on the extreme right of the allied line, on the bank of the Pei-ho River. The regiment came under a crossfire from the walls of the city and the junks in the river. After the color bearer was hit Liscum bent to retrieve the colors himself. He was hit in the abdomen as he did so and died almost immediately. His dying words, "Keep up the fire!" have become the motto of the 9th Infantry. A silver bowl, known as the Liscum Bowl, was made from ingots captured at Tientsin and is a regimental trophy. According to *Twentieth Century Biographic Dictionary*, Liscum was reappointed Brigadier General USV from 12 July 1899 to an unspecified date in 1900, but this is not confirmed by Heitman; possibly his appointment to temporary brigade command in the Philippines was misconstrued as a promotion.

Heitman, *U.S. Army*; *Twentieth Century*; F. Brown; Mueller; *New York Times*, July 16, 1900.

LITTLE, Lewis Henry, 1817–1862, Maryland-Missouri. C.S. Army, killed in action 19 September 1862 at Iuka, Mississippi.

Lewis Henry Little, or Henry Little, as he was more commonly known, had a reputation for having the most smartly turned out units, both in the Old Army and in the Confederate service, He was born and reared in Baltimore, the son of a congressman. He received a direct commission into the army in 1839, served in Mexico, where he was breveted for gallantry at Monterrey, and on the frontier. Little resigned his commission as Captain, 7th Infantry, in May 1861 and was appointed Major of artillery in the C.S. Army. He was also made Colonel in the Missouri State Guard (Confederate) and assistant adjutant general to Sterling Price, the Guard commander. He commanded a brigade of the Guard at Pea Ridge, Arkansas, in March 1862 and was commended for his action there. When the Guard entered Confederate service in April 1862 Little was commissioned Brigadier General CSA from 16 April. When Price's Army of the West moved east into Mississippi, Little commanded Price's own division and received a personal commendation from General Braxton Bragg for the fine appearance of his troops. At Iuka, Mississippi, on 19 September 1862, Little's was the only division engaged against the advancing Union forces. In the midst of the battle, while engaged in conference with Price and other officers, Little was killed by a musket ball which had passed under Price's arm and struck him (Little) in the forehead. He was buried by torchlight in Iuka that same night.

Boatner, *Civil War*; Warner, *Generals in Gray*; *B&L*, Vols. 1 & 2; *CMH*, Vol. II (Maryland).

LOWELL, Charles Russell, 1835–1864, Massachusetts, U.S. Volunteers, died 20 October 1864 of wounds received 19 October 1864 at Cedar Creek, Virginia.

Charles Russell Lowell was the nephew of the famous poet, James. He was born in Boston, graduated from Harvard at the head of his class, and traveled extensively before settling down to be manager of an iron works in Maryland. In April 1861 he went to Washington and obtained a commission as Captain in the 3rd (later 6th) U.S. Cavalry. He commanded a squadron of his regiment on the Virginia Peninsula in 1862, was breveted Major, and served on General McClellan's personal staff. At Antietam, Lowell carried messages on the battlefield and subsequently escorted captured Confederate colors to Washington. Late in 1862 he went home to recruit the 2nd Massachusetts Cavalry and became its Colonel in May 1863. Lowell commanded a cavalry brigade in the defenses of Washington until July 1864, when he joined the Cavalry Corps of the Army of the Potomac in Sheridan's Shenandoah Valley campaign. He commanded the Reserve Brigade composed of his own regiment and three regiments of regular cavalry. He participated at the battle at Winchester in September, took part in routing the Confederate cavalry at Tom's Brook in October, and fought at Cedar Creek on 19 October. In the latter battle Lowell was shot from his horse, remounted, and continued at the head of his brigade until wounded again. He died the next day at Middleton, Virginia. By the personal intercession of General Sheridan, Lowell's commission as Brigadier General was signed and presented to him on 19 October, to be effective from the same date.

Boatner, *Civil War*; Warner, *Generals in Blue*; *Twentieth Century*; *B&L*, Vol. 4.

LYON, Nathaniel, 1818–1861, Connecticut, U.S. Volunteers, killed in action 10 August 1861 at Wilson's Creek, Missouri.

Nathaniel Lyon was the first U.S. Army general killed in action in the Civil War. He was born in Ashford, now Eastford, Connecticut, and graduated from West Point in 1841. He served in Florida, on the frontier, and in Mexico, where he was wounded and breveted for gallantry. Later he served in California and in

Kansas, where his staunch abolitionist politics were hated by Southern sympathizers. In January 1861, as a Captain, Lyon was sent to St. Louis to take over command of the arsenal there in the face of secessionist threats. He was warmly welcomed by the local Republicans. Lyon saved the weapons in the arsenal by distributing them to the pro-Union Home Guard and by sending some across the river to Illinois. In May he led a force of 7,000 Home Guardsmen to disarm rebel sympathizers at Camp Jackson, outside the city. On 12 May 1861 he was commissioned Brigadier General of Missouri volunteers by the Republican governor of the state and on 17 May 1861 he became Brigadier General USV. He became commander of the Department of Missouri on 31 May. In July Lyon moved to Springfield, Missouri, and collected there a force of 6,000 to repel a Confederate advance from Arkansas. On 10 August he advanced against the army of Sterling Price emcamped at Wilson's Creek. Lyon's attack met with initial success but a counterattack by Confederate Ben McCulloch overwhelmed the Union force with a strength of two to one. Lyon was wounded in the leg and head. Sighting Price and his staff on the battlefield, Lyon personally led a charge of the 2nd Kansas against them. He was mortally wounded by a musket ball in the chest and died almost immediately. Samuel Sturgis, his successor, decided to withdraw. Lyon's body was loaded in a wagon for evacuation. However, to make room for the wounded, all of the dead were unloaded and Lyon's body was left on the field. When this was discovered later a company of cavalry was sent back to retrieve it. The Confederates duly handed it over and he was buried in a garden in Springfield to prevent being captured a second time. Ultimately he was buried in a cemetery near his birthplace.

DAB; Cullum; Boatner, *Civil War*; Warner, *Generals in Blue*; *B&L*, Vol. 1.

LYTLE, William Haines, 1826–1863, Ohio, U.S. Volunteers, killed in action 20 September 1863 at Chickamauga, Georgia.

William H. Lytle was most renowned as one of the most popular romantic poets of mid-nineteenth-century America. He was the son of a Democratic congressman who had also been Surveyor General of the United States. He was born in Cincinnati, wished to follow a military career, but accepted his father's dictum to study law. Nevertheless, he was an officer of Ohio volunteers during the Mexican War and later became Major General of Ohio militia. Before the Civil War, Lytle practiced law, sat in the state legislature, and established his fame as a poet. In May 1861 he was commissioned Colonel of the 10th Ohio, the "Bloody Tinth," composed largely of Irish immigrants from Cincinnati. In September 1861, serving under William Rosecrans, Lytle was badly wounded at Carnifax, Virginia. Later he commanded a brigade in the Army of the Ohio operating in Kentucky. At Perryville, in October 1862, Lytle was wounded again and left on the field for dead. Captured by the Confederates and restored to health, he was exchanged in February 1863. Meanwhile he had been promoted to Brigadier General USV on 29 November 1862. In April 1863 he returned to active duty and took a brigade in Phil Sheridan's division of

McCook's XX Corps. At Chickamauga, Georgia, on 20 September 1863, Lytle's brigade was part of the routed right of the Union line. As his front was overrun by Hindman's Confederate division, Lytle led a charge to clear the rear of his command, to prevent encirclement. He was mortally wounded and died the same day.

Boatner, *Civil War*; Warner, *Generals in Blue*; *B&L*, Vols. 1 & 3.

M

MANSFIELD, Joseph King Fenno, 1803–1862, New Hampshire-Connecticut, U.S. Volunteers, died 18 September 1862 of wounds received 17 September 1862 at Antietam, Maryland.

Joseph K.F. Mansfield commanded troops in combat only once in his forty-year military career and lost his life in the process. He graduated from West Point in 1822 and worked on coast defenses as an engineer officer for more than twenty years, rising to the rank of Captain. As Zachary Taylor's chief engineer in the Mexican American War he won three brevets and was wounded once. He returned to fortification duty in 1848, but in 1853 he was selected by Secretary of War Jefferson Davis to be Inspector General of the army with the rank of Colonel. When the Civil War broke out in 1861 Mansfield was appointed the first commander of the Department of Washington, charged with the defense of the nation's capital. He was made Brevet Brigadier General USA on 6 May and on 18 May promoted Brigadier General USA to rank from 14 May 1861. He remained at Washington until March 1862, when he went to the Department of Virginia and commanded a brigade at Norfolk and a division at Suffolk. Joining the Army of the Potomac in September 1862 for the Maryland campaign, Mansfield was given command of XII Corps, formerly II Corps of the Army of Virginia, recently defeated at Second Manassas. He was concurrently named a member of the FitzJohn Porter court of inquiry but attended only one session before leaving for the field. He caught up with his command in Maryland just before the battle at Antietam. Mansfield found himself on 17 September 1862 at the head of a large force of green troops with whom he was completely unacquainted, in an area with which he was unfamiliar, and with no previous experience in handling large bodies of men in combat. Acting more like a regimental colonel than a corps commander, Mansfield involved himself in encouraging individual groups of men into moving forward to face Lee's veterans. While he was doing so, his horse was shot from under him. Mansfield continued to advance on foot but was shot in the stomach while climbing over a fence. He was carried to a field hospital but died the next day. On 12 March 1863 he was posthumously confirmed as Major General USV to rank from 18 July 1862.

DAB; Cullum; Boatner, *Civil War*; Warner, *Generals in Blue*; Catton, *Mr. Lincoln's Army*; *B&L*, Vols. 1 & 2.

McBRIDE, Allan Clay, 1885–1944, Maryland, U.S. Army, died 9 May 1944 while a prisoner of war at Shirakawa, Formosa (Taiwan).

Allan C. McBride was the only U.S. Army general to die as a prisoner of war. (Other generals who died as prisoners were Revolutionary officers or in the Philippine Army.) McBride was born in Frederick, where he was the son of the county sheriff. He graduated from St. John's College in Annapolis in 1908 and went directly into the army. An artillerist, by World War I he was a Captain. Promoted Major in October 1917, McBride went to France in June 1918, was made Lieutenant Colonel in July, and commanded an artillery battalion until the end of the war. He remained with the Army of Occupation in Germany until July 1919. In 1920 he reverted to his permanent grade of Captain but subsequently was promoted through the grades to Colonel in September 1937. In the intervening years he had numerous assignments, including the Field Artillery School at Fort Sill, Oklahoma. He attended the Command and General Staff course in 1923 and was on the inspector general's staff in 1940. In February 1941 McBride went to the Far East as deputy chief of staff of the Philippine Department under General Douglas MacArthur. With the outbreak of World War II he was promoted Brigadier General on 18 December 1941 and concurrently became chief of staff of the Department. One of his principal responsibilities was the evacuation of the Department installations and materials from throughout Luzon to the Bataan Peninsula. In March 1942 McBride was named commander of the Bataan Services Area Command, a position he held until his surrender to the Japanese on 9 April 1942. Held in prison camps on Luzon until August 1942, McBride was transferred with other American generals to Formosa (Taiwan). The generals were shifted around among several camps until June 1943, when they came permanently to Shirakawa Camp. With the other generals, McBride was allowed to work in the prison garden, which he did until his death. On 9 May 1944 he died in his sleep, probably of a heart attack, and was buried at the camp. His remains were reinterred at Frederick in 1948.

Army Register, 1942–1944; *Who's Who in America*; James; L. Morton; *Maryland in the World War*, Vol. II; *Frederick News-Post*, January 13, 1945; May 26, 1948.

McCONIHE, John, 1834–1864, New York-Nebraska, U.S. Volunteers, killed in action 1 June 1864 at Cold Harbor, Virginia.

John McConihe was an outstanding example of the frenetic energy which characterized Americans in the years before the Civil War. Son of a prominent citizen of Troy, he graduated from Union College and the state University at Albany and opened a law practice in 1855. In 1857 he moved to Omaha, Nebraska, where he continued his law practice, opened a freight business, was private secretary to the governor of the territory, ran unsuccessfully for mayor of Omaha, was appointed territorial adjutant general, and led an expedition against the Pawnee Indians. In July 1861, with the outbreak of the Civil War, McConihe raised a company for the 1st Nebraska. The regiment moved to Missouri in August. In February McConihe went to Washington on official business and while there contracted typhoid. He was taken to Troy to recuperate and returned to his regiment, which had moved to Tennessee, the day before Shiloh. At that battle McConihe was wounded in the left arm and was out of action another six months. Meanwhile, in September 1862, he had resigned from the 1st Nebraska to become Lieutenant Colonel of the 169th New York, a regiment being raised in Troy. In October the regiment went to Washington, in April 1863 to Suffolk, Virginia, and subsequently to coastal operations in North and South Carolina and Florida. For bravery at the siege of Charleston McConihe was presented a sword by the citizens of Troy. In April 1864 he became Colonel of the 169th. Transferred to Fort Monroe, Virginia, the regiment went on the Ben Butler expedition to Bermuda Hundred in May. At Cold Harbor, on 1 June 1864, while leading his regiment in a charge, McConihe was shot through the heart and died instantly. He was breveted Brigadier General USV to rank from the date of his death.

Harper's; Boatner, *Civil War*; J. Morton; *OR*, Ser. I, Vols. 10, pt.1; 51, pt. 1.

McCOOK, Daniel, Jr., 1834–1864, Ohio-Kansas, U.S. Volunteers, died 17 July 1864 of wounds received 27 June 1864 at Kenesaw Mountain, Georgia.

Daniel McCook was a son of the famous "Fighting McCooks" of Ohio. Both he and his brother Robert (see below) died as Union generals in the Civil War. Daniel attended college in Alabama and Ohio before opening a law practice in Leavenworth, Kansas, with Thomas Ewing and William Tecumseh Sherman. In May 1861 he became Captain in the 1st Kansas and fought at Wilson's Creek, Missouri, in August. He was assistant adjutant general on the staff of General George Thomas at Shiloh in April 1862, but Thomas's division was not engaged. In July 1862 McCook became Colonel of the 52nd Ohio and took over a brigade in Sherman's division. He fought under Sheridan at Perryville, Kentucky, in October 1862 but was employed guarding trains at Stone's River, Tennessee, in January 1863. At Chickamauga, Georgia, in September 1863, McCook was assigned to the Reserve Corps and was barely engaged. His brigade took a more active role at Chattanooga in November and in the relief of Knoxville in December. During the Atlanta campaign McCook's brigade was a part of XIV Corps. At Kenesaw Mountain, Georgia, on 27 June 1864, McCook was selected by Sherman to lead the assault on the Confederate position. The men attacked across open ground against entrenched defenders and were repulsed with heavy loss. McCook was mortally wounded. He was carried to Ohio but died on 17 July. He had been promoted Brigadier General USV on 16 July.

Appleton's; Boatner, *Civil War*; Warner, *Generals in Blue*; *B&L*, Vol. 4.

McCOOK, Robert Latimer, 1827–1862, Ohio, U.S. Volunteers, died 6 August 1862 of wounds received 5 August 1862 near Decherd, Tennessee.

Robert L. McCook was another member of the "Fighting McCooks" of Ohio and the brother of Daniel McCook (see above). Both brothers died as Union generals during the Civil War. Robert studied and practiced law as a young man. At the beginning of the war he recruited the 9th Ohio from among the German residents of Cincinnati and became Colonel in May 1861. He joined George McClellan's army in western Virginia that summer and became a brigade commander. He did not participate in the Rich Mountain campaign, but did command his brigade at Carnifax Ferry in September. In November his brigade was transferred to Kentucky and became part of George Thomas's division. In January 1862 they were engaged in the Logan Cross Roads affair and McCook was wounded. He remained on duty with the army and was promoted Brigadier General USV on 21 March 1862. Thomas's division was not engaged at Shiloh, but McCook was actively involved in the opposition to Braxton Bragg's invasion of Kentucky in the summer of 1862. On 5 August, while advancing with his brigade, McCook was riding in a carriage because of his unhealed leg wound. As he approached a farmhouse near Decherd, Tennessee, he was attacked by a band of Southern partisans, who scattered his escort and shot McCook in the stomach after refusing his offer to surrender. He was carried into the farmhouse, where he died the next day. McCook's killer was later captured, convicted of murder, and sentenced to hang, but he was pardoned by President Andrew Johnson.

Boatner, *Civil War*; Warner, *Generals in Blue*; *B&L*, Vols. 1 & 3.

McCULLOCH, Ben, 1811–1862, Tennessee-Texas, C.S. Army, killed in action 7 March 1862 at Pea Ridge, Arkansas.

Ben McCulloch's biography is the history of the American West in the first half of the nineteenth century. He was born and reared in frontier Rutherford County, Tennessee, followed Davy Crockett to Texas, and fought with Sam Houston at San Jacinto in 1836. Remaining in the Lone Star Republic, he was a land surveyor and Indian fighter. As Captain of Texas Rangers, McCulloch served with Zachary Taylor at Monterrey and Buena Vista in the Mexican War. Later he mined gold in California, was U.S. Marshal in Texas, and U.S. Commissioner to the Mormons in Illinois. As Colonel of Texas state troops, he accepted the surrender of General David Twiggs's U.S. forces in San Antonio on 16 February 1861. McCulloch was appointed Brigadier General CSA on 11 May 1861 and given command in Arkansas. In July 1861 he advanced into

Missouri to support Sterling Price's Missouri State Guard (Confederate). At Wilson's Creek, Missouri, on 10 August, their combined forces beat the Union army of Nathaniel Lyon. McCulloch's next action was at Pea Ridge, Arkansas, on 7 March 1862. Here the Confederate army of Earl Van Dorn attempted to destroy the overextended Union force advancing into Arkansas. In an effort to exploit a withdrawal of part of the Union line McCulloch led his division in an attack on the center. He was shot in the chest by a sharpshooter and died soon after. At the time of his death he was wearing civilian clothes rather than uniform.

DAB; Boatner, *Civil War*; Warner, *Generals in Gray*; Bauer; *B&L*, Vol. 1; *CMH*, Vol. XI.

McINTOSH, James McQueen, 1828–1862, Florida-Arkansas, C.S. Army, killed in action 7 March 1862 at Pea Ridge, Arkansas.

James M. McIntosh was the son of a distinguished Georgia military family. His grandfather fought in the Revolution and his father was killed in action in the Mexican War. James was born at his father's military post at Tampa Bay, Florida. He graduated from West Point in 1849 and served on Indian fighting duty and in the border disturbances in Kansas. Promoted Captain in the 1st U.S. Cavalry in 1857, he resigned his commission in May 1861 and was appointed Captain of C.S. cavalry in Little Rock, Arkansas. He was next made Colonel of the 2nd Arkansas Mounted Rifles and commanded that regiment in Ben McCulloch's brigade in the Confederate victory at Wilson's Creek, Missouri, in August 1861. In December 1861 McIntosh was successful in breaking up Unionist Indian activities in Oklahoma, and on 24 January 1862 he was promoted Brigadier General CSA. At Pea Ridge, Arkansas, on 7 March 1862, McIntosh commanded the cavalry brigade of McCulloch's division. He was shot in the heart and killed while leading a charge of his old regiment, the 2nd Arkansas, a few minutes after the death of General McCulloch. McIntosh's brother, John Baillie McIntosh, was a graduate of Annapolis and a Union major general.

Cullum; Boatner, *Civil War*; Warner, *Generals in Gray*; *B&L*, Vol. 1; *CMH*, Vol. X (Arkansas).

McNAIR, Lesley James, 1883–1944, Minnesota, U.S. Army, killed in action 25 July 1944 near St. Lo, France.

Lesley J. McNair was the architect and organizer of U.S. ground forces in World War II. He was born in Verndale, Minnesota, to an immigrant dry goods merchant. He graduated from West Point in 1904 and entered the field artillery. He was in the Funston expedition to Vera Cruz, Mexico, in 1914 and commanded a battery under John J. Pershing in the Punitive Expedition of 1916–1917. In June 1917 McNair went to France with the operations section of the 1st Division, the first U.S. contingent to enter the World War. He later served with the training section of General Headquarters, American Expedi--

tionary Force. He rose from Major in May 1917 to temporary Brigadier General on 1 October 1918 at age thirty-five, the youngest general in the army. Reverting to his permanent grade in 1919, McNair was an instructor at the Command and General Staff School, operations officer of the Hawaiian Department, ROTC instructor at Purdue University, and commander of several artillery units. He became permanent Brigadier General in January 1937 and Major General in September 1940. McNair then became Chief of Staff of General Headquarters of the Army and began his major work of preparing the ground forces for World War II. He was promoted Lieutenant General on 9 June 1941 and was appointed Chief of Army Ground Forces in March 1942. Under his command almost 8 million men were recruited, trained, and organized into units in the U.S. Army. McNair made frequent trips to the combat zones to study tactics and conditions. In April 1943 he was seriously wounded on one such trip to Tunisia. In July 1944 he was granted his wish for a combat command and was sent to head the First U.S. Army Group in France, an organization to which no troops had yet been assigned. On 25 July 1944, while in the front lines to observe the effects of "carpet bombing" on enemy positions, he was killed when U.S. planes released their bombs short of the target. No remains were ever found except his West Point class ring. He was posthumously promoted to General by special act of Congress 19 July 1954, making him, with Simon B. Buckner, the highest ranking U.S. Army officer ever killed in combat.

DAB; *Army Register*, 1944; Cullum, Vols. 7-9; Bradley; Kahn; Weigley; *Assembly*, October 1946; *New York Times*, July 28, 1944.

McPHERSON, James Birdseye, 1828-1864, Ohio, U.S. Volunteers, killed in action 22 July 1864 at Atlanta, Georgia.

James B. McPherson, little known today, eclipsed even the meteoric rise to fame of George A. Custer in the Civil War. McPherson was the son of a blacksmith in a small village in Ohio. He was forced by economic circumstances to work in a store when he was young, but, with the help of his employer, he gained an education and graduated from West Point in 1853. He entered the Corps of Engineers, worked on coast defenses, and taught at the Military Academy. In August 1861 McPherson became Captain of Engineers and in November, Lieutenant Colonel of volunteers and assistant adjutant general to General Henry W. Halleck, commanding in Missouri. By February 1862 he was chief engineer to U.S. Grant for the campaign against Forts Henry and Donelson at Shiloh. McPherson became Colonel of volunteers in May 1862 and Brigadier General USV on the fifteenth of the same month. He commanded the engineer brigade in the Army of the Tennessee until 8 October 1862, when he was promoted Major General USV and took command of a division in XIII Corps. In January 1863 McPherson took over XVII Corps. This phenomenal rise from staff captain to corps commander was matched by no other Union officer in the Civil War. McPherson led his corps brilliantly through the Vicksburg campaign and on 1 August 1863 was rewarded with a promotion to Brigadier General USA. In March 1864 he succeeded William T. Sherman as commander of the Army of the Tennessee and led it until his death. During the advance against Atlanta that spring some questions arose over his caution in handling his troops, but he never lost Sherman's confidence. At Atlanta, on 22 July 1864, while Hardee's Confederate corps tried to get around Sherman's left, McPherson was en route to his own headquarters with his orderly when he was caught in a wood by Confederate fire and instantly killed. His body was carried on a door, for lack of a stretcher, to Sherman's headquarters. He was eventually buried in Ohio. A monument now marks the spot where he fell and a permanent U.S. military installation in Atlanta is named in his honor. In rank and position, McPherson was the highest ranking Union general killed in the Civil War.

DAB; Cullum; Boatner, *Civil War*; Warner, *Generals in Blue*; *B&L*, Vol. 4.

MERCER, Hugh, c. 1725–1777, Scotland-Virginia, Continental Army, died 11 January 1777 of wounds received 3 January 1777 at Princeton, New Jersey.

Believed by some to be one of the finest tacticians in the Continental Army, Hugh Mercer was the son of a Scottish minister. He was educated as a physician in Aberdeen and served as a surgeon with the forces of the Young Pretender in 1745. He fled to America in 1746 or 1747 and settled near Mercersburg, Pennsylvania, to practice medicine. During the French and Indian War he served with Pennsylvania troops. In 1759 he was promoted Colonel of the 3rd Pennsylvania Battalion and made commandant of Fort Pitt. After the war Mercer moved to Fredericksburg, Virginia, continued his practice of medicine, entered the Virginia militia, and became friends with George Washington, whom he had met during the war. In 1775 he was elected Colonel of militia, and in February 1776 he became Colonel of the 3rd Virginia, Continental Line. On 5 June 1776 he was promoted Brigadier General and given command of the Flying Camp, a mobile reserve of militia. Mercer took up his command in New York City in July, but he was disappointed with the number, quality, and equipment of his troops. Many of his men were captured when Forts Washington and Lee were captured by the British, and the Flying Camp went out of existence in November, when the enlistments of the rest expired. In the attack on the Hessian camp in Trenton, New Jersey, in December 1776, Mercer led a "brigade" of a few hundred men under Nathaniel Greene. Mercer was one of the officers who suggested to Washington an attack on the British post at Princeton. During the engagement on 3 January 1777 Mercer was sent with a small force to destroy a bridge, thus cutting off British reinforcements coming from Trenton. The British got to the bridge first and a full-scale firefight developed. Both sides brought up artillery and the British launched an attack which drove the Americans back. Mercer was shot and, refusing to surrender, bayoneted five times. Left on the field for dead, he was later found to be breathing and was removed to a farmhouse. He died in Princeton on 11 January. D.S. Freeman believed that Mercer ranked with Nathaniel Greene in the skill of his tactical handling of troops. Trumbull's romantic painting of "The Death of General Mercer at the Battle of Princeton" is an American classic.

DAB; Boatner, *American Revolution*; D.S. Freeman, *Washington*, Vols. 3 & 4; Wright.

MONTGOMERY, Richard, 1738–1775, Ireland-New York, Continental Army, killed in action 31 December 1775 at Quebec, Canada.

Richard Montgomery was the first American general officer killed while commanding troops in action. The son of an Irish Member of Parliament, he was educated in Dublin and entered the British army when he was eighteen. He went to Canada during the French and Indian War and served at Louisburg, Crown Point, Ticonderoga, and Montreal. In 1762 he was at the capture of Martinique and Havana. Returning to England as a Captain, Montgomery became friendly with Burke, Fox, and other liberals. In 1772 he sold his commission and came to New York, where he took up farming and married into the local aristocracy. Montgomery also espoused the colonial cause, and in May 1775 he was a delegate to New York's first provincial congress. On 22 June 1775 he became Brigadier General in the Continental Army and joined Philip Schuyler's invasion of Canada. By September he had taken over command after Schuyler fell sick. Proceeding to the head of Lake Champlain, Montgomery captured Chambly and St. John's and entered Montreal on 13 November. After resting and refitting his troops, he took command of the siege of Quebec on 2 December. He was promoted Major General on 9 December. Faced with the expiration of enlistments of his men, Montgomery decided on an assault as the only way to end the siege successfully. In the early morning hours of 31 December Montgomery and his principal subordinate, Benedict Arnold, led converging columns against Quebec's Lower Town. The British had expected just such a move. Montgomery's column of the 1st New York advanced in a howling blizzard. The general led an advance party of 50 men. With a group of only four officers and thirteen men he rushed a fortified position whose defendants held their fire until his party was almost upon them. Then a blast of cannon and musket fire cut down all but half a dozen. The attack on Quebec was aborted. Montgomery's body was recognized by former British comrades and given a decent burial. In 1818 he was reinterred in New York City. John Trumbull's painting of the "Death of General Montgomery in the Attack on Quebec" is another of his romantic classics.

DAB; *DNB*; Boatner, *American Revolution*; D.S. Freeman, *Washington*, Vols. 3 & 4; Wright.

MORGAN, John Hunt, 1825–1864, Alabama-Kentucky, C.S. Army, killed in action 4 September 1864 at Greenville, Tennessee.

John Hunt Morgan was one of the legendary cavalry leaders of the Confederacy, famed for his long-distance raids behind Union lines. He was born in

Huntsville but reared and educated near his mother's home near Lexington, Kentucky, matriculating at Transylvania College. During the Mexican War he fought at Buena Vista as an enlisted soldier. Returning to Kentucky, Morgan took over the family hemp manufactory and in 1857 organized a militia company. At the start of the Civil War he led his company to Bowling Green to join the secession forces of Simon Bolivar Buckner and was commissioned Captain in September 1861. Promoted Colonel of the 2nd Kentucky Cavalry in April 1862, he commanded a squadron at Shiloh and took over a small brigade in June. Beginning in July 1862 Morgan led a series of raids through the border and mid-western states which earned him the wrath of Union commanders and the peoples of Ohio and Indiana, but the thanks of the Confederate Congress. Morgan became Brigadier General CSA on 11 December 1862 and commanded a division of two brigades during the campaigning around Stone's River, Tennessee. His most famous raid, in July 1863, led him into Indiana and Ohio, where he was captured and imprisoned in the state penitentiary. Morgan and some of his officers escaped in November 1863 and he was given command of the Department of Southwestern Virginia in April 1864. In May he opposed the Union cavalry raids of George Crook and W.W. Averell into southwestern Virginia, and in June he conducted his own last raid to Lexington, Kentucky. On 4 September 1864, while en route to an attack on Union forces at Knoxville, Morgan was killed by a surprise attack of Union cavalry in the garden of the house in which he had been sleeping at Greenville, Tennessee. Two of Morgan's sisters were married to Confederate generals A.P. Hill and Basil W. Duke.

DAB: Boatner, *Civil War*; Warner, *Generals in Gray*; Connelly, *Autumn of Glory*; *B&L*, Vols. 3 & 4; *CMH*, Vol. IX (Kentucky).

MORTON, James St. Clair, 1829-1864, Pennsylvania, U.S. Army, killed in action 17 June 1864 at Petersburg, Virginia.

James St. Clair Morton was a professional military engineer and author of some note on contemporary military engineering topics. He was born in Philadelphia, the son of a physician, and attended the University of Pennsylvania before graduating from West Point in 1851. Before 1861 he was engaged in construction of coast defenses in South Carolina, Delaware, and New Jersey. He also taught engineering at West Point and went on an expedition to Central America. For the first fifteen months of the Civil War, Morton's duties remained unchanged as he worked on fortifications in Florida and Pennsylvania. In June 1862, he became chief engineer of the Army of Ohio, and in October took a similar position with the Army of the Cumberland. He was promoted Brigadier General USV on 29 November 1862. He was twice breveted for meritorious service—at Stone's River in January 1863 and Chickamauga in September 1863—being wounded in the latter battle. He was promoted permanent Major in the Corps of Engineers in July 1863. On 7 November 1863 Morton's volunteer commission expired and he reverted to his permanent grade. He had been commander of the pioneer brigade of the Army of the Cumberland at the time. From January to May 1864 he was assistant to the Chief of Engineers in Washington. In May 1864 Morton was assigned as chief engineer for IX Corps in the northern Virginia campaign. He was present at the battles at North Anna, Totopotomoy, and Bethesda Church. On 17 June 1864, at Petersburg, Morton was killed instantly by a shot in the chest while reconnoitering Confederate outposts. He was posthumously breveted Brigadier General USA to rank from the date of his death.

   DAB; Cullum; Boatner, *Civil War*; Warner, *Generals in Blue*; *B&L*, Vol. 3.

MOUTON, Jean Jacques Alfred Alexander, 1829–1864, Louisiana, C.S. Army, killed in action 8 April 1864 at Mansfield, Louisiana.

   Alfred Mouton, the name he usually was known by in the army, was born at Opelousas, the son of an ex-governor and U.S. senator. He spoke only French as a child and learned English after he started school. He graduated from West Point in 1850 but resigned immediately to go into railroad engineering. He also became a Brigadier General of militia. When the Civil War started Mouton raised a company of infantry for war service and became Colonel of the 18th Louisiana in October 1861. At Shiloh, in April 1862, he suffered a wound which was nearly fatal. Mouton was promoted Brigadier General CSA on 16 April 1862. He returned to duty in the summer of 1862 and led a brigade at Lafourche, Atchafalaya, Berwick Bay, and Bayou Teche. In the Red River campaign of 1864 he commanded a division under Richard Taylor. On 8 April 1864, at Mansfield, or Sabine Crossroads, Louisiana, Mouton was killed during the attack of his division on the advancing Union troops.

   Cullum; Boatner, *Civil War*; Warner, *Generals in Gray*; *B&L*, Vols. 3 & 4; *CMH*, Vol. X (Louisiana).

MULLIGAN, James Adelbert, 1830–1864, New York-Illinois, U.S. Volunteers, died 27 July 1864 of wounds received 24 July 1864 at Winchester, Virginia.

   James A. Mulligan was one of the most colorful characters of the Civil War. At various times he was a lawyer, newspaper editor, explorer, military hero, prisoner of war, and accused fraud. Mulligan was born in Utica, New York, son of an Irish immigrant family. His family moved to Chicago when he was six, and in 1850 he was the first graduate of St. Mary of the Lakes College. He interrupted his law studies to go on an expedition to Panama in 1851. On his return to Chicago he was a newspaper editor, was admitted to the bar, and in 1857 became a clerk in the U.S. Interior Department. In 1861 Mulligan raised the "Irish Brigade" for the Civil War and became its Colonel when it was mustered into service as the 23rd Illinois. The regiment went to Missouri in July and was engaged in the defense of Lexington against Sterling Price's army in September. Mulligan was forced to surrender and was taken captive, accompanied by his wife, who had been in Lexington with him. He was exchanged in November 1861 and returned to Chicago, a national hero. He was offered the rank of Brigadier General USV but refused. He reorganized his regiment at Camp Douglas, Illinois, in December 1861 and remained there until going to Indiana in July 1862. In Indiana he was arrested for deficiencies in his accounts at Camp Douglas. He was charged, among other things, with keeping insufficient records and enlisting prisoners of war. Nevertheless, Mulligan was next assigned to West Virginia, where he commanded successively a brigade and a division protecting lines of communication, although still a Colonel. In July 1864 he defended Leetown, West Virginia, against Jubal Early's attack down the Shenandoah Valley. On 24 July, when Early attacked the Union VIII Corps near Winchester, Virginia, Mulligan, at the head of the 3rd Division, was shot three times and fatally wounded. As he was being carried from the field he saw that the colors were about to be captured and ordered, "Lay me down and save the flag!" His men did as directed. Mulligan was captured before they could return to him. He died three days later in a Confederate hospital. He was posthumously breveted Brigadier General USV to rank from 23 July 1864.

Appleton's; Boatner, *Civil War*; *B&L*, Vol. 1.

MULLINNIX, Henry Maston, 1892–1943, Indiana, U.S. Navy, killed in action 24 November 1943 in the Gilbert Islands.

Henry M. Mullinnix, called by Samuel E. Morison one of the most gifted, widely experienced, and beloved of air admirals, was one of five U.S. Navy flag officers killed in action in World War II. He was born in Spencer, Indiana, attended Purdue University for a year, and graduated first in the class of 1916 from Annapolis. During World War I he served in destroyers on escort and patrol duty from Queenstown, Ireland. After additional post-war duty in destroyers, he studied aeronautical engineering at Massachusetts Institute of Technology and then took flight training. The rest of Mullinnix's naval career was connected with aviation. He served in the Bureau of Aeronautics, aboard USS *Saratoga*, as commander of a bombing squadron, and at Pensacola. He was also with the Scouting Force aircraft section and was navigator of a seaplane tender. Promoted Commander in 1936, Mullinnix was at the Pearl Harbor Air Base and subsequently aviation officer of the Battle force of the Pacific Fleet. Next he commissioned and commanded the tender USS *Albemarle*. In 1941 he was promoted Captain and commanded a patrol wing on anti-submarine duty in Newfoundland. Air Officer of the Eastern Sea Frontier from March 1942, in March 1943 Mullinnix finally got a combat command at sea as Captain of USS *Saratoga*. On 6 August 1943 he was promoted to Rear Admiral to rank from 13 November 1942 and led a task group of three escort carriers on operations in the Gilbert Islands. On 24 November 1943, while supporting the Makin Island operation, Mullinnix's flagship, the USS *Liscome Bay*, was struck by a single torpedo from a Japanese submarine. The bombs in the hold detonanted and the ship broke apart. The flight deck caved in and the *Liscome Bay* sank twenty-three minutes after being hit. Admiral Mullinnix and the ship's captain were among the 642 crew members lost.

Morison, Vol. 7; U.S. Navy Office of Information; *New York Times*, November 27, 1943.

N

NASH, Francis, c. 1742–1777, Virginia-North Carolina, Continental Army, died 7 October 1777 of wounds received 4 October 1777 at Germantown, Pennsylvania.

Francis Nash was a leader of the movement for independence in North Carolina in 1775, although he had played a leading role in suppressing anti-government dissidents only a few years before. Son of a Welshman who had come to Virginia about 1730, Nash was brought to the Hillsboro district of North Carolina while still an infant. As a young man he gained local prominence as a merchant and attorney. He served as clerk of the county court and Orange County representative to the North Carolina House of Commons. His position as a court officer brought him into frequent conflict with the "Regulators," who opposed the provincial government. As a Captain of militia he participated in the Battle of the Alamance in 1771, where the power of the Regulators was broken. Nash gained for himself a reputation for courage and military ability. In 1775 he was a delegate to the provisional congresses of North Carolina. That September he became Lieutenant Colonel of the 1st North Carolina Continentals and succeeded to regimental command in April 1776. While Nash's regiment went to the defense of Charleston he remained in North Carolina on recruiting duty to raise the nine regiments the state had been assessed by the Continental Congress. He was promoted Brigadier General on 5 February 1777 and led the North Carolina brigade to Pennsylvania for the summer campaign of 1777. At Brandywine Creek in September 1777, when Washington's army attempted to prevent the capture of Philadelphia by the British, Nash commanded his brigade in the center of the line. Late in the day, when the British turning movement around the American right became apparent, Nash was sent to that part of the line but never actually got involved in the fighting. After the British occupied Philadelphia, Washington attempted an attack on their post at Germantown on 4 October. Nash's brigade was one of two held in reserve. The attack went well at first, but the center of the American advance was held up by a British strongpoint in a stone house. Just as the North Carolinians were brought forward to join in the attack, Nash was struck in the leg by a cannon ball, which shattered his thigh. He was carried off the battlefield with the retreating Americans, but he died in camp three days later, 7 October 1777.

DAB; *Appleton's*; Boatner, *American Revolution*; D.S. Freeman, *Washington*, Vol. 4.

P

PATRICK, Edwin Davies, 1894–1945, Indiana, U.S. Army, killed in action 14 March 1945 on the Shimbu Line, Luzon, Philippine Islands.

Edwin D. Patrick was the only U.S. Army division commander killed in action in the Pacific theater in World War II. He was born in Tell City, Indiana, and attended the Universities of Indiana and Wisconsin from 1912 to 1916. In 1915 he was commissioned in the Indiana National Guard, and in June 1916 he was called to active duty on the Mexican border during Pershing's Punitive Expedition. Patrick was commissioned in the regular army in March 1917, served first in California and then, during World War I, as a company commander in France and Germany. Between the world wars Patrick was a service school instructor, served in China, attended the Command and General Staff course and the Army and Navy War Colleges. From 1938 to 1942 he was operations officer of the 8th Service Command, as Lieutenant Colonel from June 1939 and as Colonel from October 1941. In 1942 Patrick was given command of the 357th Infantry Regiment of the 90th Division. In December that year he went to the South Pacific command as war plans officer. Patrick was promoted Brigadier General on 26 April 1943 and was chief of staff of Sixth Army on New Guinea from June 1943 to April 1944. This was followed by an assignment as commander of the 158th Regimental Combat Team for the retaking of Wadke and Noemfoor. On 5 September 1944 Patrick was promoted Major General and two days later he was given command of the 6th Division. He led his division in the invasion of Luzon in January 1945 and through the fighting across the island for the next two months. On 14 March, while observing from a battalion command post an attack by the 1st Infantry Regiment on the Shimbu Line, Patrick and a group of officers were hit by a burst of Japanese machine gun fire. The regimental commander was killed and Patrick was mortally wounded. He died shortly thereafter.

Army Register, 1942 and 1945; Smith; Sixth Infantry Division; *New York Times*, March 16, 1945.

PATTEN, Henry Lyman, c. 1836–1864, Massachusetts, U.S. Volunteers, died 10 September 1864 of wounds received 16 August 1864 at Deep Bottom, Virginia.

Henry L. Patten was the third consecutive commander of the 20th Massachusetts Volunteers to be killed in action and to be breveted Brigadier General USV. He was educated at Harvard and entered service in the 20th Massachusetts as a 2nd Lieutenant in November 1861. He was wounded at Nelson's Farm on the Virginia Peninsula in June 1862 and was promoted to 1st Lieutenant in October that year. At Gettysburg in June 1863 Patten commanded two companies of his regiment as skirmishers and was wounded twice, but he remained on the field and held his position. He was made Captain in August 1863. When Henry L. Abbott was killed in action in the Wilderness, Patten was promoted Major on 7 May 1864 to succeed him. With the regimental commander also wounded, Patten was senior officer present with the regiment at Spotsylvania and Petersburg. On 22 June the 20th Massachusetts under Patten's command stopped a Confederate attack and saved a withdrawal of the entire Union position. During the action at Deep Bottom on 16 August 1864 Patten was wounded badly enough in the leg to require amputation. He was sent to a hospital in Philadelphia to recuperate but died there on 10 September. He was posthumously breveted Brigadier General USV to rank from the date of his death.

Boatner, *Civil War*; Bowen; Boston University; *OR*, Ser. I, Vols. 27, pt. 1; 40, pt. 1; 42, pt. 1.

PAXTON, Elisha Franklin, 1828–1863, Virginia, C.S. Army, killed 3 May 1863 at Chancellorsville, Virginia.

"Frank" Paxton was rated one of the best field officers in the Army of Northern Virginia by Stonewall Jackson, a stern master. Paxton was born in Rockbridge County and graduated from Washington College, Yale University, and the University of Virginia law school. He practiced law in Ohio and Virginia and was a bank president, but failing eyesight forced him to retire to his farm in 1859 or 1860. In 1861 he joined the Confederate Army at Harper's Ferry, Virginia, as a Lieutenant in the Rockbridge Rifles. He fought at Bull Run in the 4th Virginia of the Stonewall Brigade. In October he became Major in the 27th Virginia in the same brigade. Paxton was voted out of his position in the general election of field officers in the Army of Northern Virginia in the spring of 1862, but he joined Jackson's staff as assistant adjutant general. Jackson was so impressed by Paxton's talents that when Charles Winder, the Stonewall Brigade commander, was killed at Cedar Mountain in August 1862, Jackson recommended Paxton to be his successor. Paxton was duly appointed and promoted on 1 November 1862 amid the protests of the senior officers of the brigade. He commanded the brigade at Fredericksburg and through the winter and spring of 1863. At Chancellorsville, on the morning of 3 May, Paxton was killed by a shot in the chest while leading a charge on foot. He is said to have had a premonition of death after the wounding of Jackson the night before and said that he would be killed himself. He was buried in the garden of the house in which Jackson lay dying; later he was buried near Jackson in Lexington, Virginia.

Boatner, *Civil War*; Warner, *Generals in Gray*; D.S. Freeman, *Lee's Lieutenants*, Vol. 2; *B&L*, Vol. 3; *CMH*, Vol. III.

PECK, Frank Henry, 1836–1864, Connecticut, U.S. Volunteers, killed in action 19 September 1864 at Winchester, Virginia.

A native of New Haven, Peck graduated from Yale University in 1856 and practiced law. In February 1862 he entered the Union army as Major of the 12th Connecticut. The regiment was sent to Ship Island, Mississippi, the same month and was the first Union regiment to enter New Orleans as part of General Ben Butler's occupying army in April 1862. Peck went on expeditions to Lake Pontchartrain in July 1862 and Bayou Teche in January 1863. In the latter month he was promoted Lieutenant Colonel. At the attack on Port Hudson in May 1863 he was wounded in the hand. Peck served in the defenses of New Orleans until early in 1864 and was acting brigade commander at New Iberia, Louisiana. When XIX Corps was summoned from Louisiana to Virginia to participate in the Shenandoah Valley campaign in 1864, Peck commanded the 12th Connecticut in the 1st Division. At Winchester, on 19 September 1864, he was wounded by a shell fragment while preparing to go into action and died almost immediately. His last message to his family was, "Tell them I die cheerfully in the performance of my duty." He was posthumously breveted Brigadier General USV to rank from 19 September.

Boatner, *Civil War*; Croffut and Morris; *OR*, Ser. I, Vols. 15; 26, pt. 1; 43, pt. 1; 53.

PEGRAM, John, 1832–1865, Virginia, C.S. Army, killed in action 6 February 1865 at Hatcher's Run, Virginia.

A versatile officer who successfully commanded both cavalry and infantry units, John Pegram was a native of Petersburg. He graduated from West Point in 1854 and served on the frontier and in the Utah expedition of 1857. Pegram resigned from the U.S. Army in May 1861 to be appointed Lieutenant Colonel of the 20th Virginia. In the summer of 1861 he served in western Virginia, where he was captured. After his exchange he became Colonel and chief engineer to Generals Beauregard and Bragg in Mississippi in 1862. Pegram was promoted to Brigadier General CSA on 7 November 1862 and transferred to the cavalry. He commanded a brigade at Stone's River, Tennessee, in January 1863 and a division in Forrest's corps at Chickamauga in September. In

October 1863 he returned to Virginia and took command of an infantry brigade. Pegram was wounded while at the head of his brigade in the Wilderness in May 1864 but returned to duty in July. He led a brigade in Jubal Early's invasion of the Shenandoah Valley in the summer of 1864. After the battle at Winchester in September Pegram took command of a division. He exercised effective command of his division at Cedar Creek in October. His was one of the few Confederate units which did not break in the face of the Union counterattack. Pegram's division returned to Lee's main army in December and entered the Petersburg lines. At Hatcher's Run, on 6 February 1865, he was killed by a musket ball which struck him near the heart. Authorities disagree on his rank at the time of his death. Freeman flatly states that Pegram was neither nominated nor confirmed as Major General, but others report that he held that rank from 24 November 1864. Pegram's brother, William, a noted Confederate artillerist, was killed at Five Forks, Virginia, on 2 April 1865.

Cullum; Boatner, *Civil War*; Warner, *Generals in Gray*; D.S. Freeman, *Lee's Lieutenants*, Vols. 1 & 3; *B&L*, Vol. 1; *CMH*, Vol. III.

PENDER, William Dorsey, 1834–1863, North Carolina, C.S. Army, died 18 July 1863 of wounds received 2 July 1863 at Gettysburg, Pennsylvania.

William Dorsey Pender was wounded in every battle in which he participated as a general officer. Highly thought of in the Army of Northern Virginia, he had less than two months to prove his worth as a division commander before his death. Pender was reared in rural North Carolina, clerked in his brother's store, and graduated from West Point in 1854. He served in the West until he resigned his commission in March 1861. Pender first was Captain of CSA artillery and Confederate recruiting officer in Baltimore. Shortly thereafter he became Colonel of the 3rd and then the 6th North Carolina Volunteers. He fought on the Virginia Peninsula and was promoted Brigadier General CSA on 3 June 1862. Pender led his brigade through the Seven Days battles and at Second Manassas, Antietam, Fredericksburg, and Chancellorsville, being wounded or injured in every battle. On 27 May 1863 he was promoted to Major General CSA. At Gettysburg, on 2 July, Pender was riding along his line with a staff officer when he was struck in the leg by a shell fragment. The wound, although serious, was not considered life-threatening and Pender reluctantly allowed himself to be evacuated from Pennsylvania by ambulance. By the time he reached Staunton, Virginia, infection had set in and the leg was amputated on 18 July. Pender died after the operation. He was a prolific letter writer, and he has been extensively quoted by numerous authors in writing the history of the war in Virginia.

DAB; Cullum; Boatner, *Civil War*; Warner, *Generals in Gray*; D.S. Freeman, *Lee's Lieutenants*, Vols. 2 & 3; *B&L*, Vol. 3; *CMH*, Vol. IV.

PERRIN, Abner Monroe, 1827–1864, South Carolina, C.S. Army, killed in action 12 May 1864 at Spotsylvania, Virginia.

Abner M. Perrin was one of the second rank of Confederate generals thrown into high command by the vicissitudes of the Civil War. He was born in the Edgefield District of South Carolina. As a young man he first was a regular army officer in the Mexican War and then studied and practiced law in Columbia. When the Civil War started Perrin entered service as a Captain of the 14th South Carolina. After service on the coast, his regiment went to Virginia in 1862 and fought in the Seven Days battles and at Second Manassas, Antietam, and Fredericksburg. Perrin was promoted Colonel in February 1863 and commanded the regiment at Chancellorsville. When Samuel McGowan was wounded, Perrin succeeded to brigade command and led the South Carolina brigade at Gettysburg. For his work there he was promoted Brigadier General CSA on 10 September 1863 and given command of an Alabama brigade. At Spotsylvania, Virginia, on 12 May 1864, Perrin was shot from his horse with seven bullets in his body while attempting to recapture the Bloody Angle. Before the battle he is reported to have said, "I shall come out of this fight a live Major General or a dead Brigadier."

Boatner, *Civil War*; Warner, *Generals in Gray*; Coddington; *Lee's Lieutenants*, Vol. 3; *B&L*, Vol. 4; *CMH*, Vol. V.

PETTIGREW, James Johnston, 1828–1863, North Carolina, C.S. Army, died 17 July 1863 of wounds received 13 or 14 July 1863 at Falling Waters, Maryland.

Another of the bright young intellects of the South, J. Johnston Pettigrew was the son of a U.S. congressman. He was born in Tyrrell County, graduated from the University of North Carolina when he was nineteen, and accepted President Polk's appointment as assistant professor at the Naval Observatory in Washington. Pettigrew took up the study of law, traveled in Europe, and settled in Charleston. He entered the South Carolina legislature and was a Colonel of militia. When South Carolina seceded from the Union in December 1860, Pettigrew began fortification of the old defenses in Charleston harbor. Later he enlisted in Hampton's Legion. In May 1861 he was commissioned Colonel of the 12th North Carolina, and he became Brigadier General CSA on 26 February 1862. Pettigrew served on the Virginia Peninsula, where he was wounded and captured after he refused to be carried off the field at Seven Pines. Exchanged during the summer of 1862, he commanded the defenses of Petersburg before rejoining the Army of Northern Virginia with a brigade from North Carolina in May 1863. At Gettysburg, Pettigrew succeeded to the command of Henry Heth's division after the latter was wounded on 1 July. On 3 July Pettigrew led the much enfeebled unit during Pickett's charge and was wounded in the hand. On the night of 13/14 July 1863, as Lee's army was withdrawing across the Potomac, Heth's division formed the rear guard. Pettigrew, back in command of his brigade, suffered a mortal abdominal wound during an attack by Union cavalry on his position at Falling Waters, Maryland. Refusing to be left behind, he was carried into Virginia on a litter and died on 17 July.

DAB; Boatner, *Civil War*; Warner, *Generals in Gray*; D.S. Freeman, *Lee's Lieutenants*, Vols. 1–3; Coddington; *B&L*, Vols. 2 & 3; *CMH*, Vol. IV.

PIKE, Zebulon Montgomery, 1779–1813, New Jersey, U.S. Army, killed in action 27 April 1813 at York (Toronto), Ontario, Canada.

Zebulon Pike is best known for his explorations as a young officer and for the mountain peak which bears his name. He was the son of a career army officer, received his early education in the East, and accompanied his family to his father's frontier posts. In 1795 he became a Cadet in his father's company. Pike supplemented his income by acting as agent for the contractor who supplied the post, a common practice at the time. He became 1st Lieutenant in 1799, and in 1805–1806 he led an expedition to the headwaters of the Mississippi River. In July 1806 he led another expedition to find the headwaters of the Arkansas and Red Rivers and to make a reconnaissance of Spanish settlements in New Mexico. Pike moved via a circuitous route to Colorado, where he discovered Pike's Peak and was captured by the Spanish. He was taken first to Sante Fe and later to Chihuahua. His papers were confiscated, but he was allowed to return to St. Louis by way of Texas. In 1810 he published an account of his travels. Pike was promoted Major in 1808 and at the outbreak of the War of 1812 became Colonel of the 15th Infantry. He was assigned to Henry Dearborn's army for the invasion of Canada. On 12 May 1813 Pike was promoted Brigadier General USA and appointed Adjutant and Inspector General of the U.S. Army, but he stayed with Dearborn's army. In April 1813 Dearborn moved a force of 1,700 men across Lake Ontario to attack the British Post at York (Toronto). Dearborn accompanied the expedition but Pike was in immediate command. On 27 April they successfully attacked and drove the defenders out of the fort. As the British retreated they blew up their powder magazine to prevent it from falling into the hands of the Americans. Pike was struck from behind by a large rock thrown up by the explosion and his back and ribs were crushed. He was carried to a ship on the lake but died the same day.

DAB; Heitman, *U.S. Army*; Beirne; Berton.

POLK, Leonidas, 1806–1864, North Carolina-Louisiana, C.S. Army, killed in action 14 June 1864 at Pine Mountain, Georgia.

Leonidas Polk, the Bishop-General, was renowned throughout the South as clergyman and educator for years before the Civil War. He was born in Raleigh, son of a Revolutionary veteran and distant kinsman of President James K. Polk. He attended the University of North Carolina for a short time and then graduated from West Point in 1827. Polk resigned from the army six months later to enter the Episcopal ministry. In 1830 he was ordained deacon and by 1838 he was consecrated bishop. Eventually he became Bishop of the Diocese of Louisiana. He also helped to establish the University of the South at Suwanee, Tennessee. In 1861 Polk was persuaded by Jefferson Davis, his friend since cadet days, to accept a Major General's commission in the Confederate Army dated 25 June.

Polk first commanded Department Number 2 and then fought at Belmont, Missouri, Shiloh, Perryville, Stone's River, and Chickamauga. He was made Lieutenant General on 10 October 1862 and was a corps or army commander in numerous engagements. After Chickamauga he was removed from command and his court-martial ordered by Braxton Bragg, but President Davis intervened and restored him for the Atlanta campaign of 1864. At Pine Mountain, Georgia, on 14 June 1864, while in the company of Generals J.E. Johnston and W.J. Hardee, Polk was killed by a long-range shot from a Union Parrott gun. The unexploded shell passed through his chest from left to right, killing him instantly. His body was carried to Augusta, Georgia, where it was buried in the Episcopal churchyard on 29 June.

DAB; Cullum; Boatner, *Civil War*; Warner, *Generals in Gray*; Connelly, *Autumn of Glory*; *B&L*, Vols. 1, 3, 4; CMH, Vol. I; *Augusta Chronicle*, June 15 & 20, 1864.

POSEY, Carnot, 1818–1863, Mississippi, C.S. Army, died 13 November 1863 of wounds received 14 October 1863 at Bristoe Station, Virginia.

Carnot Posey was another Mississippian who traced his connections with Jefferson Davis to their shared service in the Mexican War. Posey was born in Wilkinson County, obtained a degree in Louisiana, and attended the University of Virginia law school. He settled into a life of practicing law and operating a plantation. He fought in Mexico with Davis's Mississippi Rifles and was wounded at Buena Vista. Later he was U.S. attorney for the southern district of Mississippi. In 1861 Posey raised a company of infantry for the Civil War, became its Captain, and was elected Colonel of the 16th Mississippi. He led his regiment at Bull Run and Ball's Bluff, on the Virginia Peninsula, and at Second Manassas and Antietam. He was promoted Brigadier General CSA on 1 November 1862 but was without a brigade until January 1863, when he took over the command of W.S. Featherston, who had returned to Mississippi. Posey led the brigade at Chancellorsville and Gettysburg. In the latter battle he was unable to participate in the attack on the Union center on 2 July because of the disarray of his regiments. At Bristoe Station, on 14 October 1863, while covering the flank of his division's attack, Posey received a superficial wound in the left thigh from a spherical case shot. He was carried to the home of a friend in Charlottesville to recover but died of infection on 13 November.

Boatner, *Civil War*; Warner, *Generals in Gray*; D.S. Freeman, *Lee's Lieutenants*, Vols. 2 & 3; *CMH*, Vol. VII (Mississippi).

PRATT, Don Forrester, 1892–1944, Missouri, U.S. Army, killed in action 6 June 1944 near Hiesville, Normandy, France.

Don F. Pratt was the second U.S. airborne general killed in World War II. Ironically, neither he nor Charles L. Keerans, the other combat fatality, was involved in parachute operations when killed. Pratt was born in Linn County, the son of a local judge. He attended the Universities of Minnesota and Wisconsin and was commissioned into the army in August 1917. Pratt spent the years of World War I in California. This was followed by a tour of duty in Alaska and a posting as company commander in Minnesota. He was an ROTC instructor at the University of Minnesota for five years, attended Command and General Staff School in 1931–1932, and followed this with four years in China with the 15th Infantry. Pratt returned from China as a Major, attended the Army War College course, and was an instructor at the Infantry School at Fort Benning. Promoted Lieutenant Colonel in 1940, he went to Florida to be chief of staff of the 43rd National Guard Division and was made Colonel in December 1941. In the summer of 1942 he joined the newly activated 101st Airborne Division and was promoted Brigadier General on 1 August 1942. Pratt was considered by many to be too old for airborne service, and in fact he never became parachute-qualified, but he proved himself to be a good leader and a sound tactician in ground combat training. He went to England with the division in 1943 and was expected to lead the seaborne follow-up portion of the division during the Normandy invasion. These orders were later changed, and he was designated to lead the glider troops in the first assault. On 6 June 1944, the famous D-Day, as the first American troops began to arrive in France, Pratt's glider overshot its landing strip and crashed into a tree near Hiesville. He was later found in the wreck, dead of a broken neck.

Army Register, 1944; Blair; Rapport and Northwood; Crookenden; Devlin; *New York Times*, June 22, 1944; *Time*, July 3, 1944; Don F. Pratt Museum.

PRESCOTT, George Lincoln, c. 1829–1864, Massachusetts, U.S. Volunteers, died 19 June 1864 of wounds received 18 June 1864 at Petersburg, Virginia.

George L. Prescott was another of the regimental officers who was honored in death with a promotion to Brigadier General. Prescott was a native of Concord and a lumber dealer before the Civil War. He entered service in the 5th Massachusetts, a three-month regiment, in April 1861 and was assigned to the garrison at Fort Warren in Boston harbor. In November 1861 Prescott was commissioned Captain in a regiment which was formed from the Fort Warren garrison and designated the 32nd Massachusetts. The new regiment went to Washington in May 1862. Prescott became Lieutenant Colonel in August and Colonel in December. He participated in the Maryland and Fredericksburg campaigns in 1862 but was absent providing railroad guards at Acquia Creek during Chancellorsville in May 1863. At Gettysburg, Prescott's brigade (Sweitzer's of V Corps) was nearly destroyed as a fighting unit on the second day. It suffered over 400 casualties out of slightly over 800 going into action. Prescott himself was unscathed. At Spotsylvania and Petersburg in the spring of 1864 he was temporarily in command of the brigade. On 18 June 1864, as the Union armies pressed forward against Beauregard's lines in front of Petersburg, Prescott led his regiment across an open plain in the abortive attack of V Corps. Before the advance was repulsed Prescott was shot down, mortally wounded. He died the next day. He was posthumously breveted Brigadier General USV to rank from 18 June.

Boatner, *Civil War*; Coddington; Bowen; *OR*, Ser. I, Vol. 40, pt. 1; Boston University.

PULASKI, Casimir, c. 1748–1779, Poland, Continental Army, died 11 October 1779 of wounds received 9 October 1779 at Savannah, Georgia.

Casimir Pulaski was possibly one of the most incorrigible officers ever to wear an American uniform. He was the son of a noble family and began his military career in 1767 fighting against the Russians. Later he went to Turkey and then to France. Ever the adventurer, in 1777 he came to Boston with letters of introduction from Benjamin Franklin in Paris. He joined Washington's army in time to serve as a volunteer aide at Brandywine. Pulaski spoke almost no English, but on the strength of his references Washington proposed him to Congress as commander of the dragoons. On 15 September 1777 he was appointed "Commander of the Horse" with rank of Brigadier General. Pulaski refused to recognize any authority other than Congress and insisted on dealing directly with that body. He was on continuous bad terms with his subordinates and recommended at least one for court-martial. In March 1778 Pulaski resigned as Commander of the Horse to raise his own cavalry force. He largely recruited from British prisoners and deserters despite congressional prohibitions against such practices. His first action was in October 1778 when the British surprised the sleeping infantry of the Pulaski Legion and killed more than fifty. Pulaski, with his cavalry, managed to drive off the attackers. Later his Legion served on the New York frontier as protection against Indian raiders. The Legion was moved to South Carolina in February 1779 and helped to defend Charleston against the British overland attack from Savannah in May. Pulaski was defeated in an attempt to ambush a British force, but Charleston was saved by the arrival of Benjamin Lincoln's troops from the north. In the Franco-American siege of Savannah in October 1779, Pulaski was mortally wounded in the abortive attack on the Spring Hill redoubt on 9 October. He was carried on board USS *Wasp* where a surgeon attempted to remove a grapeshot from his groin. Pulaski died as a result of his wound, probably on 11 October, and was buried either at sea or in an unmarked grave on the Georgia coast.

DAB; *Appleton's*; Boatner, *American Revolution*; D.S. Freeman, *Washington*, Vols. 4 & 5; Wright.

R

RAINS, James Edward, 1833–1862, Tennessee, C.S. Army, killed in action 31 December 1862 at Stone's River, Tennessee.

James E. Rains was a promising young attorney when the Civil War brought an end to his career. He was born in Nashville, graduated from Yale University law school, and practiced law and edited a newspaper in his native city. He was also district attorney general in the Nashville area. When the Civil War started Raines enlisted as a private in the 11th Tennessee but within a month he was elected Colonel of the regiment. He occupied Cumberland Gap during the east Tennessee campaign of 1861–1862 but was forced to withdraw before the Union advance in June 1862. Rains led a brigade in Carter Stevenson's division during Kirby Smith's invasion of Kentucky in late 1862. For his part he was rewarded with promotion to Brigadier General CSA on 4 November 1862. At Stone's River, Tennessee, on 31 December, his brigade was on the extreme left of Braxton Bragg's advancing Confederate line. Rains was killed by a musket ball while leading his men against a Union battery and was buried on the battlefield.

Boatner, *Civil War*; Warner, *Generals in Gray*; *CMH*, Vol. VIII.

RAMEY, Howard Knox, 1896–1943, Mississippi, U.S. Army Air Force, missing in action, declared dead 23 March 1943 near Port Moresby, New Guinea.

Howard K. Ramey was the third successive general commanding V Bomber Command to die in the line of duty in the South Pacific in World War II. Ramey was born in Waynesboro and attended Mississippi Agricultural and Mechanical College. He enlisted in the Army Signal Corps Aviation Section in December 1917 and was commissioned 2nd Lieutenant in April 1918. He was assigned at air bases in Florida during World War I and saw no combat service. Later he was a flying instructor, attended aerial photography school, and became commander of an observation squadron. Promoted 1st Lieutenant in July 1920, Ramey went to the Philippines in 1925 and was air intelligence officer there until 1927. Returning to the United States, he held various command and staff positions but concentrated on intelligence and aerial observation. He was promoted to Captain in 1932, attended Command and General Staff School in 1934–1936, and became Major upon graduation. Ramey next became operations officer of the 1st Wing, followed in January 1941 by an assignment as operations officer of Fourth Air Force. He had been made Lieutenant Colonel in December 1940. Promoted to Colonel in February 1942, Ramey commanded IV Bomber Command in August–September 1942 and was promoted Brigadier General on 17 September. That month he went to Hawaii to command the bomber element of Seventh Air Force. On 24 December 1942 he earned the commendation of Admiral Chester Nimitz, the Pacific theater commander, for his raid on Wake Island. In January 1943, after the death of Kenneth N. Walker, Ramey was sent to take over V Bomber Command in the South Pacific. He led his B-17s in the battle of the Bismarck Sea on 1–4 March 1943 during which twelve enemy ships were sunk. While on a reconnaissance flight to Port Moresby on 23 March Ramey's plane was lost and he was listed as missing in action. He was declared dead on 19 November 1945.

Army Register, 1943; Schnapper; Carter and Mueller; *Time*, April 12, 1943; Military Service Record.

RAMSEUR, Stephen Dodson, 1837–1864, North Carolina, C.S. Army, died 20 October 1864 of wounds received 19 October 1864 at Cedar Creek, Virginia.

S. Dodson Ramseur was one of the finest of the young officers brought to high command in the Confederate Army in the later years of the Civil War. He was born in Lincolnton, attended Davidson College for a time, and graduated from West Point in 1860. The next April he resigned his commission to enter Confederate service as Captain of North Carolina artillery. In April 1862 he was elected Colonel of the 49th North Carolina and led it in the Virginia Peninsula campaign, being wounded at Malvern Hill. Ramseur was promoted Brigadier General CSA on 1 November 1862 but was absent from his brigade at Fredericksburg. His first combat opportunity as brigade commander was at Chancellorsville in May 1863, where he distinguished himself and was wounded again but refused to leave the field. Continuing in command at Gettysburg and through 1863, he was officially cited for his actions in the Wilderness and at Spotsylvania, where he was wounded yet again at the Bloody Angle. On 1 July 1864 he was promoted to Major General CSA to take command of Jubal Early's division. Ramseur accompanied Early on the Shenandoah Valley campaign of 1864 and was present at the raid on Washington and the battle at Winchester in September. After the death of Robert Rodes, Ramseur transferred to command of that officer's division and was at its head when he was killed at Cedar Creek. Ramseur suffered a slight wound early in the battle but later took a shot in the right side which tore through both lungs. Attempts were made to carry him off the field, but he was captured by the victorious Union forces and carried to Phil Sheridan's headquarters. Despite efforts of both Union and Confederate surgeons to save him, he died on 20 October.

DAB; Cullum; Gallagher; Boatner, *Civil War*; Warner, *Generals in Gray*; D.S. Freeman, *Lee's Lieutenants*, Vols. 2 & 3; *B&L*, Vol. 4; *CMH*, Vol. IV.

RANDAL, Horace, 1831–1864, Tennessee-Texas, C.S. Army, killed in action 30 April 1864 at Jenkins's Ferry, Arkansas.

Horace Randal was never officially commissioned as a general officer by the Confederate government. He graduated from West Point in 1854 and served on the frontier before resigning his commission in February 1861. He refused a 2nd Lieutenant's commission in the C.S. Army and fought as a private in Virginia until being named Colonel of the 28th Texas Cavalry in 1862. Randal went to the Trans-Mississippi Department in September 1862 and commanded a brigade of cavalry from then on. At Milliken's Bend, Louisiana, in June 1863, his brigade fought as infantry in thwarting one of the Union attempts at Vicksburg. In November 1863 he was recommended for promotion to Brigadier General but the appointment was delayed over a bureaucratic inquiry as to whether or not his command was large enough to be called a brigade. On 8 and 9 April 1864, during the Red River campaign, Randal's brigade formed part of John G. Walker's division at the battles of Mansfield and Pleasant Hill, Louisiana. His conduct under fire was commended by General Dick Taylor, the tactical commander. On 13 April General Kirby Smith, the Department commander, assigned Randal as Brigadier General to rank from 8 April. At Jenkins's Ferry, Arkansas, on 30 April, when Taylor turned to strike the Union force at the crossing of the Sabine River, Randal was caught in a crossfire, was mortally wounded, and died the same day. According to *CMH*, he had not been informed of his promotion. This seems unlikely because Kirby Smith was with Taylor's army at the time. Randal's promotion was never sanctioned by the central government in Richmond, and many sources do not list him as a general.

Cullum; Boatner, *Civil War*; *CMH*, Vol. XI.

READ, Theodore, c. 1835–1865, Ohio-Illinois, U.S. Volunteers, killed in action 6 April 1865 at High Bridge, Virginia.

Theodore Read shares with his opponent, James Dearing, the unique fate of having been killed in personal combat with another general. Read was born in Athens, Ohio, the son of a professor at the University of Ohio. He, himself, graduated from Indiana State University, studied law, and became a clerk in the U.S. Interior Department. In 1860 he opened his own legal practice in Illinois. Read entered military service for the Civil War in July 1861 and in October was appointed Captain and assistant adjutant general on the staff of General

W.H.T. Brooks. Read remained with Brooks until the latter resigned from the army in July 1864, serving him successively as brigade, division, and department adjutant. Read was cited for gallantry at Yorktown and Williamsburg on the Virginia Peninsula in 1862 and was wounded during the Seven Days battles. He returned to duty in October 1862 and was present at Fredericksburg and Chancellorsville, where he was wounded again. From June 1863 to April 1864 Brooks commanded the Department of the Monongahela at Pittsburgh and Read accompanied him. Thereafter they returned to Virginia for the Cold Harbor campaign and Read was wounded yet again. In August 1864 he was promoted Major and became adjutant of XVIII Corps at the siege of Petersburg. In October 1864 Read's horse fell on him, breaking his leg, and while on convalescent leave, he married. In December 1864 he returned to the army as adjutant of XXIV Corps. In January 1865 Read was appointed adjutant general of the Army of the James under General Edward O.C. Ord. The records indicate that he was given the rank and pay of a Lieutenant Colonel, but the commission was never issued. On 6 April 1865 a task force of 600 mixed infantry and cavalry was formed to burn bridges to deter the retreat of Lee's army from Petersburg. Ord appointed Read to the command. At High Bridge, Virginia, they encountered a much superior force led by Confederate general James Dearing. Almost all of Read's command was captured. Read was killed by a ball above the hip while in a personal combat with Dearing, who also fell mortally wounded. Read was buried on the field. He was breveted Brigadier General USV to rank from 29 September 1864, the date of his participation in the attack on Fort Harrison at Petersburg.

Boatner, *Civil War*; *B&L*, Vol. 4; *OR*, Ser. I, Vols. 25, pt. 1; 36, pt. 1; 42, pt. 3; 46, pts. 2 & 3; 51, pt. 1; Military Service Record.

RENO, Jesse Lee, 1823–1862, Virginia-Pennsylvania, U.S. Volunteers, killed in action 14 September 1862 at South Mountain, Maryland.

Jesse Reno, born Renault, was one of two Union corps commanders killed in action during the Maryland campaign of 1862. He was a native of Wheeling (West Virginia) and moved with his family to Venango County, Pennsylvania, in 1832. He graduated from West Point in 1846 and went immediately to Mexico with Scott's army. As commander of a battery of light howitzers manned by ordnance troops he was breveted twice. Later he served as an ordnance staff officer, went on the Utah expedition, and was commander of the U.S. Arsenal at Mount Vernon, Alabama, when the Civil War started. Forced to surrender to state troops there, Reno went next to the arsenal at Fort Leavenworth, Kansas, where he was commissioned Brigadier General USV on 12 November 1861. He commanded a brigade on Burnside's North Carolina expedition and by April 1862 was commanding a division in the Department of North Carolina. Going to Virginia with the North Carolina troops in July, Reno commanded a division when they were formed into IX Corps. When Burnside, the corps commander, was elevated to lead a wing of the Army of the Potomac,

Reno took over the corps. He led it at Second Manassas, where one of his divisions, under Isaac I. Stevens, participated in the only successful action of the battle on 29 August 1862. Reno had charge of the rear guard of the army in the subsequent withdrawal toward Centerville, Virginia, and then commanded IX Corps in the Maryland campaign. On 14 September 1862, on South Mountain, Maryland, Reno was on the skirmish line to insure that his men advanced as ordered through Fox's and Turner's Gaps when he was shot by a sniper and died within a few minutes. He had been promoted Major General USV on 20 August to rank from 18 July 1862.

DAB; Cullum; Boatner, *Civil War*; Warner, *Generals in Blue*; Catton, *Mr. Lincoln's Army*; *B&L*, Vol. 2.

REVERE, Paul Joseph, 1832–1863, Massachusetts, U.S. Volunteers, died 4 July 1863 of wounds received 2 July 1863 at Gettysburg, Pennsylvania.

Paul J. Revere, named for his grandfather, was descended from one of the most renowned figures in American history. He was born in Boston, graduated from Harvard in 1852, and entered the family business. In July 1861 he was commissioned Major in the 20th Massachusetts and joined the Army of the Potomac. At Edward Baker's fiasco at Ball's Bluff, Virginia, in October 1861, Revere was wounded and captured. Taken to Libby Prison in Richmond, he was one of thirteen Union officers selected as hostages to prevent the hanging of Confederate privateers convicted of piracy. The prisoners were treated as criminals until the U.S. courts overturned the privateers' convictions. Revere was released in February 1862. He served with the 20th on the Virginia Peninsula, was absent sick for a time, and returned to the army in August 1862 as a Lieutenant Colonel, assistant adjutant general in II Corps. He was wounded again at Antietam but recovered in time to serve at Fredericksburg in December. In the spring of 1863 he took two months' sick leave and missed Chancellorsville. Promoted Colonel in April, he returned to the 20th Massachusetts in time to march to Gettysburg in June 1863. On 2 July 1863 the 20th was in reserve in rifle pits behind II Corps lines near the Clump of Trees. The officers of the regiment were standing behind the pits observing the action when Revere was hit by a shell fragment. Taken from the field to a hospital at Westminister, Maryland, he died there on 4 July. He was posthumously breveted Brigadier General USV to rank from 2 July. Paul Revere should not be confused with his brother, Brigadier General Joseph Warren Revere, who was cashiered from the army for gross dereliction at Chancellorsville, but was allowed to resign in August 1863 through the personal intervention of President Lincoln.

Boatner, *Civil War*; *Appleton's*; Catton, *Mr. Lincoln's Army*; Coddington; *OR*, Ser. I, Vols. 5; 27, pt. 1; Ser. II, Vol. 3.

REYNOLDS, John Fulton, 1820–1863, Pennsylvania, U.S. Volunteers, killed in action 1 July 1863 at Gettysburg, Pennsylvania.

John F. Reynolds was respected in the pre-Civil War U.S. Army as a professional among professionals. He was born in Lancaster, attended schools in Maryland and Pennsylvania, and graduated from West Point in 1841. He served in coast defenses and in Mexico, on the frontier, and with the Utah expedition. In 1860 he became Commandant of Cadets at West Point, the officer responsible for the discipline and professional development of the Corps of Cadets. The position carried the local rank of Lieutenant Colonel. When the regular army was expanded in May 1861 to meet the needs of the Civil War, Reynolds's rank was made permanent. He was promoted Brigadier General USV on 20 August 1861. Reynolds raised and commanded the First Brigade of the Pennsylvania Reserves which he led until June 1862. He served in the defenses of Washington, was military governor of Fredericksburg, and fought on the Virginia Peninsula in 1862. Reynolds was captured at Glendale, Virginia, in June 1862 and exchanged in August. He commanded the Pennsylvania Reserve division at Second Manassas. During the Maryland campaign he was sent to Pennsylvania to organize the state militia against Lee's invasion. At the end of September he took command of I Corps and was promoted Major General USV on 29 November 1862. Reynolds led the corps at Fredericksburg in December and at Chancellorsville the next May. In the latter battle he openly criticized Joseph Hooker, the army commander, for indecisiveness. When Hooker was relieved Reynolds was considered as a replacement but showed no interest, and George G. Meade was selected. When Union cavalry encountered Confederate forces at Gettysburg, Pennsylvania, on 1 July 1863, Reynolds and his I Corps were nearby. Reynolds rushed his divisions forward to support the cavalry and accompanied them himself. As he was personally posting regiments and batteries, and calling for reinforcements to stem the growing Confederate threat, he was struck behind the ear by a musket ball and fell from the saddle dead.

DAB; Cullum; Boatner, *Civil War*; Warner, *Generals in Blue*; Catton, *Mr. Lincoln's Army* and *Glory Road*; Coddington; *B&L*, Vols. 2 & 3.

RICE, James Clay, 1829–1864, Massachusetts-New York, U.S. Volunteers, killed in action 10 May 1864 at Spotsylvania, Virginia.

Like many other volunteer officers of the Union and Confederate armies, James C. Rice had a background in the law before entering military service. He was born in a small village in western Massachusetts, graduated from Yale in 1854, and went to Natchez, Mississippi, to teach school and write for a local newspaper. He studied law and moved to New York City, where he opened up his practice. In May 1861 he enlisted in the 39th New York, a three-month regiment, and quickly became regimental adjutant and then Captain before being mustered out in August. Rice reentered the army as Lieutenant Colonel of the 44th New York and fought through the 1862 campaign on the Virginia Peninsula. He succeeded to the colonelcy of the regiment in July 1862 and led it at Second Manassas. He was absent from the army during the Maryland and

Fredericksburg campaigns but returned in December 1862 and was again in command at Chancellorsville. Rice rendered his finest service at Gettysburg. When Strong Vincent, his brigade commander, was mortally wounded, Rice took over the brigade and held the vital left flank of the Union line at Little Round Top for two days. He was rewarded with promotion to Brigadier General USV on 17 August 1863. In the spring campaign of 1864 he commanded a brigade in V Corps. In the swirling hand-to-hand fighting at Laurel Hill near Spotsylvania, Virginia, on 10 May 1864, Rice's thigh was shattered by a musket ball. He was carried to a hospital to have his leg amputated, and when asked what position would be most comfortable for him, he requested to be placed with his face toward the enemy. Rice died the same day he was wounded.

Boatner, *Civil War*; Warner, *Generals in Blue*; Coddington.

RICE, Samuel Allen, 1828–1864, New York-Iowa, U.S. Volunteers, died 6 July 1864 of wounds received 30 April 1864 at Jenkins's Ferry, Arkansas.

Samuel Rice was the only Union general killed or mortally wounded in Arkansas during the Civil War. He was born in Cattaraugus County but moved with his family to Pennsylvania and Ohio. He attended Ohio University, and Union College in Schenectady, New York, and traveled with his father, a flatboat operator on the Ohio and Mississippi Rivers. After law school Rice settled in Iowa and opened his own practice. He subsequently became county attorney and state attorney general. Rice raised and organized the 33rd Iowa in the summer of 1862 and was mustered into service as its Colonel in October. In the spring of 1863 the regiment went to Arkansas. For the next year Rice was actively engaged in winning that state back into the Union. In command of a brigade in XIII Corps, he aided in the defense of Helena and then accompanied the expedition to capture Little Rock. He was promoted Brigadier General USV on 4 August 1863. In the spring campaign of 1864 Fred Steele's column advanced to Camden, Arkansas, in conjunction with Banks's Red River expedition, but Steele was forced to turn back to Little Rock after Kirby Smith captured his trains. Smith caught up with Steele as the latter was crossing the Sabine River at Jenkins's Ferry on 30 April 1864. The Confederates were repulsed, but Rice's ankle bone was shattered by a bullet which struck his spur. He was carried to his home in Okaloosa, Iowa, where he died of complications from his wound on 6 July 1864.

Boatner, *Civil War*; Warner, *Generals in Blue*.

RICHARDSON, Israel Bush, 1815–1862, Vermont, U.S. Volunteers, died 3 November 1862 of wounds received 17 September 1862 at Antietam, Maryland.

Israel Bush Richardson, "Greasy Dick" to his intimates, was a career officer who forsook soldiering to take up farming before the Civil War. He was born in Fairfax, Vermont, a descendant of General Israel Putnam. He graduated from West Point in 1841, fought in the Seminole and Mexican Wars, and served on the frontier. In 1855 he resigned his commission to become a farmer in Michigan, but in 1861 he raised and was appointed Colonel of the 2nd Michigan. Taking his regiment to Washington, Richardson was made a brigade commander in Irvin McDowell's army preparing to do battle in northern Virginia. His troops were roughly treated in a skirmish with Confederates a few days before Bull Run in July 1861 but were not actively engaged in the battle itself. On 9 August 1861 Richardson was promoted Brigadier General USV to rank from 17 May. He commanded first a brigade and then a division in the Army of the Potomac. Although casual in his own appearance, Richardson was a strict disciplinarian and ran a tightly organized unit. He participated creditably in the Virginia Peninsula campaign of 1862 but missed Second Manassas because his division had not yet returned from the Peninsula. Richardson was fully engaged in the Maryland campaign. While directing the fire of a supporting artillery battery on 17 September, he was struck by a single ball from a case shot. Carried to McClellan's headquarters, Richardson was at first treated as a minor casualty case. He lingered on in a field hospital for many weeks with gangrene gradually setting into the wound. He finally died on 3 November. On 5 March 1863 he was posthumously promoted to Major General USV to rank from 4 July 1862.

Cullum; Boatner, *Civil War*; Warner, *Generals in Blue*; Catton, *Mr. Lincoln's Army*; *B&L*, Vols. 1 & 2.

RODES, Robert Emmett, 1829–1864, Virginia-Alabama, C.S. Army, killed in action 19 September 1864 at Winchester, Virginia.

Robert E. Rodes was another of the fine second generation of Confederate general officers. He was born in Lynchburg, graduated from Virginia Military Institute in 1848, and taught there for three years before resigning to go into railroad engineering. He returned to VMI in 1861, but when the Civil War started he went to Alabama to raise a company of infantry for war service. He was made Colonel of the 5th Alabama in May 1861 and led his regiment so well at Bull Run that he was promoted Brigadier General CSA on 21 October 1861. Rodes commanded an Alabama brigade on the Virginia Peninsula in 1862 and was badly wounded at Seven Pines on 31 May. Nevertheless, he returned to duty to participate in the Seven Days battles. After convalescent leave, Rodes commanded his brigade at South Mountain and Antietam, Maryland, where he was wounded again, and at Fredericksburg. In January 1863 he took over the division of Daniel H. Hill, who had gone to North Carolina. At Chancellorsville, in May 1863, Rodes was the senior brigadier with II Corps and commanded the corps briefly after both Stonewall Jackson and A.P. Hill had been wounded. For his actions he was made Major General CSA on 7 May to rank from 2 May 1863. Rodes did not live up to his reputation at Gettysburg but showed considerable improvement by the spring campaign of 1864. In June 1864 he took his division to the Shenandoah Valley with Jubal Early and fought at Kernstown, in the raid on Washington, and at Monocacy Junction. During the

Confederate counterattack against the Union advance at Winchester, Virginia, on 19 September 1864, Rodes was knocked from his horse when a shell fragment hit him in the head. He died within a few minutes.

DAB; Boatner, *Civil War*; Warner, *Generals in Gray*; D.S. Freeman, *Lee's Lieutenants*, Vols. 1–3; *B&L*, Vols. 2 & 4; *CMH*, Vol. VII (Alabama).

RODMAN, Isaac Peace, 1822–1862, Rhode Island, U.S. Volunteers, died 30 September 1862 of wounds received 17 September 1862 at Antietam, Maryland.

Isaac P. Rodman was a Quaker who, in the tradition of Nathaniel Greene, forsook religious convictions to pursue his moral and political goals. He was the oldest son in a family of fourteen children and, upon attaining adulthood, entered business with his father. Later he became a prominent merchant, a member of the town council, and a state legislator. In 1861 Rodman accepted a commission as Captain in the 2nd Rhode Island. His regiment was shattered at Bull Run and he resigned his commission, but he was appointed Colonel of the 4th Rhode Island in October 1861. Rodman went to North Carolina with the Burnside expedition early in 1862 and led the charge that captured the city of New Bern in March. Taken sick, he went home to Rhode Island to recuperate and was promoted Brigadier General USV while absent from the army, to rank from 28 April 1862. Rodman returned to duty with Burnside's force, now the IX Corps, when it arrived in Virginia in the summer of 1862. He became a division commander and fought at South Mountain and Antietam in the Maryland campaign. In the latter battle, on 17 September 1862, as his division advanced against the town of Sharpsburg, it was struck by A.P. Hill's Confederate Light Division arriving on the run from Harper's Ferry. Rodman went to the assistance of one of his brigade commanders, who was trying to get his green regiments to change front. Rodman was struck in the chest by a musket ball and was carried from the field as his troops retreated. He survived in a field hospital for thirteen days before dying on 30 September.

Boatner, *Civil War*; Warner, *Generals in Blue*; Catton, *Mr. Lincoln's Army*; *B&L*, Vol. 2.

ROSE, Maurice, 1899–1945, Connecticut-Colorado, U.S. Army, killed in action 30 March 1945 near Paderborn, Germany.

Maurice Rose was one of only two U.S. division commanders killed in action in Europe in World War II and was the only American general of Jewish extraction ever killed in combat. Son of a rabbi, he was born in Middleton and moved to Denver with his family. He enlisted in the Colorado National Guard when he was seventeen but served only two months. In August 1917 he was commissioned 2nd Lieutenant in the National Army. Rose served in France where he was wounded, and was discharged in 1919. In July 1920 he entered the regular army as a 1st Lieutenant and spent ten years in the infantry. He transferred to the cavalry branch as a Captain in 1930. Promoted Major in 1936 and Lieutenant Colonel in 1940, Rose was among the group of officers who pioneered the formation of the American armored forces. In January 1942 he became chief of staff of the 2nd Armored Division and was made Colonel in February. He accompanied the division to North Africa in the Torch invasion of November 1942, and then transferred to the 1st Armored Division in Tunisia in April 1943. Rose negotiated the surrender of 40,000 German troops in Bizerte in May and was promoted Brigadier General on 2 June. He led a combat command in the 2nd Armored in Normandy in July and August 1944. In August he took command of the 3rd Armored Division and was promoted Major General on 5 September 1944. He led the division across France, Belgium, and Germany, and was engaged in the encirclement of the Ruhr in March 1945. On 30 March, while driving ahead of the division in a jeep, alone with his aide and driver, Rose encountered a German tank attempting to break out of the encirclement near Paderborn. The tank gunner ordered the Americans, in German, to surrender. Rose, in a gesture either of compliance or defiance, reached for his pistol while protesting that he did not understand. The German shot him in the head, killing him instantly.

Army Register, 1942–1946; Bradley; Harmon; McDonald; *New York Times*, April 3 & 4, 1945.

RUSSELL, David Allen, 1820–1864, New York, U.S. Volunteers, killed in action 19 September 1864 at Winchester, Virginia.

David A. Russell was the son of a New York congressman. He obtained an appointment at West Point through his father's influence and graduated in 1845. He served in the Mexican War and on frontier duty and was promoted Captain in 1854. In November 1861 he was posted to the defenses of Washington. Russell was made Colonel of the 7th Massachusetts in January 1862 and led his regiment through the Virginia Peninsula and Antietam campaigns that year. On 29 November 1862 he was promoted Brigadier General USV and took over a brigade in VI Corps. He was not heavily engaged at Fredericksburg in December 1862, but his brigade was one of those in the attack on Marye's Heights at Chancellorsville in May 1863. Russell's brigade formed part of the infantry support for the cavalry clash at Brandy Station, Virginia, in June 1863, but was barely involved in the fighting at Gettysburg in July. The high point of his Civil War career occurred at the crossings of the Rappahannock on 7 November 1863. Commanding a division if VI Corps, Russell overran a supposedly impregnable Confederate bridgehead on the north side of the river, capturing four guns, eight colors, and over 1,600 prisoners. Russell was wounded in the action but led a delegation to Washington to present the colors to the Secretary of War, who inexplicably refused to receive him. Thereafter he was hospitalized for more than sixty days and was saved only through the influence of Generals Meade, Sedgwick, and H.G. Wright from being mustered out of service for exceeding the legally permissible time away from his command, a rule rarely, if ever, enforced. In the spring 1864 campaign he was permanent division commander in VI Corps and fought in the Wilderness and at Cold Harbor and

Petersburg. In July he went with the corps to defend Washington against Early's raid. At Winchester, Virginia, on 19 September 1864, Russell was wounded in the chest but remained on his horse, directing one of his brigades until killed by a shell fragment in the heart. He had been breveted Brigadier General USA for his actions in the Wilderness and was posthumously breveted Major General USA and USV to rank from 19 September.

Cullum; Boatner, *Civil War*; Warner, *Generals in Blue*; *B&L*, Vol. 4.

S

SACKETT, William, 1838–1864, New York, U.S. Volunteers, died 14 June 1864 of wounds received 11 June 1864 at Trevilian Station, Virginia.

William Sackett was commander of one of the regiments of cavalry which opened the battle of Gettysburg on the Union side on 1 July 1863. He was the son of a U.S. senator from New York and was in legal practice in Albany when the Civil War started. Sackett became Major in the 9th New York Cavalry in November 1861. The regiment served variously in the Department of Washington, John Pope's Army of Virginia in the summer of 1862, XI Corps for the Maryland and Fredericksburg campaigns, and the Cavalry Corps of the Army of the Potomac after it was formed in the spring of 1863. Sackett was advanced to Lieutenant Colonel in June 1862 and Colonel in May 1863. At Gettysburg the 9th New York was part of T.C. Devin's brigade, which was thrown into the line to delay the Confederate advance until Union infantry could come up. In the extremely confused fighting at Trevilian Station on 11 June 1864, during Sheridan's raid against that place, Sackett was mortally wounded while leading a charge against a house and orchard occupied by enemy forces. He was captured and died in Confederate hands three days later. In a poignant aftermath to his death, his wife came to Grant's headquarters under her father-in-law's aegis, seeking news of her husband. In response to Grant's personal request for news, Robert E. Lee returned Sackett's sword with the message that Sackett had died and been buried. Sackett was breveted Brigadier General USV to rank from 14 June 1864.

Harper's; Boatner, *Civil War*; Weygant; Phisterer, *New York in the War*; Starr, Vols. 1 & 2; *B&L*, Vol. 3; *OR*, Ser. I, Vols. 27, pt. 1; 36, pt. 1; 40, pt. 3.

SANDERS, John Caldwell Calhoun, 1840–1864, Alabama, C.S Army, killed in action 21 August 1864 near Petersburg, Virginia.

John C.C. Sanders was the youngest Confederate general killed in action during the Civil War. He was born in Tuscaloosa, the son of a physician, and spent three years at the state university before leaving his studies to enlist in the 11th Alabama in 1861. Elected Captain of his company, Sanders went to Virginia, fought in the Peninsula campaign of 1862, and was wounded in the leg at Frayser's Farm. Returning to duty in August 1862, Sanders was promoted Colonel of the 11th after Antietam, having already commanded the regiment in that battle, where he was wounded in the face. He led the regiment at Fredericksburg, Chancellorsville, and Gettysburg, where he was wounded yet again, this time in the knee. Sanders was at the head of his regiment in the Wilderness in May 1864 and took command of the brigade after the death of Abner Perrin at Spotsylvania. He was promoted Brigadier General CSA on 7 June to rank from 31 May 1864 and led a brigade in the Petersburg defenses, notably at the battle of the Crater on 30 July. On 21 August 1864, while in action along the Weldon Railroad outside Petersburg, Sanders was shot through both thighs and died of arterial bleeding within a few minutes.

Boatner, *Civil War*; Warner, *Generals in Gray*; D.S. Freeman, *Lee's Lieutenants*, Vol 3; *CMH*, Vol. VII (Alabama).

SANDERS, William Price, 1833–1863, Kentucky-Mississippi, U.S. Volunteers, died 19 November 1864 of wounds received 18 November 1864 near Knoxville, Tennessee.

William P. Sanders was one of that small group of Southern officers in the Old Army who held true to their allegiance to the Union and served in the Northern armies during the Civil War. He was the son of a lawyer and was born near Frankfort, Kentucky, but reared near Natchez, Mississippi. He graduated from West Point in 1856, served on the frontier and on the Utah expedition, and became Captain of the 6th U.S. Cavalry in 1861. He participated in the Virginia Peninsula and Maryland campaigns of 1862. After a period of sick leave, Sanders became Colonel of the 5th Kentucky Cavalry and moved to the western theater in March 1863. He joined in the hunt after Confederate raider John Hunt Morgan that summer and in September and October was chief of cavalry of the Department of the Ohio. He was promoted Brigadier General USV on 18 October 1863. Sanders briefly commanded an infantry brigade in XXIII Corps and then the 1st Division, Cavalry Corps, a mixed force of cavalry and mounted infantry. In the Knoxville campaign that November he was called upon to delay Longstreet's Confederate advance while the defenses of Knoxville were made ready. For two days his two small brigades, fighting dismounted, held out against Longstreet's assaults. Sanders continually exposed himself to hostile fire as an example to his own men. On the afternoon of 18 November his luck ran out and he was mortally wounded. As soon as he fell his line broke. By that time the defenses of the city were ready. Sanders was carried to a hotel room in Knoxville, where he died the next day.

Cullum; Boatner, *Civil War*; Warner, *Generals in Blue*; *B&L*, Vol. 3.

SCOTT, Norman, 1889–1942, Indiana, U.S. Navy, killed in action 12 November 1942 off Guadalcanal, Solomon Islands.

Norman Scott was one of two flag officers killed in the battle of Savo Island near Guadalcanal in November 1942, both of whom were posthumously awarded the Medal of Honor. He was born in Indianapolis, graduated from Annapolis in 1911, and served two years in the USS *Idaho*. As was the custom of the day, he was commissioned Ensign in 1912, after his first tour of sea duty. Later he served in destroyers and was executive officer of USS *Jacob Jones* when she was sunk by a German submarine near Queenstown, Ireland, in December 1917. He spent the remainder of World War I in Washington in the Office of the Chief of Naval Operations. For seven months he was naval aide to President Wilson. He spent almost a year commanding motor patrol boats, including a trip to Constantinople from the east coast of the United States. From 1922 to 1924 Scott was at the Fourteenth Naval District in Honolulu. Then he was an instructor at the Naval Academy and later commanded a destroyer in the Asiatic Fleet. In 1935 he attended the Naval War College and from 1937 to 1939 was a member of a naval mission to Brazil. On 7 December 1941 Scott was commander of the heavy cruiser USS *Pensacola*, escorting an Army convoy to Manila. After news of the Japanese attack on Pearl Harbor was received, the convoy was diverted to Australia. On 11 May 1942 Scott was promoted Rear Admiral and given command of a task force in the South Pacific. During the battle for Guadalcanal from August to November 1942 his force consisted of the light cruiser USS *Atlanta* and five destroyers. Scott's immediate commander was Rear Admiral Daniel Callaghan. On the night of 12–13 November 1942 Callaghan and Scott met and defeated a far superior Japanese force off Savo Island. Early in the action *Atlanta* was hit by several salvoes which killed Scott and others on the bridge and rendered the ship dead in the water. Despite heroic salvage efforts, *Atlanta* sank the night of 13 November. Callaghan was also killed in the action. Both were posthumously awarded the Medal of Honor, Scott's for his action at Cape Esperance as well as for Guadalcanal.

Morison, Vols. 3–5; *MOH*; Office of Navy Information; *New York Times*, November 18, 1942.

SCURRY, William Read, 1821–1864, Tennessee-Texas, C.S. Army, killed in action 30 April 1864 at Jenkins's Ferry, Arkansas.

William R. Scurry was one of the many Americans who went to Texas to seek their fortunes after the founding of the Lone Star Republic. He was born in Gallatin, Tennessee, and migrated to San Augustine, Texas, when he was sixteen. He enlisted as a private in the Texas volunteers for the Mexican War and was mustered out as a Major. Prominent politically, Scurry served on a Texas-New Mexico boundary commission and was a delegate to the state secession convention in February 1861. Commissioned Lieutenant Colonel of the 4th Texas Mounted Rifles, he fought at Val Verde, New Mexico, under Henry H. Sibley in February 1862 and was *de facto* commander of Confederate forces at Glorieta Canyon in March because Sibley had reported himself sick. Scurry was promoted Brigadier General CSA on 12 September 1862 and commanded a brigade at the capture of Galveston on 1 January 1863. During the Red River campaign his brigade was in the division of John G. Walker in the battles at Mansfield and Pleasant Hill, Louisiana, on 8 and 9 April 1864. At Jenkins's Ferry, Arkansas, on 30 April, Scurry was mortally wounded in Kirby Smith's attack on the retreating Union column. Refusing to be carried to the rear, he bled to death on the battlefield. Scurry and Horace Randal were two of three brigade commanders in Walker's division killed at Jenkins's Ferry.

Boatner, *Civil War*; Warner, *Generals in Gray*; *B&L*, Vols. 2 & 3; *CMH*, Vol. XI.

SEARBY, Edmund Wilson, 1896–1944, California, U.S. Army, killed in action 14 September 1944 at Meurthe-et-Moselle, France.

"Ned" Searby was the only artillery general killed while commanding his troops in World War II. He was born in Berkeley and attended the University of California before graduating from West Point in November 1918 in the so-called War Emergency Course. He went to Germany with the Army of Occupation in 1919 and then attended the French artillery school before returning to the United States. Searby served with troop units as a young officer and was an instructor at West Point. He served briefly in the Army Air Corps and then returned to the field artillery as a course instructor for eight years. He was promoted Captain in 1934 and Major in 1940. During that time he commanded artillery battalions, attended the Command and General Staff course, and served on the staff of the General Headquarters of the Army and the Army Ground Forces. Searby became Lieutenant Colonel in 1941 and Colonel in June 1942. In February 1943 he went to Tennessee to take command of the artillery of the 80th Infantry Division then in training. He was promoted Brigadier General on 19 March 1943. The division went to England in July 1944 and landed in France the first week in August. Thrown into combat immediately, the 80th was involved in the pursuit of the retreating Germans across France and in September successfully secured bridgeheads across the Moselle River near Toul. On 14 September, during a fierce German counterattack on the American position near Meurthe-et-Moselle, Searby was killed in action with his guns.

Army Register, 1944; Cullum, Vols. 7–9; Cole, *Forward, 80th!*; *Assembly*, September 1978; *St. Augustine Record*, September 26, 1944.

SEDGWICK, John, 1813–1864, Connecticut, U.S. Volunteers, killed in action 9 May 1864 at Spotsylvania, Virginia.

"Uncle John" Sedgwick was universally loved and respected during the Civil War as the most humane and compassionate Union commander. He was born in northwestern Connecticut, received an early education normal for the times, taught school for two years, and then graduated from West Point in 1837. He served in the artillery and cavalry in Florida and Mexico, on the frontier, and in the Utah expedition of 1857. By virtue of the resignation of senior officers of Southern birth as their states seceded from the Union, Sedgwick became Colonel of the 1st (later 4th) U.S. Cavalry in March 1861. He was appointed Brigadier General USV on 31 August 1861 and served as a brigade and division commander in the defenses of Washington before taking the field with a division in II Corps for the Virginia Peninsula campaign of 1862. He was wounded at Frayser's Farm during the Seven Days fighting and was promoted Major General USV on 25 July 1862 to rank from 4 July. At Antietam, on 17 September, Sedgwick led his division with such gallantry that he was wounded three times and had to be carried off the field unconscious. After recovering from his wounds he briefly commanded II Corps and IX Corps before becoming permanent commander of VI Corps. At Chancellorsville he led the left wing of the army, but at Gettysburg he had practically no command, as his brigades were all attached to other corps as they arrived on the field. In November 1863 he was in overall command of the successful action of V and VI Corps at Rappahannock Bridge. In the spring of 1864 Sedgwick was mentioned for the command in the Shenandoah Valley, which eventually went to Phil Sheridan. Grant felt that Sedgwick was a competent corps commander but afraid of the responsibility of higher authority. At Spotsylvania, on the morning of 9 May 1864, Sedgwick was assisting the commander of a battery of guns located near his headquarters position the guns while under sniper fire. Sedgwick commented to the gunners that "they couldn't hit an elephant at this distance." Within a minute he was struck dead by a single bullet under the left eye. Statues in his honor have been erected at Gettysburg and West Point.

DAB; Cullum; Boatner, *Civil War*; Warner, *Generals in Blue*; Catton, *Mr. Lincoln's Army* and *Stillness at Appomattox*; Coddington; *B&L*, Vols. 2–4.

SEGUNDO, Fidel Ventura, 1894–1945, Philippines, Philippine Army, executed by the Japanese, probably on 6 January 1945, at Manila.

Fidel Segundo, or "Smoke" as he was known to his army compatriots, was born in Ilocos Norte Province on the island of Luzon. He was a pre-medical student at the University of the Philippines before graduating from West Point in 1917. Segundo was commissioned 2nd Lieutenant in the Philippine Scouts (PS) of the U.S. Army, but during World War I he became Major in the Philippine National Guard. In December 1918 he reverted to his regular rank of 1st Lieutenant. He commanded a PS artillery battery, became an air observer, and returned to the United States in 1924 for artillery and cavalry schooling. Segundo continued with artillery assignments after his return to the Islands and was also an ROTC instructor at the university there from 1929 to

1936, ultimately becoming Commandant of Cadets. He was promoted Major in the PS in 1936 and concurrently became Colonel in the Philippine Army (PA) and assistant chief of staff for intelligence, operations, and training. He was made Lieutenant Colonel PS in July 1940 and in August took command of the 2nd Infantry Regiment PA. This was followed in 1941 by an assignment as commander 24th Artillery Regiment PS and then as Superintendent of the Philippine Military Academy. On 18 December 1941 Segundo was promoted to Brigadier General PA and became commander of the 1st Regular Division PA. He fought on Bataan and surrendered on 9 April 1942. After the Death March he was paroled but remained active as an adviser to the resistance movement. In December 1944 Segundo and his oldest son were arrested by the Japanese. Both were executed in Manila, probably on 6 January 1945. General Segundo was officially declared dead on 11 March 1946.

Army Register, 1942 and 1947; Cullum, Vols. 7–9; L. Morton; *Intelligence Activities*; *Assembly*, June 1986.

SEMMES, Paul Jones, 1815–1863, Georgia, C.S. Army, died 10 July 1863 of wounds received 2 July 1863 at Gettysburg, Pennsylvania.

Paul Semmes was the lesser known brother of Raphael Semmes of CSS *Alabama* fame. Paul was born in Wilkes County, educated at the University of Virginia, and settled in Columbus, where he became a banker, planter, and businessman. Active in the militia, Semmes was Captain of the Columbus Guards for fifteen years. When the Civil War started Semmes was elected Colonel of the 2nd Georgia and went to Virginia. He was promoted Brigadier General CSA on 11 March 1862 and led his brigade creditably during the Virginia Peninsula campaign and at Antietam and Fredericksburg. Personal business or illness kept Semmes away from the Army of Northern Virginia so long during the winter of 1862–1863 that a replacement for command of his brigade was considered, but he returned in April 1863 and fought at Chancellorsville. At Gettysburg, on 2 July 1863, during Longstreet's attack on the Round Tops, Semmes was mortally wounded as his brigade moved forward to support Joseph Kershaw's advance. He was evacuated by ambulance with the other wounded but died at Martinstown, West Virginia, on 10 July. His last words were, "I consider it a privilege to die for my country."

Boatner, *Civil War*; Warner, *Generals in Gray*; D.S. Freeman, *Lee's Lieutenants*, Vols. 2 & 3; Coddington; *B&L*, Vol. 3; *CMH*, Vol. VI.

SIGERFOOS, Edward, 1868–1918, Ohio, U.S. Army, died 7 October 1918 of wounds received 30 September 1918 in the Meuse-Argonne, France.

Edward Sigerfoos was the only American general officer killed in combat during World War I, although one former general was killed in France in 1918. Sigerfoos was the son of a businessman. He attended public schools and graduated from Ohio State University in 1891. He entered service as 2nd Lieutenant, 5th Infantry, the same year and became 1st Lieutenant in 1898 and Captain in

1902. He was a graduate of the Infantry and Cavalry Schools and fought in the Santiago campaign in Cuba in 1898. He served at various posts, was Commandant of Cadets in the University of Minnesota ROTC program, and in 1915 he attended the Command and General Staff course. Sigerfoos was promoted Major in 1913. By April 1917 he was Lieutenant Colonel of the 15th Infantry in Tientsin, China. He was called to the United States on the outbreak of World War I to train newly raised recruits, and in August 1917 he was promoted Colonel in the National Army and given command of the 152nd Brigade, 77th Division, at Camp Upton, New York. Sigerfoos accompanied the brigade to France in March 1918, but after arrival there General Pershing appointed him Commandant of the Army School of the Line at Langres. He was awarded a Distinguished Service Medal for his work in organizing the school. In September 1918, when wholesale replacement of National Guard commanders by regular army officers took place in the divisions at the front, Sigerfoos, on the basis of his Command and General Staff training, was assigned to the 56th Brigade, 28th Division. He had already been selected and nominated for promotion to Brigadier General. On his way to the front in the Meuse-Argonne on 30 September 1918, Sigerfoos's car was caught in an artillery barrage and he was mortally wounded. He died on 7 October and was posthumously confirmed as Brigadier General to rank from that date.

Army Register, 1916, 1918; Heitman, *U.S. Army*; *Darke County*; Martin; Stallings; Adler; Coffman; *CMH, DSC, DSM*; *New York Times*, October 25, 1918; *Greenville Democrat*, October 23, 1918.

SILL, Joshua Woodrow, 1831–1862, Ohio, U.S. Volunteers, killed in action 31 December 1862 at Stone's River, Tennessee.

Joshua Sill was the officer for whom Fort Sill, the U.S. Army's Field Artillery Center, was named. Sill was born in Chillicothe, the son of an attorney. He was tutored by his father before graduating from West Point in 1853. Sill became an ordnance officer, served in various arsenals, and was an instructor at West Point. In January 1861 he resigned his commission to become a professor at Brooklyn Polytechnic Institute in New York. When the Civil War broke out he returned to Ohio and became assistant state adjutant general. Sill served in West Virginia as an unattached volunteer in the early summer of 1861 and then became Colonel of the 33rd Ohio in August. Later he served in the occupation of northern Alabama and eastern Tennessee as a brigade commander. On 16 July 1862 he was promoted Brigadier General USV and given command of a division in the Army of the Ohio during Braxton Bragg's Confederate invasion of Kentucky. Sill's division was in garrison at Frankfort and missed the battle at Perryville on 8 October 1862. When the Army of the Ohio was reorganized after William B. Rosecrans succeeded Don Carlos Buell as commander, Sill became a brigade commander in the division of his West Point classmate Phil Sheridan. At Stone's River, Tennessee, on 31 December 1862, when Bragg's army surprised Rosecrans, Sill was killed while ordering a counterattack against the first Confederate assault of the day. At the time of his death he was wearing Sheridan's coat, which he had mistakenly taken from the latter's tent the night before. In 1869 Sheridan named the newly built cavalry post in Indian Territory for his fallen comrade.

Cullum; Boatner, *Civil War*; Warner, *Generals in Blue*; *B&L*, Vols. 2 & 3.

SLACK, William Yarnell, 1816–1862, Kentucky-Missouri, C.S. Army, died 21 March 1862 of wounds received 7 March 1862 at Pea Ridge, Arkansas.

William Y. Slack was one of four division commanders of the Missouri State Guard (Confederate) who were later killed in combat in the Civil War. He was born in Mason County, Kentucky, but moved to Missouri with his family when he was a young child. He was reared and educated near Columbia, studied law, and opened his own practice. He was Captain of Missouri volunteers under Sterling Price in the Mexican War. He returned to his law practice in 1848. When Price organized the State Guard in 1861 to swing Missouri into the Confederacy, Slack became a Brigadier General to rank from about 18 June 1861. Slack fought under Price in the Wilson's Creek campaign and was severely wounded in the hip. He returned to the field in October, probably prematurely, and remained with the army through the Pea Ridge campaign. On 7 March 1862 he was wounded again in the same place while at the head of his brigade. He was taken to a house near the battlefield but had to be moved to avoid capture, thereby aggravating his condition. Slack gradually weakened, and died on 21 March. At the time of the Pea Ridge campaign, the State Guard was being assimilated into the Confederate Army. On 17 April 1862 Slack was posthumously appointed Brigadier General CSA to rank from 12 April. Historians suggest that his death might not have been known in Richmond at the time of his confirmation.

Boatner, *Civil War*; Warner, *Generals in Gray*; Bevier; *B&L*, Vol. 1; *OR*, Ser. I, Vols. 3, 8, 53.

SMITH, Preston, 1823–1863, Tennessee, C.S. Army, killed in action 19 September 1863 at Chickamauga, Georgia.

Preston Smith was another officer who fell victim to mistaken identity on the battlefield. He was born in Giles County, graduated from Jackson College in Columbia, Tennessee, and settled in Memphis to practice law. On the outbreak of the Civil War he was commissioned Colonel of the 154th Tennessee, a militia regiment which retained its old designation when mustered into Confederate service. At Shiloh, in April 1862, Smith succeeded to brigade command after General Bushrod Johnson was wounded, only to be seriously wounded himself. After recovery he became permanent commander of the brigade and led it through the Kentucky invasion. At Perryville, on 8 October, he led Cleburne's division after the latter was wounded at Richmond although still only a Colonel. Smith was rewarded with promotion to Brigadier General CSA on 27 October 1862. He led his brigade through the next year's fighting until the battle at Chickamauga, Georgia. There, on 19 September 1863, Smith was mortally wounded when he rode into a Union force in the dark, mistaking it for the Confederate brigade of James Deshler. Carried to the rear of his own lines, Smith died within the hour.

Boatner, *Civil War*; Warner, *Generals in Gray*; *B&L*, Vol. 3; *CMH*, Vol. VIII.

SMYTH, Thomas Alfred, 1832–1865, Ireland-Delaware, U.S. Volunteers, died 9 April 1865 of wounds received 7 April 1865 at Farmville, Virginia.

Thomas A. Smyth had as varied a career as almost any officer in the Union army in the Civil War: farmer, woodworker, adventurer, and coachmaker. He was born in County Cork and worked on his father's farm until coming to Philadelphia in 1854. He worked there as a woodcarver until he went to Nicaragua with the William Walker expedition in 1857. Upon his return he settled in Wilmington as a coachmaker. In 1861 Smyth raised a company of Irish immigrants in Wilmington for war service, but the Delaware government refused to accept them. Smyth crossed the state line and had his men mustered into the 24th Pennsylvania, a three-month regiment. Smyth reentered the army as Major of the 1st Delaware in October 1861. The regiment was at Suffolk, Virginia, in July 1862. It joined II Corps in northern Virginia in time for the Maryland campaign, where it suffered one third casualties at Antietam. Smyth commanded the 1st Delaware at Fredericksburg and became Lieutenant Colonel on 30 December 1862; he was promoted Colonel in February 1863. He led the regiment at Chancellorsville and succeeded to brigade command at Gettysburg. On 3 July he was wounded by a shell fragment but returned to duty the next day. He continued in command of the brigade until the end of the war, being made Brigadier General USV on 1 October 1864. In the final pursuit of Lee's army to Appomattox in 1865, Smyth, serving as divisional commander, was riding his horse along his skirmish line near Farmville, Virginia, on 7 April when he was shot in the mouth by a sniper. He was carried to the nearby Burke residence, where he lived for two days, dying on the day of Lee's surrender. Smyth was posthumously breveted Major General USV to rank from 7 April.

Boatner, *Civil War*; Warner, *Generals in Blue*; Coddington.

STAFFORD, Leroy Augustus, 1822–1864, Louisiana, C.S. Army, died 8 May 1864 of wounds received 5 May 1864 in the Wilderness, Virginia.

Leroy Stafford was representative of the planter class of the Deep South who came forward to fight during the Civil War. He was born in Rapides Parish, attended school in Tennessee and Kentucky, and became a planter. He was also sheriff of Rapides Parish and an enlisted volunteer during the Mexican War. At the outbreak of war in 1861 Stafford raised a company of infantry and then became Lieutenant Colonel of the 11th Louisiana. Going to Virginia with his regiment, he became Colonel in October 1861 and fought in Jackson's famed Valley campaign of 1862, in the Seven Days battles on the Virginia Peninsula, at Second Manassas, and at Antietam. In the latter battle he temporarily commanded the Stonewall Brigade until he injured his foot. During Richard Taylor's protracted illness Stafford remained in command of the Louisiana brigade in Jackson's division. He led his own regiment through all the battles of 1863 until finally becoming Brigadier General CSA on 8 October 1863 with concurrent command of the 2nd Louisiana Brigade. Stafford was mortally wounded while leading his brigade in the first day of fighting in the Wilderness, on 5 May 1864. He was taken to a hotel in Richmond, where he died on 8 May.

Boatner, *Civil War*; Warner, *Generals in Gray*; D.S. Freeman, *Lee's Lieutenants*, Vols. 2 & 3; *CMH*, Vol. X.

STARKE, William Edwin, 1814–1862, Virginia-Louisiana, C.S. Army, killed in action 17 September 1862 at Antietam, Maryland.

A successful businessman who also became a successful battlefield commander, William E. Starke was born in Brunswick County. As a young man he operated a stage line with his brothers and later became a successful cotton broker in Mobile and New Orleans. At the outbreak of war in 1861 he went to Virginia to become aide to Richard S. Garnett in western Virginia. After Garnett was killed Starke became Colonel of the 60th Virginia and served in North Carolina and on the Virginia Peninsula. He was once wounded and twice commended for his actions. Stark was promoted Brigadier General CSA on 6 August 1862 and given command of a Louisiana brigade in Stonewall Jackson's own division. He actually commanded that division at Second Manassas three weeks later and distinguished himself again. At Antietam he took over the division yet again after the previous commander had retired from the field. Starke performed admirably in repulsing Hooker's Union attack on 17 September 1862, but while rallying his men on the field he was shot three times through the body and died.

Boatner, *Civil War*; Warner, *Generals in Gray*; D.S. Freeman, *Lee's Lieutenants*, Vol. 2; *B&L*, Vol. 2; *CMH*, Vol. III.

STEDMAN, Griffin Alexander, Jr., 1838–1864, Connecticut, U.S. Volunteers, died 6 August 1864 of wounds received 5 August 1864 near Petersburg, Virginia.

Griffin A. Stedman was yet another young lawyer who entered military service at the start of the Civil War. A native of Hartford and a graduate of Trinity College, he was reading law in 1861. He was commissioned Captain in the 5th Connecticut in July 1861 and went to the Shenandoah Valley. In November 1861 he became Major in the 11th Connecticut and went on the Burnside expedition to North Carolina in February 1862. In June Stedman became Lieutenant Colonel of the 11th Connecticut and returned to Virginia with Burnside's corps for the Second Manassas and Maryland campaigns. He was seriously wounded at the Stone Bridge at Antietam in September 1862. Stedman was made Colonel the same month and commanded the regiment at Fredericksburg. The regiment went to the Department of Virginia and North

Carolina in 1863, and Stedman was engaged at Suffolk in April and in the demonstration against Richmond in July. He commanded a brigade in XVIII Corps in Ben Butler's advance up the Virginia Peninsula in the spring of 1864 and fought at Drewry's Bluff and Cold Harbor. On 5 August 1864, in the lines in front of Petersburg, Stedman was mortally wounded in the stomach. He had just finished reconnoitering the ground in front of his brigade when the Confederate mine was exploded. Accounts differ as to whether he was struck by a fragment of flying metal or by a sniper's bullet. He was carried from the field and died the next day. His posthumous brevet as Brigadier General USV to rank from the date of his wound was sent to his mother. A statue in his honor was erected in Hartford.

Boatner, *Civil War*; *Johnson, Stedman*; Croffut and Morris; Nivens; *B&L*, Vol. 4; *OR*, Ser. I, Vols. 18; 36, pt. 2; 42, pts. 1 & 2; 51, pt. 1.

STEEN, Alexander Early, 1827–1862, Missouri, Missouri State Guard, killed in action 7 December 1862 at Prairie Grove, Arkansas.

Of the generals of the Missouri State Guard who were later killed in combat in the Confederate service, only Alexander Steen did not achieve equivalent rank in the C.S. Army. He was born in St. Louis, possibly the son of an army officer. He entered the army himself as 2nd Lieutenant in 1847, went to Mexico with Scott's army, and was breveted for gallantry. He was mustered out of service in 1848 but returned in 1852. Steen served with the 3rd Infantry in New Mexico and Texas until 1861. He was a victim of the Twiggs surrender to state forces in Texas in February 1861 and was home in St. Louis on parole when he resigned his commission. He became Lieutenant Colonel in the Missouri State Guard (MSG) in May 1861, Captain in the regular C.S. Army in June, and Brigadier General in the MSG on 18 June. Steen joined Sterling Price's Army as commander of the 5th Division and participated in the Wilson's Creek and Lexington campaigns in 1861 and at Pea Ridge in 1862. In March 1862, as the MSG was being amalgamated into the Confederate Army, Price recommended Steen to be Brigadier General CSA, but the appointment was denied because Steen's brigade was not fully formed. When Earl Van Dorn led Price's Army of the West east of the Mississippi in April 1862, Steen went as far as Memphis, where he fell ill and was left behind. After his recovery he was ordered to the Trans-Mississippi Department at Little Rock in his regular C.S. rank. When the unregimented Missouri volunteers in Arkansas were formed into a brigade under Mosby M. Parsons in November 1862, Steen was appointed Colonel of the 10th Missouri. At Prairie Grove, Arkansas, on 7 December 1862, Steen was killed by a bullet through the brain while leading a charge of the Missouri brigade. Although his death was noted in Union reports of the battle, it was not even mentioned by the Confederate commanders on the field.

Boatner, *Civil War*; Heitman, *U.S. Army*; Bevier; *CMH*, Vol. IX (Missouri); *OR*, Ser. I, Vols. 3, 8, 13, 22, 53; Ser. II, Vol. 4; Missouri National Guard; Records of the Adjutant General's Office (RG 94); Military Service Record.

STEVENS, Clement Hoffman, 1821–1864, Connecticut-South Carolina, C.S. Army, died 25 July 1864 of wounds received 20 July 1864 at Atlanta, Georgia.

Clement H. Stevens, known to his men as "Rock" for his unflinching nerve in combat, was born in Norwich, Connecticut, the son of an officer in the U.S. Navy. The family later moved to Florida and then to South Carolina. As a youth Stevens was naval secretary to Commodores William Shubrick and William Bee, both of them his mother's kinsmen. Later he went into banking in Charleston and dabbled with inventions of military hardware of different kinds. In July 1861 Stevens was present at Bull Run as a volunteer aide to his brother-in-law, Barnard Bee, and was wounded when Bee was killed. When he returned to South Carolina he became Colonel of the 24th South Carolina and served in coast defenses until May 1863. Stevens went to Mississippi with the brigade of States R. Gist for the Vicksburg campaign and was wounded at Chickamauga, Georgia, in September 1863. He was promoted Brigadier General CSA on 20 January 1864 and commanded a brigade in W.H.T. Walker's division in the Atlanta campaign of 1864. At Peach Tree Creek, on 20 July 1864, Stevens was mortally wounded at the head of his brigade. He died in Atlanta five days later.

DAB; Boatner, *Civil War*; Warner, *Generals in Gray*; *B&L*, Vol. 4; *CMH*, Vol. V.

STEVENS, Isaac Ingalls, 1818–1862, Massachusetts, U.S. Volunteers, killed in action 1 September 1862 at Chantilly, Virginia.

Isaac I. Stevens was a man of great talents but contradictory opinions. He was born in Andover, attended Phillips-Andover Academy, and graduated first in his class from West Point in 1839. He worked on coast defenses, went to Mexico with Scott's army, where he was wounded and received two brevets, and wrote a history of the war. In 1853 he resigned his commission as 1st Lieutenant to become governor of the Washington Territory. His major goal was to increase emigration there from the eastern states and the means he used had him in constant trouble with the Justice Department, the War Department, and the commander of the army's Department of the Pacific. In 1857 he became territorial delegate to Congress. In 1860 Stevens was campaign manager for Southern Democratic and pro-slavery Presidential candidate John C. Breckenridge. This undoubtedly raised the suspicions of the Republicans, and when Stevens offered his services in April 1861 he was refused. Finally, on 30 July 1861, he became Colonel of the 79th New York. On 28 September 1861 he was promoted Brigadier General USV and took over a brigade in the defenses of Washington. In October he went to Port Royal, South Carolina, where he was part of the occupying force and later division commander. Under protest, he also led the disastrous assault at Secessionville, South Carolina, in July 1862. When the troops from the Department of the South were transferred to Virginia as IX Corps in August 1862, Stevens was a division commander. He participated in the only successful Union operation at Second Manassas, the turning of Stonewall Jackson's left flank on 29 August, and was involved in the fight at

Chantilly on 1 September. There, in an incident markedly similar to Phil Kearny's, Stevens was leading his men forward in the rain and the dark when he ran into Confederate lines and was killed by a bullet in the temple. On 12 March 1863 he was posthumously confirmed as Major General USV to rank from 18 July 1862.

DAB; Cullum; Boatner, *Civil War*; Warner, *Generals in Blue*; Catton, *Mr. Lincoln's Army*; D.S. Freeman, *Lee's Lieutenants*, Vol. 2; *B&L*, Vol. 2.

STEVENSON, Thomas Greely, 1836–1864, Massachusetts, U.S. Volunteers, killed in action 10 May 1864 at Spotsylvania, Virginia.

Thomas G. Stevenson, a Bostonian by birth, was interested in military affairs from his childhood and became an officer and drillmaster in the Massachusetts militia. At the outbreak of the Civil War he raised the 24th Massachusetts with his militia battalion as nucleus and became Colonel in December 1861. He went to North Carolina with Burnside's expedition in February 1862, became a brigade commander in April 1862, and fought at New Bern, Washington, Goldsboro, and Kinston. Stevenson was promoted Brigadier General 24 December 1862, but the Senate failed to confirm the nomination. On 9 April he was reappointed to rank from 14 March 1863. Stevens led a brigade in the siege of Charleston in 1863 and commanded a division in the assault on Morris Island in July. He was sick with malaria during the winter of 1863–1864 and in April was assigned to command a brigade in IX Corps for the advance on Richmond. On 10 May 1864, at Spotsylvania, as IX Corps moved forward to support the Union attack on the Confederate salient, Stevenson was killed instantly by a sharpshooter.

Boatner, *Civil War*; Warner, *Generals in Blue*; *B&L*, Vol. 4.

STRAHL, Otho French, 1831–1864, Ohio-Tennessee, C.S. Army, killed in action 30 November 1864 at Franklin, Tennessee.

Otho Strahl was one of six Confederate generals killed or mortally wounded at the disastrous battle of Franklin. He was born in McConellsville and attended Ohio Wesleyan College, but studied law and went into practice in Tennessee at the behest of Daniel Reynolds, another future Confederate general, whom he had met in college. In 1861 Strahl entered Confederate service as Captain in the 4th Tennessee. In early 1862 he became Lieutenant Colonel of the regiment and fought at Shiloh in April and Stone's River in December. Strahl was promoted Colonel in January 1863 and Brigadier General CSA on 28 July 1863. He commanded a Tennessee brigade in the Chickamauga-Chattanooga campaign of 1863 and the Atlanta campaign of 1864. He went on Hood's invasion of Tennessee in the fall of 1864 in the division of John C. Brown. At Franklin on 30 November, Strahl was reduced to the role of an infantry private loading and handing muskets to men on the parapet when his brigade disintegrated in a ditch below the Union breastworks. As he directed an observer to take post, he was shot three times and killed. Of the five general officers in Brown's division, three were killed, one wounded, and one captured.

Boatner, *Civil War*; Warner, *Generals in Gray*; McDonough and Connelly; *B&L*, Vol. 4; *CMH*, Vol. VIII.

STRONG, George Crockett, 1832–1863, Vermont-Massachusetts, U.S. Volunteers, died 30 July 1863 of wounds received 18 July 1863 at Battery Wagner, Charleston, South Carolina.

George C. Strong was as much a victim of the medical practices of the day as he was of the wound to which his death is attributed. He was born in Stockbridge, Vermont, but after the death of his father he was adopted and reared by an uncle in Easthampton, Massachusetts. He graduated from West Point in 1857 as an ordnance officer and served in arsenals in New York, Pennsylvania, Alabama, and Virginia until the Civil War. Strong was Irvin McDowell's ordnance officer at Bull Run in July 1861 and later was assistant ordnance officer on McClellan's staff. In October 1861 he was promoted Major and named assistant adjutant general Ben Butler. Strong helped to organize the expedition to New Orleans in April 1862 and later became Butler's chief of staff and ordnance officer. Strong's health was poor and he was on extended sick leave for several months in 1862 and 1863. On 23 March 1863 he was promoted Brigadier General USV to rank from 29 November 1862, and in June he took command of U.S. forces at St. Helena Island, South Carolina. On 10 July 1863 he led his brigade in an assault on Morris Island near Charleston. The attack was successful for the most part but Fort, or Battery, Wagner held out. On 18 July an attack on the fort was repulsed with heavy Union loss. Strong was wounded in the hip or thigh and was evacuated to a hospital at Beaufort. He insisted on going to New York City but developed lockjaw on the ship en route and died in New York on 30 July. On 31 July he was nominated and confirmed as Major General USV to rank from 18 July.

Cullum; Boatner, *Civil War*; Warner, *Generals in Gray*; *B&L*, Vol. 4.

STUART, James Ewell Brown, 1833–1864, Virginia, C.S. Army, died 12 May 1864 of wounds received 11 May 1864 at Yellow Tavern, Virginia.

"Jeb" Stuart is probably the best known of all Confederate generals after Robert E. Lee and Stonewall Jackson. His cavalry exploits have thrilled and regaled generations of soldiers and historians. Stuart was born in Patrick County, the son of a congressman. He was a law clerk, attended Emory and Henry College, and graduated from West Point in 1854. He served on the frontier in the cavalry, was seriously wounded in Indian fighting, and was Lee's aide during John Brown's capture at Harper's Ferry, Virginia, in 1859. When the Civil War started Stuart resigned his commission to become Lieutenant Colonel of Virginia infantry and then Colonel of the 1st Virginia Cavalry in May 1861. Stuart's biography is a history of Confederate cavalry in Virginia. For his exploits at Bull Run he was promoted Brigadier General CSA on 24 September 1861. An outstanding intelligence officer, he kept Lee well informed of Union movements on the Virginia Peninsula and was made Major General CSA on 25 July 1862. He led the cavalry division of the Army of Northern Virginia at Second Manassas, Antietam, Fredericksburg, and Chancellorsville. In the latter battle Stuart was temporary successor as corps commander to the fallen Stonewall Jackson. At Gettysburg he was criticized for being absent when the army most needed him. For the spring campaign of 1864 the cavalry was organized under Stuart into a corps of three small divisions. By this time, however, the Union cavalry had grown in size and skill and received a new commander in Phil Sheridan. At Yellow Tavern, on 11 May, while opposing Sheridan's raid on Richmond, Stuart was shot in the stomach by a dismounted trooper of Custer's Michigan brigade. Stuart was taken by ambulance to Richmond, where he died the next day.

DAB; Cullum; Boatner, *Civil War*; Warner, *Generals in Gray*; D.S. Freeman, *Lee's Lieutenants*, Vols. 1–3; Thomason; *CMH*, Vol. III.

T

TALLMAN, Richard Joseph, 1925–1972, Pennsylvania, U.S. Army, killed in action 9 July 1972 at An Loc, Vietnam.

Richard J. Tallman was the last American general killed in combat. He was born in Honesdale and enlisted in the army after graduating from high school in 1943. He was a machine gun squad leader in the 242nd Infantry Regiment, 42nd Division, in the Ardennes and Rhineland campaigns in Germany and received a battlefield commission in February 1945. Tallman resigned his commission to enter West Point in July 1945 and graduated in 1949. During the Korean War he was platoon leader and company commander in the 65th Infantry, 3rd Division. After Korea he served with the 8th Division in Germany, was a tactical officer at West Point, and attended the Command and General Staff College, the Armed Forces Staff College, and the Army War College. Promoted Major in 1959, Lieutenant Colonel in 1963, and Colonel in 1968, Tallman also served on the army staff in Washington and as Deputy Commandant of Cadets at West Point from 1967 to 1971. His career included three tours of duty in Vietnam. In 1964 he was an adviser to a Vietnamese infantry division; from 1967 to 1969 he commanded a battalion of the 101st Airborne Division and was on the staff at Long Binh; and in 1971 and 1972 he commanded a brigade of the 101st and was chief of staff and then deputy commander of the Third Regional Assistance Command. Tallman was promoted Brigadier General on 29 June 1972. On 9 July, while visiting An Loc, he was mortally wounded when an enemy shell burst among a group of officers running from a helicopter to a bunker. Although he was immediately transported to a hospital in Saigon, he died a few hours later.

Army Register, 1972; *New York Times,* July 11, 1972; *Wayne Independent,* January 30, 1969; June 15, July 11, 1972; Military Service Record.

TAYLOR, George William, 1808–1862, New Jersey, U.S. Volunteers, died 31 August 1862 of wounds received 27 August 1862 near Manassas Junction, Virginia.

George Taylor fell victim to one of the soldier's deadliest sins: acting with insufficient knowledge of the enemy. He was born in Hunterdon County and graduated from Partridge's Military Academy in Connecticut in 1827. He was a Midshipman in the Navy for four years, took up farming in New Jersey, and then served as Lieutenant and Captain in the 10th U.S. Infantry during the Mexican War. After he was mustered out Taylor joined the Forty-niners in California but returned to New Jersey in 1851 to open an iron mining and smelting business. In 1861 he became Colonel of the 3rd New Jersey, which guarded lines of communication during the Bull Run campaign. In the spring of 1862 Taylor became commander of the New Jersey brigade in succession to General Phil Kearny and was himself promoted to Brigadier General USV on 9 May 1862. During the Virginia Peninsula campaign the New Jersey brigade distinguished itself at Gaines's Mill and White Oak Swamp when it was twice used to fill in gaps which had been created in the Union line. In August Taylor and his brigade were among the first units sent back to northern Virginia to bolster John Pope's army defending Washington. After disembarking at Alexandria the brigade was sent by train on 27 August to advance along the Orange and Alexandria Railroad toward Manassas Junction to drive off what were thought to be Confederate raiders. An obstruction halted the train but Taylor continued the advance on foot. Near Manassas they ran into, not raiders, but the lead division of Stonewall Jackson's advancing corps. Taylor's brigade disintegrated, his train was captured, and he was mortally wounded. This was the opening round in the second battle at Manassas. Taylor was carried back to Alexandria, where he died on 31 August. Warner gives his date of death as 1 September.

Boatner, *Civil War*; Warner, *Generals in Blue*; Catton, *Mr. Lincoln's Army*; D.S. Freeman, *Lee's Lieutenants*, Vol. 2; *B&L*, Vol. 2.

TERRILL, James Barbour, 1838–1864, Virginia, C.S. Army, killed in action 30 May 1864 at Bethesda Church, Virginia.

The case of the Terrills is a tragic example of the brother-against-brother motif of the American Civil War and provides one of two incidents of two brothers being killed while American general officers. James B. Terrill was born at Warm Springs and graduated from Virginia Military Institute in 1858. He took up the practice of law in his hometown. In May 1861 he became Major in the 13th Virginia under Colonel A.P. Hill and fought at Bull Run, in the Valley of Virginia, on the Peninsula, and at Second Manassas, Antietam, and Fredericksburg. Terrill was successively promoted to Lieutenant Colonel in 1862 and Colonel in May 1863. He won frequent commendations from his superiors, including comment on his part at Gettysburg in July 1863. Terrill commanded his regiment through the fall campaign of 1863 and in the battles in the Wilderness in May 1864. He was killed at Bethesda Church, on 30 May 1864, in the opening engagement of the battles around Cold Harbor. Terrill had already been nominated to be Brigadier General CSA and was confirmed as such on 31 May to rank from 1 June 1864. Terrill's older brother was Union Brigadier General William R. Terrill (see below).

Boatner, *Civil War*; Warner, *Generals in Gray*; *CMH*, Vol. III.

TERRILL, William Rufus, 1834–1862, Virginia, U.S. Volunteers, killed in action 8 October 1862 at Perryville, Kentucky.

William R. Terrill was one of two brothers killed while serving on opposite sides in the Civil War. Son of a lawyer and state legislator, he was born in Covington and reared in Warm Springs. He graduated from West Point in 1853. While a cadet he was involved in the notorious fighting incident in which Phil Sheridan was turned back one year for threatening Terrill with a bayonet and then attacking him physically. Terrill was commissioned in the artillery, and served in Florida, on recruiting duty, as an instructor at West Point, and in Kansas. In 1861, after family consultations, he opted to stay with the Union and was made Captain in the 5th U.S. Artillery. Terrill became acting inspector general of the Department of Washington and then went to Kentucky to command a camp of instruction for new recruits. In January 1862 he was assigned to the Army of the Ohio and commanded a battery at Shiloh in April and Corinth during the summer. He was promoted to Brigadier General USV on 9 September 1862 and given command of a brigade of newly recruited regiments in the division of James S. Jackson. On 8 October 1862, when Buell's Army of the Ohio met Braxton Bragg's Confederates at Perryville, Kentucky, Terrill's brigade formed the extreme left of the Union line. Under the full weight of the attack of Cheatham's division Terrill's brigade was crushed. Jackson was killed in the first rush. Terrill tried for over an hour to rally his troops but to no avail. He was finally struck in the side by a shell fragment and died that night in a field hospital. The other brigade commander of Jackson's division, Colonel George Webster, was also killed. Terrill's younger brother was Confederate Brigadier General James B. Terrill (see above).

Cullum; Boatner, *Civil War*; Warner, *Generals in Blue*; *B&L*, Vols. 1 & 3.

THOMPSON, Wiley, 1781–1835, Virginia-Georgia, Georgia Militia, murdered by Indians 28 December1835 at Fort King, Florida.

Wiley Thompson was the son of a Revolutionary soldier. As a child he moved with his family from Virginia to frontier Georgia and settled near Elberton. He gained local prominence at an early age and was commissioner of Elbert Academy by 1808. Thompson's military career began with service in the War of 1812, and in November 1817 he was appointed Major General of the 4th Division of Georgia militia. He served in the state senate in 1817–1819 and was a member of a commission to determine the Georgia-Florida boundary after the former Spanish territory was annexed. Thompson was elected to the U.S. Congress as a Democrat in 1820 and served until 1833. He resigned from the militia in 1824, but he continued his interest in military affairs. As chairman of the House Committee on Military Affairs he obtained payment for claims for activation of the Georgia militia in 1793 and 1824. Thompson was a delegate to the state constitutional convention in 1833 and was then appointed agent to the Seminole Indians by President Andrew Jackson. He supported Jackson's Indian removal policy and, as Superintendant of Emigration, successfully negotiated the transfer of several Seminole groups in 1834. Other chiefs, notably Osceola, were less amenable to removal, and a confrontation developed over the next eighteen months. Thompson called for troops and cut off Indian trade. Osceola was imprisoned and then released, in May 1835; thereafter he apparently agreed to emigrate. This was only a cover to his real intentions. On 28 December 1835 Thompson was walking outside the enclosure at Fort King with his aide when Osceola and sixty warriors, who had been waiting two days for such an opportunity, rose from the brush and fired on the pair, killing both. Thompson was struck by fourteen musket balls and allegedly stabbed in the chest after he was dead. Both bodies were scalped. This and the Dade Massacre were the opening incidents in the Second Seminole War.

DAB; *BDAC*; Mahon; Peithmann; *Elbert County*.

TILGHMAN, Lloyd, 1816–1863, Maryland-Kentucky, C.S. Army, killed in action 16 May 1863 at Champion's Hill (Vicksburg) Mississippi.

Lloyd Tilghman was another professionally trained military officer who spent much of his life in civilian pursuits. He was a descendant of a prominent Maryland family and was born in Talbot County. He graduated from West Point in 1836 but resigned his commission the same year to go into railroad construction. Tilghman returned to active duty during the Mexican War as Captain in the Maryland and District of Columbia Battalion and as aide to General David Twiggs. After the war he engaged in railroad work all over the South and in Panama. Eventually he settled in Paducah, Kentucky. On 18 October 1861 Tilghman was commissioned Brigadier General CSA, made responsible for the defenses of Forts Henry and Donelson, and placed in command of the latter. Aware of his post's defects, he put up as strong a defense as possible before surrendering to U.S. Grant in January 1862. Tilghman became a prisoner and was not exchanged until the fall of that year. At that time he was given command of a brigade in the Army of the West at Corinth, Mississippi. Transferred to Vicksburg, Tilghman was killed at Champion's Hill on 16 May 1863 while his brigade was covering the road over which Pemberton's army was to withdraw into the city. He was directing the fire of his artillery when he was struck in the chest by a shell fragment which passed completely through his body.

Cullum; Boatner, *Civil War*; Warner, *Generals in Gray*; *B&L*, Vols. 1 & 3; *CMH*, Vol. II (Maryland).

TINKER, Clarence Leonard, 1887–1942, Oklahoma, U.S. Army Air Force, missing in action declared dead 7 June 1942 near Wake Island in the Pacific Ocean.

Clarence Tinker was the first general killed in action in the history of the U.S Army Air Force or U.S. Air Force. Part Osage Indian, he was born in northeastern Oklahoma near the Kansas border and graduated from Wentworth Military Academy in Lexington, Missouri, in 1908. He entered the army as 2nd Lieutenant of Philippine Scouts and served for four years before receiving a commission in the regular army in 1912. Tinker spent most of the next five years in Hawaii with the 25th Infantry Regiment, a black unit, and then returned to the United States at the outbreak of World War I as a Captain. He saw no combat duty during the war. In 1920 he entered the Air Service as a Major, took flight training, and commanded a number of aero squadrons. Tinker went to London in 1926 as assistant military attache. While there he won the Soldier's Medal, an award for non-combat bravery, for rescuing an American naval officer from a burning plane. He held a number of staff and command positions before being promoted to Lieutenant Colonel in 1935 and Colonel in 1936. Tinker became chief of the Aviation Division of the National Guard Bureau in 1937 and chief of the Supply Division of the Air Corps in 1939. Later that same year he took command of the 27th Bombardment Group. With the pre-World War II expansion of the Air Corps, Tinker was promoted Brigadier General on 1 October 1940 and given command of the 3rd Bomb Wing in January 1941. In November 1941 he became commander of the 3rd Interceptor Command. After the attack on Pearl Harbor, Tinker was sent to Hawaii to command the Seventh Air Force and was promoted Major General on 14 January 1942. On 6 June 1942, during the battle of Midway, Tinker took personal command of a flight of four LB-30 long-range Liberator bombers which had arrived that very day in Hawaii and led them on a bombing mission against Japanese-held Wake Island. An overcast sky prevented accurate navigation and the flight never found Wake. Tinker's plane disappeared from the flight early in the mission and was never seen again. He was listed as missing in action on 7 June 1942 and declared dead on 7 June 1943.

Army Register, 1942–1944; Morison, Vol. 3; Prange; Carter and Mueller; *Current Biography, 1942; New York Times,* June 13, October 25, 1942; *Newsweek,* June 22, 1942; Military Service Record.

TRACY, Edward Dorr, 1833–1863, Georgia-Alabama, C.S. Army, killed in action 1 May 1863 at Port Gibson, Mississippi.

Edward D. Tracy was born in Macon, the son of a judge. As a young man he moved to Huntsville and opened a law practice. He was active in politics and strongly supported the Southern Democratic ticket in the election of 1860. When the Civil War started, Tracy became Captain in the 4th Alabama and fought at Bull Run in Virginia. He refused an appointment as Major of the 12th

Alabama but became Lieutenant Colonel of the 19th Alabama in October 1861. At Shiloh, in April 1862, Tracy's horse was killed under him but he was personally unharmed. He went with his regiment to eastern Tennessee and was promoted Brigadier General CSA on 16 August 1862 on the recommendation of General E. Kirby Smith. Smith formed a brigade of the five Alabama regiments in his army and gave the command to Tracy. Early in 1863 Tracy's brigade was sent to the Mississippi theater and assigned to Carter Stevenson's division. At Port Gibson, Mississippi, on 1 May 1863, Tracy was shot in the breast while near the front line and died instantly without making a sound.

Boatner, *Civil War*; Warner, *Generals in Gray*; *CMH*, Vol. VII (Alabama).

TYLER, Robert Charles, c. 1832–1865, Maryland-Tennessee, C.S. Army, killed in action 16 April 1865 at West Point, Georgia.

Robert C. Tyler was the last Confederate general killed in action, as opposed to those who died of wounds, in what was the last Civil War action east of the Mississippi River. Although little is known about his early life, he was probably born in Baltimore. He accompanied William Walker on his first expedition to Nicaragua in 1857 and later settled in Memphis. Tyler enlisted in the 15th Tennessee as Quartermaster Sergeant in 1861, was promoted to Major on the staff of General Benjamin Cheatham, and was Lieutenant Colonel commanding the 15th at Belmont, Missouri, by November 1861. Still in command of the regiment, he was wounded at Shiloh in April 1862. He was provost marshal to Braxton Bragg during the latter's invasion of Kentucky but was promoted Colonel and returned to his regiment after the battle at Corinth, Mississippi, in October 1862. He remained in command of the 15th for the next year and was wounded again at Chickamauga and Chattanooga in 1863. At Chattanooga, while temporarily in command of a brigade, Tyler lost his leg in the defense of Missionary Ridge and was permanently invalided from the army in the field. He was promoted Brigadier General CSA on 23 February 1864 and sent on convalescent leave to West Point, Georgia. He was still there in the closing weeks of the war. On 16 April 1865 Tyler scraped together a handful of men to defend an earthwork called Fort Tyler against a brigade of Union cavalry advancing eastward from Alabama. In a desperate fight on the west side of the town Tyler was killed by a rifle shot by a sharpshooter.

Boatner, *Civil War*; Warner, *Generals in Gray*; *B&L*, Vol. 4; *CMH*, Vol. VIII.

V

VINCENT, Strong, 1837–1863, Pennsylvania, U.S. Volunteers, died 7 July 1863 of wounds received 2 July 1863 at Gettysburg, Pennsylvania.

To Strong Vincent, more than to any other man, may be due the Union victory at Gettysburg in 1863. His quick appreciation of the situation and good tactical sense led him to occupy a key area on the battlefield at a critical moment. Vincent was born in Waterford, the son of a foundryman, attended Trinity College, and graduated from Harvard in 1859. He was admitted to the bar and opened a law practice in Erie in 1860. He volunteered for military service at the start of the Civil War and was adjutant of the three-month Erie Regiment of militia until July. In September 1861 he became Lieutenant Colonel of the 83rd Pennsylvania. He went to the Virginia Peninsula in 1862 but contracted malaria in May and was away from duty until December. In the meantime he had been made Colonel of the regiment in June and commanded it at Fredericksburg and Chancellorsville. He became a brigade commander in May 1863. At Gettysburg, on 2 July 1863, Vincent was about to lead his brigade into battle when he encountered his corps commander's aide looking for a unit to occupy Little Round Top, the vital point on the Union left flank. Recognizing the importance of the knoll, Vincent took it upon himself to move to its defense and by doing so formed the extreme left of the Union position. His men occupied the top of the knoll just as advancing Confederates came up its west face. Vincent's brigade sucessfully beat off repeated attacks, but as he tried to rally the faltering right of his line he was shot down. He lingered in a field hospital for five days before dying on 7 July. He was posthumously promoted Brigadier General USV to rank from 3 July 1863.

Boatner, *Civil War*; Warner, *Generals in Blue*; Catton, *Glory Road*; *B&L*, Vol. 3.

W

WADSWORTH, James Samuel, 1807–1864, New York, U.S. Volunteers, died 8 May 1864 of wounds received 6 May 1864 in the Wilderness, Virginia.

James S. Wadsworth was one of the wealthiest men in the North to enter the Union army during the War between the States. His father was one of the largest landowners in New York state. His uncle William was a general of New York militia in the War of 1812 and was captured by the British at Queenstown Heights in 1812. James was born in Geneseo and reared with the intent of taking over his father's philanthropic and manorial responsibilities. He attended Harvard, studied law, and was admitted to the bar, although he never practiced. He devoted his time to Democratic politics and the conservance of his estates. Later he became a Free Soiler and then a Republican and was a Presidential elector in 1856 and 1860. In 1861 he was one of the moderates who tried to work out the differences between the North and South at the Washington Peace Conference. When war broke out Wadsworth went to Washington and was volunteer aide to General Irvin McDowell at Bull Run. On McDowell's recommendation Wadsworth was commissioned Brigadier General USV on 9 August 1861 and took over a New York brigade in the Army of the Potomac. In March 1862 he became military governor of the District of Columbia. That fall he ran for governor of New York but lost to the Democrat, Horatio Seymour. In December he returned to the army as division commander in I Corps. At Chancellorsville, in May 1863, he was not engaged, but at Gettysburg, in July, his division fought continuously for three days, being among the first to open the engagement. In March 1864, with the consolidation of old units of the Army of the Potomac, Wadsworth took command of a division in V Corps which included most of his old division. On 6 May 1864, in the opening days of the Wilderness campaign, Wadsworth, while rallying his division and adjacent units for an attack, was shot off his horse with a bullet in the brain. He was captured and lingered in a Confederate field hospital for two days before dying on 8 May. He was posthumously breveted Major General USV to rank from the date of his wound. Some two months after his death his personal effects were returned to his widow by General Lee.

DAB; Boatner, *Civil War*; Warner, *Generals in Blue*; Catton, *Glory Road* and *Stillness at Appomattox*; Coddington; *New York at Gettysburg*; *B&L*, Vols. 1, 3 & 4.

WALKER, Kenneth Newton, 1898–1943, New Mexico-Colorado, U.S. Army Air Force, missing in action, declared dead 5 January 1943 at Rabaul, New Britain Island.

Kenneth N. Walker was the second of three successive generals commanding V Bomber Command to lose his life in the line of duty. His predecessor, Harold H. George, was killed in a bizarre airplane accident at Darwin, Australia, in 1942. His successor, Howard Ramey, was downed a few weeks after Walker. Walker was born in Cerrillos and enlisted in the Signal Corps Air Service in December 1917. He entered on active duty in March 1918 and saw no combat service in World War I but was commissioned 2nd Lieutenant in November 1918. After several years as a flying instructor Walker went to the Philippines as staff intelligence officer. Promoted 1st Lieutenant in 1924, he returned to the United States in 1925 and held staff, command, and instructor positions for the next eight years. From 1933 to 1935 he attended the Command and General Staff course and was promoted Captain and Major in August and October 1935. Walker carried out command and staff assignments in California and Hawaii until 1941. In January that year he reported to the Plans Division of the Air Corps in Washington and was promoted Lieutenant Colonel in July. In March 1942 he became a Colonel and took a position on the War Department General Staff. He was promoted Brigadier General on 17 June 1942 and transferred to Australia, where he took over V Bomber Command in September. Walker flew seventeen raids with his B-17s, the last on 5 January 1943. On that raid to Rabaul, a major Japanese naval base on New Britain, Walker's planes scored hits on nine vessels in the harbor. Walker's plane was hit and forced down, the only one lost on the mission. He was listed missing in action and was officially declared dead on 12 December 1945. Walker was posthumously awarded the Medal of Honor "for conspicuous leadership" of the raid on Rabaul.

Army Register, 1943 and 1946; *Congressional Record*, 78th Congress, 1st Session; *MOH*; Carter and Mueller; *Time*, April 5, 1943; Military Service Record.

WALKER, Nelson Macy, 1891–1944, Massachusetts, U.S. Army, died 10 July 1944 of wounds received 9 July 1944 near Lessay, Normandy, France.

Killed in Normandy in July 1944, Nelson M. Walker was a victim of the need for higher level commanders to overcome the inexperience of American troops in their first combat. Walker was born in Pittsfield, attended local schools and then went into the lumber business. In 1917 he entered Officers' Training Camp and was commissioned 2nd Lieutenant in August that year. He went to France with the 47th Infantry Regiment of the 4th Division, fought in the Argonne, and was gassed there. Walker remained in the regular army after World War I and was promoted Captain in 1920. His career included duty as aide to the Chief of Staff of the Army, General John L. Hines, service in China, and ROTC instructor duty at Manlius Military Academy in New York. He attended the Command and General Staff course in 1930 and the Army War College in 1933. Walker was promoted Major in 1935 and Lieutenant Colonel in 1940. He served on the War Department General Staff and with Army Ground Forces Headquarters. Promoted Colonel in December 1941, he was assigned to the 84th Division as assistant commander in August 1942 and was promoted Brigadier General on 11 September 1942. Walker went to England with the 8th Division in February 1944 and was with them when they landed in France the first week in July. The division was inserted in the line for the final mop-up of the Contentin Peninsula on the right of the Normandy beachhead. The 8th Division suffered from inexperience and from indecisive leadership in its early days in the *bocage* country of Normandy. The division commander was relieved soon after their arrival at the front. On the division's second day in action, 9 July, as Walker was touring the front, he observed an anti-tank company that had been halted by enemy fire. He personally reorganized the company and led it forward until he was mortally wounded by machine gun fire. He died during the early hours of 10 July.

Army Register, 1944; Blumenson; Griesbach; *New York Times*, July 21, 1944; *Berkshire Eagle*, July 21, 1944.

WALKER, William Henry Talbot, 1816–1864, Georgia, C.S. Army, killed in action 22 July 1864 at Atlanta, Georgia.

A courageous and accomplished professional soldier, W.H.T. Walker was also an ardent states' rights advocate and a man of extremely touchy personal pride. He was born in Augusta, son of the sometime mayor and U.S. senator, attended local schools, and graduated from West Point in 1837. In his first military action, against the Seminoles at Lake Okeechobee, Florida, on 25 December 1837, Walker was severely wounded and left on the field for dead. Through his own superhuman efforts he later recovered. Continuing in the army he was again seriously wounded and twice breveted for gallantry in Mexico. Later he was Commandant of Cadets at West Point. With seriously impaired health he took extended leave of absence as a Major in 1856 and never returned to the U.S. Army. When South Carolina seceded from the Union in 1860, Walker, who was living on his estate in Augusta, hurried to

Charleston to attend the secession convention, and resigned his commission on secession day, the first officer of the Old Army to do so. Successively Colonel and Major General of Georgia state troops, he became Brigadier General CSA on 25 May 1861. Walker was first assigned at Pensacola and later went to Virginia, but resigned in October 1861 over a question of being passed over for promotion by younger men. Walker accepted a commission as Brigadier General of Georgia state troops from Governor Joseph Brown in November 1861 and commanded a brigade at Savannah. On 9 February 1863 he was recommissioned in the C.S. Army. In May 1863 he took his own brigade and that of General S.R. Gist from the coast defenses of the Southeast to aid in the defense of Vicksburg. He was cited by General Joseph Johnston as the only general in Johnston's army fit to command a division and was duly promoted Major General CSA on 23 May 1863. Walker commanded a division under Johnston in Mississippi, took his troops to Tennessee, and commanded the Reserve Corps at Chickamauga, Georgia, in September 1863. He was a leader of the opposition to General Patrick Cleburne's suggestion to draft black troops into the Confederate army in the winter of 1864 and led a division in the Atlanta campaign. On 22 July 1864, in the attempt of John Bell Hood to turn the left flank of Sherman's army above Atlanta, Walker's division went astray as it felt for the Union left in the woods of what is now East Atlanta. As Walker rode ahead of his troops to reconnoiter the ground he was shot and killed by an unseen sniper. His body was recovered after the battle and carried to Augusta, where it was buried on the grounds of the arsenal, now Augusta College.

DAB; Cullum; Boatner, Civil War; Warner, Generals in Gray; Connelly, Autumn of Glory; Kurtz; B&L, Vols. 3 & 4; CMH, Vol. VI.

WALLACE, William Harvey Lamb, 1821–1862, Ohio-Illinois, U.S. Volunteers, died 10 April 1862 of wounds received 6 April 1862 at Shiloh, Tennessee.

W.H.L. Wallace lost his own life in the course of trying to save the lives of the members of his command. He was born in Urbana, Ohio, but was taken to Illinois as a young child. He studied law and was admitted to the bar, served in the Illinois volunteers in the Mexican War, and then returned to his legal practice. In May 1861 Wallace entered service in the Union army as Colonel of the 11th Illinois, a three-month regiment. The regiment was posted to southeastern Missouri, where it reenlisted for three years after the expiration of its initial term. Wallace was not present at U.S. Grant's victory at Belmont in November 1861, but he commanded a brigade in the Forts Henry and Donelson campaign in the winter of 1862. He was promoted Brigadier General USV on 21 March 1862 and was given command of one of Grant's infantry divisions on 2 April. At Shiloh, four days later, Wallace's division formed the center of the Union defensive position set up after the initial Confederate attack. This line withstood twelve assaults during the day, but Wallace's division was finally surrounded late in the afternoon. Wallace attempted to change front and march to the rear, but only two regiments got away. The rest were forced to surrender. Wallace was mortally wounded and died at Grant's headquarters at Savannah, Tennessee, on 10 April. His defense at Shiloh has been acclaimed by friend and foe alike. Even Beauregard, the Confederate commander on the field, characterized it as "unflinching."

Boatner, *Civil War*; Warner, *Generals in Blue*; Catton, *Grant Moves South*; *B&L*, Vol. 1.

WARD, George Hull, c. 1825–1863, Massachusetts, U.S. Volunteers, killed in action 2 July 1863 at Gettysburg, Pennsylvania.

George H. Ward was one of four Union colonels killed at Gettysburg who were posthumously breveted as brigadier generals. Involved in only two battles in his career, he lost a leg in one and his life in the other. Ward was a native of Worcester, and before the Civil War he was a farmer and was active in the militia. By 1861 he had risen to Brigadier General, but he was mustered into service in July as Lieutenant Colonel of the 15th Massachusetts. He served in garrison along the Potomac and fought at Ball's Bluff, Virginia, in October 1861. There Ward was seriously wounded in the leg and later lost his limb to amputation. He was absent from the army on sick leave for over a year but became Colonel of the 15th in April 1862. He returned late in December 1862 and briefly commanded a brigade in February and March 1863. Ward was absent again during the Chancellorsville campaign but returned in time for the march into Pennsylvania. At Gettysburg, on 2 July 1863, the 15th was one of two regiments posted in front of their division to provide flank protection for the division on their left. The men erected a breastwork of fence rails, and Ward walked up and down the line on his wooden leg with a cane in one hand and a sword in the other. Under a heavy Confederate attack the neighboring regiment broke. As Ward tried to conduct an orderly withdrawal he was wounded by a musket ball and died shortly after. One official report says he was mounted when he was shot. Possibly this was preparatory to retiring. Ward was posthumously breveted Brigadier General USV to rank from 2 July.

Boatner, *Civil War*; Catton, *Glory Road*; Coddington; Bowen; *B&L*, Vol. 2; *OR*, Ser. I, Vols. 5, pt. 1; 27, pt. 1; 29, pt. 2; Boston University.

WARE, Keith Lincoln, 1915–1968, Colorado-California, U.S. Army, killed in action 13 September 1968 near Binh Long, Vietnam.

Keith L. Ware was the first U.S. Army general killed in Vietnam. He was born in Denver and was a city employee in Glendale, California, when he was drafted into the army in 1941. He graduated from Officer Candidate School at Fort Benning in 1942 and participated in combat operations in North Africa, Sicily, Italy, France, and Germany in World War II. On 26 December 1944 Ware, while commanding 1st Battalion, 15th Infantry, 3rd Division, as a Lieutenant Colonel, was awarded a Medal of Honor for action at Sigolsheim, France. Reconnoitering alone in front of his battalion, he then personally led an assault force of only twelve men and one tank in the reduction of four German machine guns which had been holding up his advance. Although wounded he refused to leave the field until his companies were free to move forward. After the war Ware remained in the regular army. Although he had no formal education beyond high school, he held some of the most sensitive positions on the army staff. Promoted Colonel in 1953, he was chief of legislative liaison for the army, chief of emergency planning in Europe, and deputy chief and chief of public information. He attended the Command and General Staff College, the Armed Forces Staff College, and the National War College. On 1 May 1963 he was promoted Brigadier General and on 1 July 1966, Major General. In November 1967 Ware volunteered for duty in Vietnam. During the Tet Offensive of 1968 he commanded an *ad hoc* task force of nine infantry battalions which sucessfully defended Saigon. Subsequently he commanded the 1st Infantry Division west of Saigon. On 13 September 1968 the helicopter in which Ware and his staff were flying was hit by enemy ground fire and crashed and burned in Binh Long Province near the Cambodian border. There were no survivors.

Army Register, 1968; Abbott; *MOH*; *New York Times*, September 14 & 15, 1968; Military Service Record.

WARREN, Joseph, 1741–1775, Massachusetts, Massachusetts Army, killed in action 17 June 1775 at Bunker Hill, Massachusetts.

Joseph Warren was the first American general killed in action. He was the son of a prosperous farmer, graduated from Harvard College when he was eighteen, and became a successful Boston physician. As early as 1767 Warren became involved in the struggle against British taxation. He was on the committee to demand withdrawal of British troops after the Boston Massacre, possibly participated in the Boston Tea Party, and drafted the Suffolk Resolves urging the people of Massachusetts to form their own government. Warren later became head of the Boston Committee of Safety and dispatched the news of the British movement toward Lexington and Concord in April 1775. He was present in the fighting on 19 April and helped to rally the militia on the Lexington road. On 24 April Warren became President of the Massachusetts Provincial Congress and in May he took personal charge of the committee organizing the provincial army. On 14 June, at his own request, Warren was elected Major General of the Massachusetts Army. Before his commission could be issued the battle of Bunker Hill developed and Warren went out to join the defenders as a civilian volunteer. Upon his arrival on the scene he was offered the command but he refused. He remained in the redoubt on Breed's Hill through all three British charges and was one of the group of thirty men who covered the retreat of the others back to Bunker Hill. Warren was bayoneted in the arm but held his rear guard together long enough for the main body to get safely away. In a final British volley Warren was shot behind the ear as he turned to rally his followers and he fell to the ground dead. The British buried

Warren in an unmarked grave, but the body was recovered and reinterred after their evacuation of Boston.

DAB; Boatner, *American Revolution*; D.S. Freeman, *Washington*, Vol. 3; Fleming; Wright.

WASHBURN, Francis, c. 1838–1865, Massachusetts, U.S. Volunteers, died 22 April 1865 of wounds received 6 April 1865 at High Bridge, Virginia.

A native of Lancaster, Francis Washburn was a student in Germany when the Civil War began. He returned to the United States to become 2nd Lieutenant of the 1st Massachusetts Cavalry in December 1861 and was promoted 1st Lieutenant in March 1862. The regiment served first in the Sea Islands of South Carolina. In August 1862 it was transferred to Virginia to form part of Pleasanton's division for the Maryland campaign. After losing many of its horses to disease and its colonel to drunkenness, the 1st Massachusetts was in Averill's brigade at Fredericksburg. In January 1863 Washburn became Captain in the 2nd Massachusetts Cavalry. He was appointed Lieutenant Colonel of the 4th Massachusetts Cavalry in February 1864 and was promoted Colonel in February 1865. The regiment was assigned first to XVIII Corps around Fort Monroe, Virginia, then to X Corps around Petersburg, and eventually as headquarters troops for the Army of the James. On 6 April 1865 Washburn's regiment formed part of the small force under General Theodore Read sent to destroy the High Bridge across the Appomattox to prevent Lee's retreat from Petersburg. In the action that ensued Washburn was shot in the head and, falling from his horse, sabered. He was captured and held two days without medical care, which was non-existent in the Confederate army. When Lee surrendered on 9 April 1865, Washburn was returned to Union control but died of his wounds on 22 April. He was posthumously breveted Brigadier General USV to rank from 6 April.

Boatner, *Civil War*; Bowen; *B&L*, Vol. 4; *OR*, Ser. I, Vols. 42, pt. 3; 46, pt. 1; Boston University.

WEED, Stephen Hinsdale, 1834–1863, New York, U.S. Volunteers, killed in action 2 July 1863 at Gettysburg, Pennsylvania.

Stephen H. Weed earned his military reputation as an artillerist but died in command of an infantry brigade. He was born in Potsdam but moved to New York City with his family while still a child. He graduated from West Point in 1854, served on the frontier in Kansas, and on the Utah expedition. Weed was promoted Captain in the newly formed 5th U.S. Artillery Regiment in May 1861 and remained at Harrisburg, Pennsylvania, raising and training his battery until the spring of 1862. He subsequently served on the Virginia Peninsula, at Second Manassas, and at Antietam. At the latter battle Weed's battery fired what James Longstreet later called "the second best artillery shot I ever saw." At a distance of about one mile Weed fired a single shell at a group of Confederate officers composed of Longstreet, R.E. Lee, and D.H. Hill. The shot took the legs off Hill's horse. Weed commanded all of the artillery of his division at

Fredericksburg and all of the artillery of V Corps at Chancellorsville in May 1863. In recognition of his fine record he was made Brigadier General USV on 6 June 1863. Henry J. Hunt, Chief of Artillery of the Army of the Potomac, wryly remarked, "[Weed showed] such special aptitude and fitness for large artillery commands that he was immediately promoted from captain to brigadier general and transferred to the infantry." On the second day at Gettysburg Weed's brigade of V Corps was rushed to the defense of Little Round Top in time to repel the initial Confederate attack. After they had set up their positions Weed was standing in the Devil's Den with Lieutenant Charles Hazlett, his battery commander, when he was shot through the arm and chest. As Hazlett bent over Weed's body, he, too, was shot and fell across Weed. Hazlett died immediately, Weed lingered a few hours before expiring, four weeks from the date of his promotion. Today there is a marker on Little Round Top designating it as Weed's Hill. Warner gives Weed's year of birth as 1831 based on what may be erroneous pension records.

Cullum; Boatner, *Civil War*; Warner, *Generals in Blue*; Catton, *Glory Road*; Coddington; *B&L*, Vol. 3.

WELLS, George Duncan, c. 1827–1864, Massachusetts, U.S. Volunteers, killed in action 13 October 1864 at Fisher's Hill, Virginia.

George D. Wells was a judge in Boston before the Civil War. He entered the army as Lieutenant Colonel of the 1st Massachusetts in May 1861 and fought at Bull Run, where he commanded the skirmishers at Blackburn's Ford. He served on the Virginia Peninsula in 1862 and was twice cited for meritorious conduct by his brigade commander. After its colonel was wounded at Fair Oaks, Wells was assigned to temporary command of the 26th Pennsylvania for the balance of the Seven Days battles, a highly unusual step in a time of intense unit loyalty to its own commanders. Wells was rewarded with promotion to Colonel of the 34th Massachusetts in July 1862. This regiment was assigned to the defenses of Washington from August 1862 to July 1863. For part of this time Wells commanded a brigade at Fort Lyon. Wells was so highly thought of as a field officer that when General Joseph Hooker took over the Army of the Potomac in February 1863 he asked for Wells to be returned to his army but without avail. In July 1863 Wells was transferred to the defenses of Harper's Ferry, Virginia. There he was active in skirmishing around the post and in demonstrating against Confederate forces. He commanded a brigade in the Army of West Virginia in the spring of 1864 and fought at New Market and Winchester. In the latter battle he commanded the army's rear guard as it retreated. He commanded a brigade in VIII Corps at the next battle at Winchester in September. On 13 October 1864, while making a reconnaissance toward Fisher's Hill, Wells failed to get an order to withdraw, was caught in an enfilading fire, and was mortally wounded. He was captured, and died on the field. His body was returned under a flag of truce the next day. Wells was breveted Brigadier General USV to rank from 12 October 1864.

Boatner, *Civil War*; Bowen; *B&L*, Vol. 4; *OR*, Ser. I, Vols. 11, pts. 1 & 2; 29, pts. 1 & 2; 37, pt. 1; 43, pts. 1 & 2; 51, pt. 1; Boston University.

WHARTON, James Edward, 1894–1944, New Mexico, U.S. Army, killed in action 12 August 1944 near Sourdeval, Normandy, France.

James E. Wharton was an officer who showed versatility and talent in every assignment he was given. He was a native of Elk and graduated from New Mexico Agricultural and Mechanical College. He was commissioned 2nd Lieutenant in August 1917 and rose to Captain by the end of World War I. After the war he served in the Philippines and at Fort Snelling, Minnesota. Wharton was an instructor at the Infantry School, attended the Command and General Staff course in 1931–1933, and was an instructor there in 1934–1935. Later he attended the Army War College and the Army Industrial College. Promoted Major in 1935 and Lieutenant Colonel in 1940, Wharton became an expert in army personnel matters and headed the officers' branch of the Army Personnel Division and was director of personnel for the Services of Supply. He was made Colonel in December 1941 and advanced to Brigadier General on 15 March 1942. In March 1943 he went to Tennessee to organize and train the 80th Division, and in October 1943 he went to England to be assistant commander of the 9th Division for the upcoming invasion of France. In May 1944, less than one month before D-Day, Wharton was directed to take over and shake up the 1st Engineer Special Brigade, which had performed poorly in pre-invasion rehearsals. Sixty minutes after the first infantry units landed on Utah Beach in Normandy on 6 June 1944 Wharton came ashore with the lead elements of his 15,000-man brigade, whose mission it was to organize the beachhead in support of the combat units. So successful had he been in the rehabilitation of the engineer brigade that when the 28th Division became bogged down in fighting toward a link-up with British forces, the XIX Corps commander gave Wharton command of the division. His tenure was brief. A few hours after taking command near Sourdeval on 12 August 1944, while visiting one of his regiments to become familiar with the situation, Wharton was mortally wounded by a sniper and died the same day.

Army Register, 1944; Beck; Blumenson; Ruppenthal; *28th Division in World War II*; *New York Times*, August 18, September 22, 1944; *Staunton Leader*, August 16, 1944.

WHIPPLE, Amiel Weeks, 1816–1863, Massachusetts, U.S. Volunteers, died 7 May 1863 of wounds received 4 May 1863 at Chancellorsville, Virginia.

An engineer officer who ranged widely across the American West in the years before the Civil War, Amiel Whipple was born in Greenwich, taught school, and studied at Amherst College before he graduated from West Point in 1841. Whipple was assigned to the Topographical Engineers, a now defunct branch of the army, which was responsible for surveying and mapmaking. He surveyed the United States-Mexican border, the United States-Canadian border, and a southern railroad route to California. He became the chief topographical engineer on General McDowell's staff at Bull Run in 1861 and retained that position until he was promoted Brigadier General USV on 14 April 1862. Whipple commanded a brigade and a division in the defenses of Washington until November 1862. Thereafter his division was assigned to the Army of the Potomac and was present but only slightly engaged at Fredericksburg in December. Whipple spent the winter of 1863 converting his men from garrison to field troops, and by the spring they were rated with the best in the army. On 4 May 1863, at Chancellorsville, Whipple was sitting on his horse writing out an order to have a Confederate sniper dislodged from a tree when he was shot in the stomach by the man he was attempting to eliminate. The bullet exited cleanly but the wound proved fatal. Whipple was carried to Washington, where he died on 7 May. On the day of his death he was promoted to Major General USV to rank from 3 May, breveted Brigadier General USA to rank from 4 May, and breveted Major General USA to rank from 7 May.

Cullum; Boatner, *Civil War*; Warner, *Generals in Blue*; *B&L*, Vol. 3.

WHITING, William Henry Chase, 1824–1865, Mississippi-North Carolina, C.S. Army, died 10 March 1865 of wounds received 15 January 1865 at Fort Fisher, North Carolina.

William H.C. Whiting's career in the Confederate army was one of promise unfulfilled. Although he was among the most highly rated of the Old Army officers who joined the Confederacy, his saga was that of one lost opportunity after another. He was the son of an army officer, born at his father's post at Biloxi. He attended Georgetown College in the District of Columbia before graduating first in his class at West Point in 1845. He worked as an engineer on coast defenses and waterway improvements until 1861, when he resigned. Whiting was commissioned Major in the C.S. army and was General J.E. Johnston's engineer at Harper's Ferry and Bull Run. After the latter battle he was promoted to Brigadier General CSA to rank from 21 July 1861. He commanded a brigade and an informal division through the fall and winter of 1861–1862 and a division on the Virginia Peninsula in the spring of 1862. The bad feeling which sprang up over his inability or unwillingness to cooperate with other commanders led to a controversy with Stonewall Jackson and a certain animosity on the part of President Davis, who blocked Whiting's promotion to Major General. Whiting was on sick leave for several months in 1862, but in November he took command of the District of Wilmington in North Carolina. There he developed Fort Fisher into the strongest coastal fortress in the South and was finally promoted to Major General CSA on 22 April 1863. He once again showed his obstinacy by refusing to cooperate in Longstreet's attempt against New Bern in 1863. In May 1864 Whiting took command at Petersburg, Virginia, in the face of Union general Ben Butler's advance on Richmond. There, through either indecision or inability, he did not cooperate in Beauregard's attack on Butler on 16 May. Some accused him of being under the influence of alcohol or narcotics. Whiting voluntarily relinquished his command and returned to North Carolina. He commanded at Fort Fisher during the two Union assaults in December 1864 and January 1865 and was shot twice on the day the fort fell, 15 January. He was carried as a prisoner to Governor's Island, New York, where he died of his wounds on 10 March 1865.

Cullum; Boatner, *Civil War*; Warner, *Generals in Gray*; D.S. Freeman, *Lee's Lieutenants*, Vols. 1–3; *B&L*, Vol. 4; *CMH*, Vol. IV.

WILLIAMS, Thomas, 1815–1862, New York-Michigan, U.S. Volunteers, killed in action 5 August 1862 at Baton Rouge, Louisiana.

Noted throughout the regular and volunteer armies as a stern disciplinarian, Thomas Williams was born in Albany and moved to Michigan with his family while still a child. He served as a volunteer in the Black Hawk War in 1832 and graduated from West Point in 1837. Williams served in Florida as an instructor at West Point. He was also aide to the Commanding General of the Army, Winfield Scott, for six years and won two brevets for gallantry while with Scott in Mexico. He continued on frontier duty until 1861, when he became Major in the newly raised 5th U.S. Artillery Regiment. Williams was inspector general of the Department of Virginia until the fall of 1861, when he became Brigadier General USV on 28 September and went to Hatteras, North Carolina, with General Ben Butler's expedition. Williams remained in North Carolina until April 1862, when he accompanied Butler to the capture of New Orleans. Williams was posted to Baton Rouge and assisted in Flag Officer Porter's attempt on Vicksburg that summer. He was commanding at Baton Rouge when the Confederate forces of Earl Van Dorn and John C. Breckenridge assaulted his post on 5 August 1862. The initial Confederate attack was successful, but Williams was able to re-form his command and drive Van Dorn from the town. Williams was shot in the chest and killed just as his counterattack started. Despite, or because of, his experience as a youthful volunteer, Williams had long had the regular's contempt for the volunteer forces, but by the time of Baton Rouge he had begun to realize what fine material he had to work with.

Cullum; Boatner, *Civil War*; Warner, *Generals in Blue*; *B&L*, Vols. 1 & 3.

WILSON, Russell Alger, 1905–1944, Illinois, U.S. Army Air Force, missing in action, declared dead 6 March 1944 near Berlin, Germany.

Russell A. Wilson was one of the young bomber generals killed over Europe in World War II. He was born in Dixon Springs, the son of the school superintendent. After attending Southern Illinois Normal School he graduated from West Point in 1928 and entered the Signal Corps. In 1930 he obtained a master's degree in communications engineering from Yale University. Wilson transferred to the Army Air Corps in 1931 and served in a number of units, primarily as a communications officer. He was promoted to 1st Lieutenant in 1934 and Captain in 1935. Between 1938 and 1941 he commanded the 1st Communications Squadron and the 13th Reconnaissance Squadron. Promoted

Major in 1941, he was assigned to headquarters of the Army Air Forces Combat Command and, as a Lieutenant Colonel in 1942, to the War Department Operations Division in the Latin American Section. Wilson became Colonel in March 1942, and in April 1943 he went to England as executive officer of the 4th Bomb Wing. In May he was made commander of the 403rd Provisional Wing to replace the missing Nathan Bedford Forrest, and in July he took over the 4th Bomb Wing as commander. Wilson's service in the Eighth Air Force was notable. On 8 October 1943 he led a precision daylight attack by several hundred B-17s bombers which destroyed the Fock Wolf factory at Marienburg. He was promoted Brigadier General on 6 March 1944 to rank from 29 February. On the very day of his promotion Wilson led the first daylight raid on Berlin. On what has been termed the bloodiest day in the history of the Eighth Air Force, Wilson commanded the 3rd Air Division and flew as co-pilot in a Pathfinder B-17 at the front of the formation. Near Berlin his plane was hit by flak, but he continued on his bomb run with one engine on fire. After dropping out of formation his plane exploded and eight of the twelve crewmen were killed. Wilson was listed as missing in action from 6 March and declared dead on 7 August 1945. In 1956 his remains were recovered from a mass grave of "unknown British airmen" and reinterred in Illinois.

Army Register, 1944–1946; Cullum, Vols 7–9; R. Freeman; *New York Times*, March 20, 1944; *Marion Republican*, February 21, April 17, 1956; Military Service Record.

WINDER, Charles Sidney, 1829–1862, Maryland, C.S. Army, killed in action 9 August 1862 at Cedar Mountain, Virginia.

Charles S. Winder was one of a number of Maryland officers who sided with the South during the Civil War. He was born in Talbot County and graduated from West Point in 1850. En route to California on a troop ship in 1854, he showed such great heroism during and after a hurricane in the Atlantic that he was rewarded with a captaincy in the new 9th Infantry Regiment in March 1855. He was engaged in Indian fighting in Washington Territory when the southern states began to secede and he resigned his commission effective 1 April 1861. Winder was appointed Major in the regular Confederate artillery and assisted in the reduction of Fort Sumter in Charleston Harbor. He became Colonel of the 6th South Carolina in July 1861 and took his regiment to Virginia, but he arrived too late to participate in the battle at Bull Run. Winder was promoted Brigadier General CSA on 1 March 1862 and took command of the Stonewall Brigade in Jackson's division after the arrest of Richard B. Garnett. With them he fought in the Valley and Peninsula campaigns of 1862. Beginning with the Seven Days battles, when Jackson was elevated to informal corps command, Winder led Jackson's division. At Cedar Mountain, on 9 August 1862, when the action shifted from the Peninsula back to northern Virginia, Winder was so sick he had to be carried to the field in an ambulance. During the artillery duel preceding the action he was struck in the left side by a shell and his body was horribly mangled. He was carried to a house nearby and lived only until sundown the same day. His death was not lamented by the men of his brigade and division, who considered him a martinet, but he was mourned generally throughout the South.

Cullum; Boatner, *Civil War*; Warner, *Generals in Gray*; D.S. Freeman, *Lee's Lieutenants*, Vols. 1 & 2; *B&L*, Vol. 2; *CMH*, Vol. II (Maryland).

WINTHROP, Frederick, 1839–1865, New York, U.S. Volunteers, killed in action 1 April 1865 at Five Forks, Virginia.

Little is known about Frederick Winthrop beyond the outline of his military career. He was a native of New York City and enlisted in the 71st New York, a three-month regiment, in April 1861. In October 1861 he was commissioned Captain in the 12th U.S. Infantry, a new regular regiment, and raised his own company at Fort Hamilton in Brooklyn. He joined the Army of the Potomac in April 1862 and fought on the Virginia Peninsula, where he was cited for gallantry, and at Second Manassas, Antietam, and Fredericksburg. At Gettysburg, Winthrop was assistant adjutant general of one of the regular brigades in V Corps, and he continued in that position until the spring of 1864. In the Wilderness, in May 1864, Winthrop assumed command of the 12th Infantry, although still a Captain, and remained in command until after Cold Harbor. Then he became assistant adjutant general of a division in V Corps and was recommended by General Meade for appointment as a Brigadier General of volunteers. Winthrop became Colonel of the 5th New York Veteran Volunteers, a reenlisted regiment, in August 1864 and was breveted Brigadier General USV from 1 August, both on the recommendation of General Governor K. Warren, the corps commander. Winthrop commanded a brigade in V Corps from August to October 1864 and remained in the Petersburg lines with his regiment through the winter of 1865. When Sheridan attempted to force Lee's army out of its defenses on 1 April 1865, Winthrop was killed while leading a charge against the Confederate breastworks at Five Forks. His brigade captured 1,000 prisoners and four stands of colors. As he died he inquired about the success of the attack. Winthrop bore a physical resemblance to Sheridan, and the army was thrown into temporary consternation when it was first reported that Sheridan, and not Winthrop, had been killed. Winthrop was posthumously breveted Brigadier General USA to rank from 20 February 1865 and Major General USV to rank from 1 April.

Appleton's; Boatner, *Civil War*; Phisterer, *New York in the War*; *B&L*, Vol. 4; *OR*, Ser. I, Vols. 21; 36, pt. 3; 40, pt. 3; 42, pts. 1 & 3; 46, pts. 1 & 2; 51, pt. 1.

WOODFORD, William, 1734–1780, Virginia, Continental Army, died 17 November 1780 while a prisoner of war in New York City.

William Woodford, known to his friends as "Beau," was the son of an English officer who settled in Virginia. He received a better than average education, and then entered the militia for the French and Indian War. He was a member of his county Committee of Correspondence and an alternate to the Virginia Convention in 1774 and 1775. In August 1775 Woodford became Colonel of the 3rd Virginia State Regiment and helped to repel Lord Dunsmore's attempts to regain control of the state for the British. Woodford was appointed Colonel of the 2nd Virginia Continentals in February 1776 and was promoted Brigadier General on 21 February 1777 to replace the fallen Hugh Mercer. He commanded a brigade and was wounded at Brandywine in September 1777, but was able to return to the field in time for Germantown the next month. He suffered through the winter at Valley Forge with his men and fought at Monmouth in June 1778. Woodford's was one of the brigades selected in early 1780 to march to the aid of Charleston, South Carolina, threatened by a British siege. Leaving New Jersey in March, they arrived at Charleston the first week in April, covering 505 miles in thirty days. The city was already under attack. Ten days after Woodford's arrival it was encircled. Sir Henry Clinton slowly reduced the defenses by regular approaches, and General Benjamin Lincoln, the American commander, surrendered on 12 May. Woodford was one of nine American generals captured. Most of the captives remained in Charleston to await parole or exchange, but Woodford was transported to New York and imprisoned. He survived only six months and died 13 November 1780. He was buried in Trinity Churchyard in New York.

   DAB; Boatner, *American Revolution*; D.S. Freeman, *Washington*, Vols. 4 & 5; Stewart; Wright.

WOODHULL, Nathaniel, 1722–1776, New York, New York Militia, died 10 September 1776 of wounds received 28 August 1776 at Jamaica, New York.

   Nathaniel Woodhull had a long career as soldier and politician before the American Revolution. He was born at Mastic, Long Island, the son of a farmer, and farmed himself for many years. He was an officer of New York Provincials during the French and Indian Wars, serving as Major at Crown Point in 1758, Lieutenant Colonel in the campaigns of 1759, and Colonel of the 2nd New York in the expedition to Montreal in 1760. Woodhull represented Suffolk County in the New York Assembly from 1769 to 1775, was a member of the convention which chose delegates to the Second Continental Congress, and was President of the New York Provincial Congress in 1775–1776. In August 1776, with New York threatened by William Howe's British army, Woodhull was appointed Brigadier General of Queens and Suffolk County militia and sent to eastern Long Island to protect the local inhabitants. After Howe's victory at Brooklyn the militia became badly demoralized and Woodhull moved his men to Jamaica, New York, to await orders and reinforcements. On 28 August he was captured by a British force rounding up stray militiamen in the Jamaica swamps. Either at the time of his capture or shortly thereafter Woodhull was severely wounded in the arm by the sword slash of a British officer, supposedly Sir James Baird, and was said to be saved from further mistreatment by the intervention of Oliver DeLancey, the New York loyalist. Woodhull was imprisoned, first on a prison hulk, later at New Utrecht. He was refused treatment for his wound until the arm required amputation. He died of the aftereffects on 10 September while still in prison. Campbell and Sabine present evidence to refute the charges against Baird.

DAB; *Appleton's*; Boatner, *American Revolution*; D.S. Freeman, *Washington*, Vol. 4; Campbell; Sabine.

WOOSTER, David, 1711–1777, Connecticut, Connecticut State Troops, died 2 May 1777 of wounds received 27 April 1777 at Ridgefield, Connecticut.

David Wooster was the oldest American general ever killed in action. He was the son of a mason and graduated from Yale College in 1738. He entered the militia and was captain of an armed sloop in 1742. He went on the expedition to Louisburg, Nova Scotia, during King George's War in 1745 and became Captain in Pepperell's 49th Foot, a British regiment raised in North America, the same year. He remained on the regiment's rolls on half pay until he retired in 1774. Wooster was Colonel of a Connecticut regiment during the French and Indian War and was present when Ticonderoga was captured. In 1763 he became Collector of Customs for the port of New Haven. In June 1775 Wooster was made Major General of Connecticut state troops and commanded the forces sent to garrison, New York and Long Island while Washington's army besieged the British in Boston. On 22 June Wooster was appointed Brigadier General in the Continental Army and was assigned to Philip Schuyler's army for the invasion of Canada. When Schuyler fell sick, Wooster found himself subordinated to Schuyler's replacement, Richard Montgomery, who was his junior by date of rank. Wooster solved this dilemma by admitting that he personally was subject to Montgomery's orders but his men were not. After Montgomery was killed at Quebec, Wooster became senior American commander in Canada but he undertook no active operations. In the spring of 1776 he returned to Connecticut and never again commanded Continental troops, although he retained his congressional commission. In January 1777 Wooster led Connecticut militia against German garrisons at King's Bridge, New York. In April 1777 he took the field for the last time to repel British raiders into Connecticut. In concert with Benedict Arnold, Wooster led the militia which harassed the British column as it retreated from Danbury back toward its ships. On 27 April Wooster attacked the camp of the British as they were eating breakfast and captured forty prisoners. Emboldened by this success, he tried the same tactic against the moving column several hours later. This time the British were ready. As his men wavered before the enemy's volleys, Wooster rode to the front and called for another charge. Suddenly he clutched his side and fell from the saddle. Carried to a house in Danbury, Wooster died on 2 May while his wife sat at his bedside.

DAB; Boatner, *American Revolution*; D.S. Freeman, *Washington*, Vols. 3 & 4; Sellers; Wright.

WORLEY, Robert Franklin, 1919–1968, California, U.S. Air Force, killed in action 23 July 1968 near Hue, Vietnam.

Robert F. Worley was the first general of the U.S. Air Force killed in action. Son of a government employee, he was born in Riverside and graduated from Riverside Junior College in 1937. Worley was first interested in a maritime career and spent three years in the Merchant Marine, including four trips to the Far East. In 1940 he enlisted in the Air Corps and completed flight training in 1941. During World War II Worley flew one hundred combat missions in P-40 and P-47 fighters in North Africa, Sicily, Italy, and the Pacific. On his first mission he was shot down in the desert and walked back to his unit through enemy lines. He was wounded once, and by war's end he was Lieutenant Colonel and squadron commander. In 1947 he became a member of the independent U.S. Air Force and served as squadron and wing commander. Promoted Colonel in January 1951, he was vice commander of the 27th Air Division in 1952 and served extensively at bases in the American West and in Germany. Worley was promoted Brigadier General on 24 September 1964 and was commander of the 831st Air Division and on the staff of Tactical Air Command. He was promoted Major General on 1 October 1966 and was assigned as Vice Commander, Seventh Air Force in Vietnam in July 1967. On 23 July 1968, two weeks before the end of his tour of duty in Vietnam, Worley was flying an RF-4C reconnaissance plane in the northern part of the country not far from Hue when it was hit and downed by enemy ground fire. The co-pilot ejected safely but Worley, either overcome by smoke or trapped in his seat, went down with the plane. At the time he was acting commander of Seventh Air Force.

New York Times, July 24, 1968; *Riverside Press*, July 23 & 24, 1968; Air Force Records Center.

Z

ZOLLICOFFER, Felix Kirk, 1812–1862, Tennessee, C.S. Army, killed in action 19 January 1862 at Logan Cross Roads, Kentucky.

Felix Zollicoffer was a politician-turned-soldier whose military ineptitude led to his own death. He was born in Maury County, received a rudimentary education, and became a printer at age sixteen. He served as a Lieutenant of volunteers in the Second Seminole War and then returned to journalism as an editor. Zollicoffer, a Whig, became a political power in Tennessee, held several offices, was state senator, and was elected to Congress in 1852. He supported the Constitutional Unionist party in the Presidential election of 1860, hoping for mediation of sectional disputes, and was a delegate to the Washington Peace Conference of 1861, as was James Wadsworth of New York. Nevertheless, on 9 July 1861 Zollicoffer accepted a commission as Brigadier General CSA. He was sent to eastern Tennessee in an unsuccessful attempt to win support from the strongly pro-Union inhabitants. In September 1861 Zollicoffer occupied Cumberland Gap and in November crossed the Cumberland River into Kentucky. He was ordered to withdraw into Tennessee but refused to do so, thereby precipitating the battle at Logan Cross Roads. On 19 January 1862 the Confederate force moved forward from its base to confront the advancing Union army. In a remarkable episode, Colonel Speed Fry of the 4th (Union) Kentucky rode to the flank of his regiment for a reconnaissance and was approached by an officer wearing an unmarked raincoat. The two came close enough for their knees to touch and the stranger warned Fry against the dangers of firing into his own men. Fry agreed when another man came up behind the stranger and shot Fry's horse. Fry wheeled and he and several of his men shot the first stranger. He fell from his horse, killed by a pistol shot and two musket balls. It was Zollicoffer.

DAB; *BDAC*; Boatner, *Civil War*; Warner, *Generals in Gray*; Connelly, *Army of the Heartland*; *B&L*, Vol. 1; *CMH*, Vol. VIII.

ZOOK, Samuel Kosciuszko, 1821–1863, Pennsylvania-New York, U.S. Volunteers, died 3 July 1863 of wounds received 2 July 1863 at Gettysburg, Pennsylvania.

Samuel K. Zook was killed while rushing his brigade forward to plug a gap in the Union line at Gettysburg. He was born in Chester City and reared near Valley Forge. Zook entered the Pennsylvania militia as a youth and also took a job in Philadelphia with the New York and Washington Telegraph Company. Later he moved to the company's New York office and transferred to the New York militia. In 1861 he was mustered into service as Lieutenant Colonel of the 6th New York militia, occupied Annapolis, Maryland, in July, and served as military governor of the city. After the expiration of his regiment's enlistment Zook returned to New York, where he raised and became Colonel of the 57th New York in October. The regiment fought in the Virginia Peninsula campaign of 1862 but was not at Second Manassas. Zook was absent from the army during the Maryland campaign. He returned in October 1862 to take command of a brigade and led it in the wasteful attacks on the Confederate positions at Fredericksburg in December. During the winter of 1863 Zook was in temporary command of a division and was promoted Brigadier General USV on 23 March 1863 to rank from 29 November 1862. Zook served in Winfield Hancock's division at Chancellorsville, Virginia, in May 1863 and remained in II Corps for the Gettysburg campaign. On 2 July 1863, while leading his brigade forward at the Wheatfield to stem the flood of Longstreet's advance, Zook was shot in the abdomen. He was carried to a small house which was being used as a field hospital, but he survived only until the early morning hours of 3 July.

Boatner, *Civil War*; Warner, *Generals in Blue*; Catton, *Glory Road*; Coddington; *B&L*, Vol. 3.

APPENDIX A
General Officer Data

TABLE 1
General Officer Deaths by War or Campaign

American Revolution	**12**
Indian Wars	**4**
War of 1812	**2**
Civil War (Union)	**80**
Civil War (Confederate)	**80**
Philippine Insurrection	**2**
Boxer Rebellion	**1**
World War I	**2**
World War II	**30**
Vietnam	**8**

TABLE 2
General Officer to Total Fatality Ratio

	BATTLE DEATHS	GENERALS	RATIO
American Revolution (Army)	5,992	12	1:499
War of 1812	1,950	2	1:975
Civil War (UnionArmy)	138,154	80	1:1,727
Civil War (Confederate total)	74,524	80	1:932
World War I (Army)	50,510	2	1:25,255
World War II (Army) (includes Army Air Force)	234,874	25	1:9,395
(Navy)	36,950	5	1:7,390
Vietnam (Army)	30,839	5	1:6,168
(Marines)	13,053	1	1:13,053
(Air Force)	1,708	2	1:854

Source for Battle Deaths: *The World Almanac and Book of Facts 1983.*

TABLE 3
Highest Rank Held

UNITED STATES ARMY		CONFEDERATE ARMY		OTHER SERVICES	
General*	2	General	2	Rear Adm USN	5
Maj Gen	27	Lt Gen	3	Maj Gen USAF	1
Brig Gen	71	Maj Gen	7	Maj Gen USMC	1
Bvt Brig Gen	33	Brig Gen	69	Brig Gen USAF	1

*Both Lt Gen at time of death

TABLE 4
Place of Death or Mortal Wound

Belgium	1	Arkansas	7	Missouri	1
Canada	3	California	1	Montana	1
China	1	Connecticut	1	New Jersey	1
France	7	Florida	1	New York	2
Germany	4	Georgia	16	North Carolina	2
Italy	4	Hawaii	1	Ohio	1
Okinawa	2	Kentucky	3	Pennsylvania	15
Pacific	6	Louisiana	6	South Carolina	4
Philippines	8	Maryland	9	Tennessee	18
Taiwan	1	Massachusetts	1	Virginia	<u>78</u>
Vietnam	<u>8</u>	Mississippi	7		176
	45				

TABLE 5
General Officer Combat Deaths by
Branch of Service

Infantry	171
Cavalry	22
Armor	1
Artillery	4
Air Force & Army Air Force	9
Engineers	3
Staff	5
Navy & Marines	<u>6</u>
Total	221

TABLE 6
Place of Birth

State				Foreign Country	
New York	26	Mississippi	4	Ireland	5
Virginia	25	California	3	Philippines	3
Ohio	17	New Hampshire	3	England	2
Massachusetts	15	New Jersey	3	Germany	2
North Carolina	12	Rhode Island	3	France	1
Pennsylvania	11	Texas	3	Poland	1
Tennessee	11	Vermont	3	Scotland	1
Connecticut	9	Louisiana	2		
Kentucky	8	Michigan	2		
South Carolina	8	Missouri	2		
Maryland	7	New Mexico	2		
Georgia	6	Arkansas	1		
Alabama	5	Colorado	1		
Illinois	4	Florida	1		
Indiana	4	Kansas	1		
Maine	4	Minnesota	1		

TABLE 7
Principal Occupation

Professional Military	93
Legal Profession	48
Politician	26
Businessman	24
Farmer	20
Student	10
Engineer	6
Government Employee	5
Educator	3
Banker	2
Physician	2
Frontiersman	2
Newspaperman	1
Clergyman	1
Unknown	7
	251*

*Some officers counted in more than one category

TABLE 8
Rank Status at Time of Death

United States Forces

Serving Generals and Admirals	93
Serving Brevet Generals	2
Posthumous Generals	8
Posthumous Brevet Generals	31
Former General Posthumously Breveted as General	1
Former Generals Killed While Serving in Lower Grades	3
Serving Officer Killed Before Accepting General's Commission	1
Civil Official Killed Before Accepting General's Commission	1
Civil Official Killed After Resigning General's Commission	1
	141

Confederate States Army

Serving Generals	73
Posthumous Generals	4
Serving General Not Formally Commissioned	1
Died After Discharge as General	2
	80

TABLE 9
Educational Status

U.S. Military Academy Graduates	65
U.S. Naval Academy Graduates	5
Other Military School Graduates	10
Other College Graduates	<u>43</u>
	123
Former Cadets, U.S. Military Academy	3
Former College Students, Non-Graduate	<u>22</u>
Total College Attendees	148

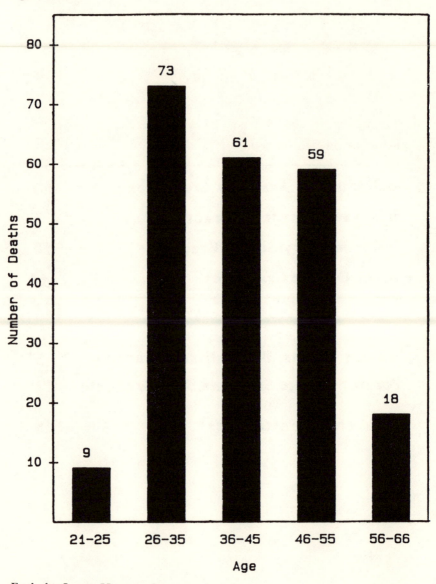

FIGURE 1
Age at Death

Excludes James Hogun whose age is unknown

APPENDIX B

American General and
Flag Officer Combat Fatalities

NAME AND RANK	DATE OF DEATH AND PLACE WOUND INCURRED
American Revolution	
1. Maj. Gen. Joseph Warren	17 June 1775, Bunker Hill, Mass.
2. Maj. Gen. Richard Montgomery	31 December 1775, Quebec, Canada
3. Brig. Gen. Nathaniel Woodhull	20 September 1776, Jamaica, N.Y.
4. Brig. Gen. Hugh Mercer	11 January 1777, Princeton, N.J.
5. Maj. Gen. David Wooster	2 May 1777, Ridgefield, Conn.
6. Brig. Gen. Nicholas Herkimer	16 August 1777, Oriskany, N.Y.
7. Brig. Gen. Francis Nash	7 October 1777, Germantown, Pa.
8. Brig. Gen. Casimir Pulaski	11 November 1779, Savannah, Ga.
9. Maj. Gen. Johann Kalb	19 August 1780, Camden, S.C.
10. Brig. Gen. William Woodford	13 November 1780, Charleston, S.C.
11. Brig. Gen. James Hogun	4 January 1781, Charleston, S.C.
12. Brig. Gen. William Lee Davidson	1 February 1781, Cowan's Ford, N.C.
Indian Wars	
1. Maj. Gen. Richard Butler	4 November 1791, St. Mary's, Ohio

2. Maj. Gen. Wiley Thompson   28 December 1835, Ft. King. Fla.
3. Bvt. Maj. Gen. Edward
   R.S. Canby   11 April 1873, Lava Beds, Calif.
4. Bvt. Maj. Gen. George A. Custer   25 June 1876, Little Big Horn, Mont.

War of 1812

1. Brig. Gen. Zebulon M. Pike   27 April 1813, York, Ontario, Canada
2. Brig. Gen. Leonard Covington   14 November 1813, Chrysler's Farm,
                                        Ont.

Civil War, Union

1. Brig. Gen. Nathaniel Lyon   10 August 1861, Wilson's Creek Mo.
2. Maj. Gen. Edward D. Baker   21 October 1861, Ball's Bluff, Va.
3. Brig. Gen. William H.L. Wallace   10 April 1862, Shiloh, Tenn.
4. Brig. Gen. Thomas Williams   5 August 1862, Baton Rouge, La.
5. Brig. Gen. Robert L. McCook   6 August 1862, Dechard, Tenn.
6. Brig. Gen. Henry Bohlen   22 August 1862, Freeman's Ford, Va.
7. Brig. Gen. George W. Taylor   31 August 1862, Manassas, Va.
8. Maj. Gen. Philip Kearny   1 September 1862, Chantilly, Va.
9. Maj. Gen. Isaac I. Stevens   1 September 1862, Chantilly, Va.
10. Bvt. Brig. Gen. Thornton
    F. Brodhead   2 September 1862, Manassas, Va.
11. Maj. Gen. Jesse L. Reno   14 September 1862, South Mountain,
                                        Md.
12. Maj. Gen. Joseph K.F. Mansfield 18 September 1862, Antietam, Md.
13. Brig. Gen. Isaac P. Rodman   30 September 1862, Antietam, Md.
14. Brig. Gen. Pleasant A. Hackleman 3 October 1862, Corinth, Miss.
15. Brig. Gen. James S. Jackson   8 October 1862, Perryville, Ky.
16. Brig. Gen. William R. Terrill   8 October 1862, Perryville, Ky.
17. Brig. Gen. Israel B. Richardson 3 November 1862, Antietam, Md.
18. Brig. Gen. Conrad F. Jackson   13 December 1862, Fredericksburg,
                                        Va.
19. Brig. Gen. George D. Bayard   13 December 1862, Fredericksburg,
                                        Va.
20. Brig. Gen. Joshua W. Sill   31 December 1862, Stone's River,
                                        Tenn.

21. Maj. Gen. Hiram G. Berry	3 May 1863, Chancellorsville, Va.
22. Maj. Gen. Amiel W. Whipple	7 May 1863, Chancellorsville, Va.
23. Brig. Gen. Edwin P. Chapin	27 May 1863, Port Hudson, La.
24. Brig. Gen. Edmund Kirby	28 May 1863, Chancellorsville, Va.
25. Maj. Gen. John F. Reynolds	1 July 1863, Gettysburg, Pa.
26. Bvt. Brig. Gen. George H. Ward	2 July 1863, Gettysburg, Pa.
27. Brig. Gen. Stephen H. Weed	2 July 1863, Gettysburg, Pa.
28. Bvt. Brig. Gen. A. Van Horne Ellis	2 July 1863, Gettysburg, Pa.
29. Brig. Gen. Samuel K. Zook	3 July 1863, Gettysburg, Pa.
30. Brig. Gen. Elon J. Farnsworth	3 July 1863, Gettysburg, Pa.
31. Bvt. Brig. Gen. Paul J. Revere	4 July 1863, Gettysburg, Pa.
32. Brig. Gen. Strong Vincent	7 July 1863, Gettysburg, Pa.
33. Bvt. Brig. Gen. Louis R. Francine	16 July 1863, Gettysburg, Pa.
34. Brig. Gen. Edward N. Kirk	29 July 1863, Stone's River, Tenn.
35. Maj. Gen. George C. Strong	30 July 1863, Charleston, S.C.
36. Brig. Gen. William H. Lytle	20 September 1863, Chickamauga, Ga.
37. Brig. Gen. William P. Sanders	19 November 1863, Campbell's Station, Tenn.
38. Brig. Gen. Stephen G. Champlin	24 January 1864, Fair Oaks, Va.
39. Bvt. Brig. Gen. Lewis Benedict	9 April 1864, Pleasant Hill, La.
40. Bvt. Maj. Gen. Alexander Hays	5 May 1864, Wilderness, Va.
41. Bvt. Brig. Gen. Henry L. Abbott	6 May 1864, Wilderness, Va.
42. Bvt. Maj. Gen. James S. Wadsworth	8 May 1864, Wilderness, Va.
43. Maj. Gen. John Sedgwick	9 May 1864, Spotsylvania, Va.
44. Brig. Gen. Thomas G. Stevenson	10 May 1864, Spotsylvania, Va.
45. Brig. Gen. James C. Rice	10 May 1864, Laurel Hill, Va.
46. Bvt. Brig. Gen. William N. Green	14 May 1864, Pleasant Hill, La.
47. Bvt. Brig. Gen. Henry. H. Giesy	28 May 1864, Dallas, Ga.
48. Bvt. Brig. Gen. John McConihe	1 June 1864, Cold Harbor, Va.
49. Bvt. Brig. Gen. Arthur H. Dutton	5 June 1864, Bermuda Hundred, Va.
50. Bvt. Brig. Gen. Thomas W. Humphrey	10 June 1864, Guntown, Miss.
51. Bvt. Brig. Gen. William Sackett	14 June 1864, Trevilian Station, Va.
52. Bvt. Brig. Gen. James S. Morton	17 June 1864, Petersburg, Va.
53. Bvt. Brig. Gen. George L. Prescott	19 June 1864, Petersburg, Va.

54. Bvt. Brig. Gen. William Blaisdell   23 June 1864, Petersburg, Va.
55. Brig. Gen. Charles G. Harker   27 June 1864, Kenesaw Mountain,
                                            Ga.
56. Brig. Gen. Samuel A. Rice   6 July 1864, Jenkins's Ferry, Ark.
57. Brig. Gen. Daniel McCook   17 July 1864, Kenesaw Mountain, Ga.
58. Bvt. Brig. Gen. George A.
    Cobham   20 July 1864, Peachtree Creek, Ga.
59. Maj. Gen. James B. McPherson   22 July 1864, Atlanta, Ga.
60. Bvt. Brig. Gen. James A. Mulligan   26 July 1864, Winchester, Va.
61. Bvt. Brig. Gen. Griffin A. Stedman   5 August 1864, Petersburg, Va.
62. Bvt. Brig. Gen. George R. Elstner   8 August 1864, Atlanta, Ga.
63. Bvt. Brig. Gen. Daniel Chaplin   20 August 1864, Deep Bottom, Va.
64. Bvt. Brig. Gen. Henry L. Patten   10 September 1864, Deep Bottom,
                                            Va.
65. Bvt. Maj. Gen. David A. Russell   19 September 1864, Winchester, Va.
66. Bvt. Brig. Gen. Frank H. Peck   19 September 1864, Winchester, Va.
67. Brig. Gen. Hiram Burnham   30 September 1864, Ft. Harrison, Va.
68. Bvt. Brig. Gen. Willoughby
    Babcock   6 October 1864, Winchester, Va.
69. Bvt. Brig. Gen. Alexander
    Gardiner   7 October 1864, Opequan Creek, Va.
70. Bvt. Brig. Gen. George D. Wells   13 October 1864, Cedar Creek, Va.
71. Brig. Gen. Daniel D. Bidwell   19 October 1864, Cedar Creek, Va.
72. Brig. Gen. Charles R. Lowell   20 October 1864, Cedar Creek, Va.
73. Bvt. Brig. Gen. Sylvester G. Hill   16 December 1864, Nashville,
                                            Tenn.
74. Bvt. Brig. Gen. J. Howard
    Kitching   10 January 1865, Cedar Creek, Va.
75. Bvt. Maj. Gen. Frederick
    Winthrop   1 April 1865, Five Forks, Va.
76. Bvt. Brig. Gen. George W.
    Gowen   2 April 1865, Petersburg, Va.
77. Bvt. Brig. Gen. Theodore Read   6 April 1865, High Bridge, Va.
78. Bvt. Maj. Gen. Thomas A. Smyth   9 April 1865, Farmville, Va.
79. Bvt. Brig. Gen. Francis Washburn   22 April 1865, High Bridge, Va.
80. Bvt. Brig. Gen. Cleveland J.
    Campbell   13 June 1865, Petersburg, Va.

Civil War, Confederate

1.	Brig. Gen. Robert S. Garnett	13 July 1861, Carrick's Ford, Va.
2.	Brig. Gen. Barnard E. Bee	22 July 1861, Bull Run, Va.
3.	Brig. Gen. Felix K. Zollicoffer	22 January 1862, Logan Cross Roads, Ky.
4.	Brig. Gen. Ben McCulloch	7 March 1862, Pea Ridge, Ark.
5.	Brig. Gen. James M. McIntosh	7 March 1862, Pea Ridge, Ark.
6.	Brig. Gen. William Y. Slack	21 March 1862, Pea Ridge, Ark.
7.	Gen. Albert S. Johnston	6 April 1862, Shiloh, Tenn.
8.	Brig. Gen. Adley H. Gladden	12 April 1862, Shiloh, Tenn.
9.	Brig. Gen. Robert H. Hatton	31 May 1862, Seven Pines, Va.
10.	Brig. Gen. Turner Ashby	6 June 1862, Harrisonburg, Va.
11.	Brig. Gen. Richard Griffith	30 June 1862, Savage's Station, Va.
12.	Brig. Gen. Charles S. Winder	9 August 1862, Cedar Mountain, Va.
13.	Brig. Gen. Samuel Garland	14 September 1862, South Mountain, Md.
14.	Brig. Gen. L. O'Brien Branch	17 September 1862, Antietam, Md.
15.	Brig. Gen. William E. Starke	17 September 1862, Antietam, Md.
16.	Brig. Gen. Lewis H. Little	19 September 1862, Iuka, Miss.
17.	Brig. Gen. George B. Anderson	16 October 1862, Antietam, Md.
18.	Brig. Gen. Alexander E. Steen	7 December 1862, Prairie Grove, Ark.
19.	Brig. Gen. Thomas R.R. Cobb	13 December 1862, Fredericksburg, Va.
20.	Brig. Gen. Maxcy Gregg	13 December 1862, Fredericksburg, Va.
21.	Brig. Gen. James E. Rains	31 December 1862, Stone's River, Tenn.
22.	Brig. Gen. Roger W. Hanson	4 January 1863, Stone's River, Tenn.
23.	Brig. Gen. Edward D. Tracy	1 May 1863, Port Gibson, Miss.
24.	Brig. Gen. Elisha F. Paxton	3 May 1863, Chancellorsville, Va.
25.	Lt. Gen. Thomas J. Jackson	10 May 1863, Chancellorsville, Va.
26.	Brig. Gen. Lloyd Tilghman	16 May 1863, Champion's Hill, Miss.
27.	Brig. Gen. Ishom W. Garrott	17 June 1863, Vicksburg, Miss.

28. Brig. Gen. Martin E. Green	27 June 1863, Vicksburg, Miss.
29. Brig. Gen. William Barksdale	3 July 1863, Gettysburg, Pa.
30. Brig. Gen. Richard B. Garnett	3 July 1863, Gettysburg, Pa.
31. Brig. Gen. Lewis A. Armistead	5 July 1863, Gettysburg, Pa.
32. Brig. Gen. Paul J. Semmes	10 July 1863, Gettysburg, Pa.
33. Brig. Gen. J. Johnston Pettigrew	17 July 1863, Falling Waters, Md.
34. Maj. Gen. W. Dorsey Pender	18 July 1863, Gettysburg, Pa.
35. Brig. Gen. Preston Smith	19 September 1863, Chickamauga, Ga.
36. Brig. Gen. James Deshler	20 September 1863, Chickamauga, Ga.
37. Brig. Gen. Benjamin H. Helm	20 September 1863, Chickamauga, Ga.
38. Brig. Gen. Carnot Posey	13 November 1863, Bristoe Station, Va.
39. Brig. Gen. J.J.A. Alexander Mouton	8 April 1864, Mansfield, La.
40. Brig. Gen. Thomas Green	12 April 1864, Mansfield, La.
41. Brig. Gen. Horace Randal	30 April 1864, Jenkins's Ferry, Ark.
42. Brig. Gen. William R. Scurry	30 April 1864, Jenkins's Ferry, Ark.
43. Brig. Gen. John M. Jones	5 May 1864, Wilderness, Va.
44. Brig. Gen. Micah Jenkins	6 May 1864, Wilderness, Va.
45. Brig. Gen. Leroy A. Stafford	8 May 1864, Wilderness, Va.
46. Maj. Gen. James E.B. Stuart	12 May 1864, Yellow Tavern, Va.
47. Brig. Gen. Abner M. Perrin	12 May 1864, Spotsylvania, Va.
48. Brig. Gen. Junius Daniel	13 May 1864, Spotsylvania, Va.
49. Brig. Gen. James B. Gordon	18 May 1864, Meadow Bridge, Va.
50. Brig. Gen. Albert G. Jenkins	21 May 1864, Cloyd's Mountain, Va.
51. Brig. Gen. James B. Terrill	30 May 1864, Bethesda Church, Va.
52. Brig. Gen. George P. Doles	2 June 1864, Bethesda Church, Va.
53. Brig. Gen. William E. Jones	5 June 1864, Piedmont, Va.
54. Lt. Gen. Leonidas Polk	14 June 1864, Pine Mountain, Ga.
55. Maj. Gen. William H.T. Walker	22 July 1864, Atlanta, Ga.
56. Brig. Gen. Clement H. Stevens	25 July 1864, Peachtree Creek, Ga.
57. Brig. Gen. Samuel Benton	28 July 1864, Atlanta, Ga.
58. Brig. Gen. John R. Chambliss	16 August 1864, Deep Bottom, Va.

59. Brig. Gen. Victor J.B. Girardey 16 August 1864, Deep Bottom, Va.

60. Brig. Gen. John C.C. Sanders 21 August 1864, Weldon Railroad, Va.

61. Brig. Gen. John H. Kelly 4 September 1864, Franklin, Tenn.

62. Brig. Gen. John H. Morgon 4 September 1864, Greenville, Tenn.

63. Maj. Gen. Robert E. Rodes 19 September 1864, Winchester, Va.

64. Brig. Gen. Archibald C. Godwin 19 September 1864, Winchester, Va.

65. Brig. Gen. John Dunovant 1 October 1864, Vaughan Road, Va.

66. Brig. Gen. John Gregg 7 October 1864, Darbytown Road, Va.

67. Maj. Gen. Stephen D. Ramseur 20 October 1864, Cedar Creek, Va.

68. Maj. Gen. Patrick R. Cleburne 30 November 1864, Franklin, Tenn.

69. Brig. Gen. John Adams 30 November 1864, Franklin, Tenn.

70. Brig. Gen. States R. Gist 30 November 1864, Franklin, Tenn.

71. Brig. Gen. Hiram B. Granbury 30 November 1864, Franklin, Tenn.

72. Brig. Gen. Otho F. Strahl 30 November 1864, Franklin, Tenn.

73. Brig. Gen. Archibald Gracie 2 December 1864, Petersburg, Va.

74. Brig. Gen. John C. Carter 10 December 1864, Franklin, Tenn.

75. Brig. Gen. John Pegram 6 February 1865, Hatcher's Run, Va.

76. Maj. Gen. William H.C. Whiting 10 March 1865, Fort Fisher, N.C.

77. Lt. Gen. Ambrose P. Hill 2 April 1865, Petersburg, Va.

78. Brig. Gen. Robert C. Tyler 16 April 1865, West Point, Ga.

79. Brig. Gen. James Dearing 23 April 1865, High Bridge, Va.

80. Brig. Gen. Stephen Elliott 21 March 1866, Petersburg, Va.

Far East Wars

1. Brig. Gen. Harry C. Egbert 26 March 1899, Malinta, Luzon, P.I.

2. Maj. Gen. Henry W. Lawton 19 December 1899, San Mateo, Luzon, P.I.

3. Brig. Gen. Emerson H. Liscum 13 July 1900, Tientsin, China

World War I

1. Brig. Gen. Edward Sigerfoos 7 October 1918, Argonne, France

2. Brig. Gen. Henry R. Hill 16 October 1918, Montfaucon, France

World War II

1. Rear Adm. Isaac C. Kidd	7 December 1941, Pearl Harbor, Hawaii
2. Maj. Gen. Clarence L. Tinker	7 June 1942, near Wake Island
3. Brig. Gen. Guy O. Fort	9 or 13 November 1942, Lanao, P.I.
4. Rear Adm. Daniel J. Callaghan	13 November 1942, Solomon Islands
5. Rear Adm. Norman Scott	13 November 1942, Solomon Islands
6. Brig. Gen. Kenneth N. Walker	5 January 1943, Rabaul
7. Brig. Gen. Howard K. Ramey	26 March 1943, New Britain
8. Brig. Gen. Nathan B. Forrest	13 June 1943, Kiel, Germany
9. Brig. Gen. Charles L. Keerans	11 July 1943, Sicily
10. Rear Adm. Henry M. Mullinnix	24 November 1943, Gilbert Islands
11. Brig. Gen. Davis D. Graves	8 February 1944, San Stefano, Italy
12. Brig. Gen. Russell A. Wilson	6 March 1944, Berlin, Germany
13. Brig. Gen. Allan C. McBride	9 May 1944, Bataan, P.I.
14. Brig. Gen. Don F. Pratt	6 June 1944, Normandy, France
15. Brig. Gen. Nelson M. Walker	10 July 1944, Normandy, France
16. Gen. Lesley J. McNair	25 July 1944, St. Lo, France
17. Brig. Gen. James E. Wharton	12 August 1944, near Sourdeval, France
18. Brig. Gen. Edmund W. Searby	14 September 1944, Moselle River, France
19. Brig. Gen. Frederick W. Castle	24 December 1944, Liege, Belgium
20. Brig. Gen. Vicente Lim	6 January (?) 1944, Manila, P.I.
21. Brig. Gen. Fidel Segundo	6 January 1944, Manila, P.I.
22. Rear Adm. Theodore E. Chandler	7 January 1945, Lingayen Gulf, P.I.
23. Maj. Gen. Edward D. Patrick	15 March 1945, Luzon, P.I.
24. Brig. Gen. Gustav J. Braun	17 March 1945, near Bologna, Italy
25. Maj. Gen. Maurice Rose	30 March 1945, Paderborn, Germany
26. Brig. Gen. Lloyd H. Gibbons	7 April 1945, Kassel, Germany
27. Brig. Gen. William O. Darby	30 April 1945, Lake Garda, Italy
28. Brig. Gen. James L. Dalton	16 May 1945, Balete Pass, Luzon, P.I.
29. Gen. Simon B. Buckner	18 June 1945, Okinawa
30. Brig. Gen. Claudius M. Easley	19 June 1945, Okinawa

Vietnam War

1. Maj. Gen. Bruno A. Hochmuth   14 November 1967, Hue
2. Brig. Gen. Edward B. Burdett   18 November 1967, North Vietnam
3. Maj. Gen. Robert F. Worley   23 July 1968, Hue
4. Maj. Gen. Keith L. Ware   13 September 1968, Binh Long
5. Brig. Gen. William R. Bond   1 April 1970, War Zone D
6. Maj. Gen. John A.B. Dillard   14 May 1970, Pleiku
7. Brig. Gen. Carroll E. Adams   14 May 1970, Pleiku
8. Brig. Gen. Richard J. Tallman   9 July 1972, An Loc

APPENDIX C

American General and Flag Officer Non-Combat Fatalities During Time of Hostilities

NAME AND RANK	DATE AND PLACE OF DEATH	CAUSE OF DEATH
American Revolution		
1. Maj. Gen. John Thomas	2 June 1776 Sorel, Canada	Smallpox
2. Brig. Gen. Frederick William, Baron de Woedtke	28 July 1776 Lake George, N.Y.	Liver ailment
3. Brig. Gen. James Moore	9 April 1777 Wilmington, N.C.	Stomach ailment
4. Maj. Gen. Philippe C.J.B. Tronson de Coudray	15 September 1777 Philadelphia, Pa.	Drowned
5. Brig. Gen. Enoch Poor	8 September 1780 Paramus, N.J.	Typhus
6. Brig. Gen. William Campbell (Virginia militia)	22 August 1781 Rocky Mills, Va.	Sickness
7. Brig. Gen. William Thompson	3 September 1781 Carlisle, Pa.	Natural causes
8. Brig. Gen. Andrew Lewis (Virginia militia)	26 September 1781 Virginia	Natural causes
9. Brig. Gen. John Ashe (North Carolina militia)	7 October 1781 Sampson County, N.C.	Smallpox

10. Maj. Gen. William Alexander   15 January 1783   Gout
                                               Albany, N.Y.

Mexican War

Brig. Gen. Thomas L. Hamer   2 December 1846   Disease
                                         Monterrey, Mexico

Civil War, Union

1. Bvt. Brig. Gen. John Garland	5 June 1861 New York City	Natural causes
2. Bvt. Maj. Gen. George Gibson	29 September 1861 Washington, D.C.	Natural causes
3. Brig. Gen. Frederick W. Lander	5 March 1862 Camp Chase, Va.	Pneumonia
4. Maj. Gen. Charles F. Smith	25 April 1862 Savannah, Tenn.	Infection
5. Brig. Gen. William H. Keim	8 May 1862 Harrisburg, Pa.	Fever
6. Brig. Gen. Joseph B. Plummer	9 August 1862 Corinth, Miss.	Exposure
7. Maj. Gen. William Nelson	29 September 1862 Louisville, Ky.	Murdered
8. Maj. Gen. Ormsby M. Mitchell	30 October 1862 Beaufort, S.C.	Yellow fever
9. Brig. Gen. Charles D. Jameson	6 November 1862 Old Town, Me.	Fever
10. Brig. Gen. Francis E. Patterson	6 November 1862 Fairfax, Va.	Accidental self-inflicted gunshot wound
11. Bvt. Brig. Gen. Sylvester Churchill	7 December 1862 Washington, D.C.	Natural causes
12. Maj. Gen. Edwin V. Sumner	21 March 1863 Syracuse, N.Y.	Natural causes
13. Brig. Gen. James Cooper	28 March 1863 Columbus, Ohio	Fever
14. Rear Adm. Andrew H. Foote	26 June 1863 New York City	Bright's disease
15. Commo. Henry W. Morris	14 August 1863 New York City	Poor health

16.	Brig. Gen. Thomas Welsh	14 August 1863 Cincinnati, Ohio	Malaria
17.	Maj. Gen. John Buford	16 December 1863 Washington, D.C.	Exposure
18.	Brig. Gen. Michael Corcoran	22 December 1863 Fairfax, Va.	Horse fell on him
19.	Bvt. Maj. Gen. Joseph G. Totten	22 April 1864 Washington, D.C.	Natural causes
20.	Commo. William D. Porter	1 May 1864 New York City	Poor health
21.	Brig. Gen. Friend Rutherford	20 June 1864 Alton, Ill.	Exposure
22.	Brig. Gen. Joseph P. Taylor	29 June 1864 Washington, D.C.	Natural causes
23.	Brig. Gen. Daniel P. Woodbury	15 August 1864 Key West, Fla.	Yellow fever
24.	Brig. Gen. Joshua B. Howell	14 September 1864 Petersburg, Va.	Fall from horse
25.	Brig. Gen. Thomas J.C. Amory	7 October 1864 Beaufort, S.C.	Yellow fever
26.	Maj. Gen. David B. Birney	18 October 1864 Philadelphia, Pa.	Malaria
27.	Bvt. Maj. Gen. Thomas E.G. Ransom	29 November 1864 near Rome, Ga.	Typhoid
28.	Bvt. Brig. Gen. Charles Wheelcock	21 January 1865 Washington, D.C.	Disease
29.	Bvt. Brig. Gen. David P. Shunk	21 February 1865 place unknown	Disease

Civil War, Confederate

1.	Brig. Gen. John P. Grayson	21 October 1861 Tallahassee, Fla.	Lung disease
2.	Brig. Gen. Philip S. Cocke	26 December 1861 Powhatan County, Va.	Suicide
3.	Brig. Gen. Joseph L. Hogg	16 May 1862 Corinth, Miss.	Dysentery
4.	Maj. Gen. David E. Twiggs	15 July 1862 Augusta, Ga.	Lung infection

5. Brig. Gen. William D. Smith	4 October 1862 Charleston, S.C.	Yellow fever
6. Brig. Gen. Allison Nelson	7 October 1862 Austin, Ark.	Fever
7. Brig. Gen. John P. Villepigue	9 November 1862 Port Hudson, La.	Fever
8. Brig. Gen. Johnson K. Duncan	18 December 1862 Knoxville, Tenn.	Typhoid
9. Brig. Gen. David R. Jones	15 January 1863 Richmond, Va.	Heart attack
10. Brig. Gen. Daniel S. Donelson	17 April 1863 Montvale, Tenn.	Natural causes
11. Maj. Gen. Earl Van Dorn	17 May 1863 Spring Hill, Miss.	Murdered
12. Maj. Gen. John S. Bowen	13 July 1863 Raymond, Miss.	Dysentery
13. Brig. Gen. John B. Floyd	26 August 1863 Abingdon, Va.	Poor health
14. Brig. Gen. Lucius M. Walker	7 September 1863 Little Rock, Ark.	Killed in a duel
15. Brig. Gen. Claudius C. Wilson	27 November 1863 Ringgold, Ga.	Camp fever
16. Brig. Gen. William E. Baldwin	19 February 1864 Mobile, Ala.	Fall from horse
17. Brig. Gen. James J. Archer	24 October 1864 Richmond, Va.	Exhaustion
18. Brig. Gen. John H. Winder	7 February 1865 Florence, S.C.	Exhaustion
19. Maj. Gen. John A. Wharton	6 April 1865 Houston, Tex.	Murdered

Spanish-American War

| Brig. Gen. John S. Poland | 8 August 1898 Ashville, N.C. | Typhoid |

World War I

| 1. Brig. Gen. Robert E.L. Michie | 4 June 1918 Rouen, France | Sudden illness |

2. Brig. Gen. Charles A.   6 October 1918   Influenza
   Doyen, USMC   Quantico, Va.

3. Rear Adm. William A. Gill   10 October 1918   Exposure
                                Bridgeport, Conn.

World War II

1. Maj. Gen. Herbert A. Dargue   12 December 1941   Air crash
                                  California

2. Rear Adm. John W. Wilcox   27 March 1942   Lost at sea
                                  North Atlantic

3. Vice Adm. Arthur L. Bristol   20 April 1942   Heart attack
                                  North Atlantic

4. Brig. Gen. Harold H. George   21 April 1942   Hit by airplane
                                  Australia

5. Maj. Gen. Frank C. Mahin   24 July 1942   Air crash
                                  Tennessee

6. Brig. Gen. Albert K.B. Lyman   13 August 1942   Heart attack
                                  Hawaii

7. Brig. Gen. Asa N. Duncan   17 November 1942   Missing aircraft
                                  Bay of Biscay

8. Brig. Gen. Alfred J. Lyon   1 December 1942   Exposure
                                  Washington, D.C.

9. Maj. Gen. Alexander E.   24 December 1942   Heart attack
   Anderson   Texas

10. Brig. Gen. Carlyle H. Wash   26 January 1943   Air crash
                                  Mobile, Ala.

11. Brig. Gen. Clinton W. Russell 24 March 1943   Natural causes
                                  New York City

12. Maj. Gen. Robert Olds   28 April 1943   Pneumonia
                                  Tucson, Ariz.

13. Lt. Gen. Frank M. Andrews   3 May 1943   Air crash
                                  Iceland

14. Brig. Gen. Charles H. Barth   3 May 1943   Air crash
                                  Iceland

15. Maj. Gen. William P.   21 July 1943   Air crash
    Upshur, USMC   Alaska

16. Commo. James A. Logan	4 September 1943 Northern Ireland	Air crash
17. Brig. Gen. William D. Powell	6 October 1943 Kunming, China	Stroke
18. Maj. Gen. Charles D. Barrett, USMC	8 October 1943 Pacific area	Vehicle accident
19. Maj. Gen. Stonewall Jackson	13 October 1943 Camp Polk, La.	Air crash
20. Rear Adm. Frank T. Leighton	23 November 1943 Newport, R.I.	Illness
21. Brig. Gen. Arthur B. McDaniel	26 December 1943 Birmingham, Ala.	Illness
22. Rear Adm. Robert H. English	21 January 1944 California	Air crash
23. Brig. Gen. Donald A. Davison	6 May 1944 Bangalore, India	Natural causes
24. Brig. Gen. Theodore Roosevelt, Jr.	12 July 1944 Normandy, France	Heart attack
25. Maj. Gen. Paul W. Newgarden	14 July 1944 Chattanooga, Tenn.	Air crash
26. Rear Adm. Charles P. Cecil	31 July 1944 Pacific area	Air crash
27. Rear Adm. Don P. Moon	5 August 1944 England	Suicide
28. Brig. Gen. James F.C. Hyde	7 August 1944 Valley Forge, Pa.	Heart attack
29. Brig. Gen. Gordon D. Carrington	21 August 1944 Washington, D.C.	Natural causes
30. Brig. Gen. Thomas E. Roderick	21 September 1944 North Africa	Illness
31. Brig. Gen. Harry D. Chamberlain	29 September 1944 San Francisco	Illness
32. Brig. Gen. John H. Gardner	11 November 1944 Washington, D.C.	Heart attack
33. Rear Adm. Ernest G. Small	26 December 1944 New York City	Illness
34. Maj. Gen. Jose de los Reyes (Philippine Constabulary)	December 1944 Malolos, P.I.	Murdered

35. Brig. Gen. William H. Eaton	6 February 1945 France	Air crash
36. Maj. Gen. Edwin M. Watson	20 February 1945 at sea	Heart attack
37. Lt. Gen. Millard F. Harmon	26 February 1945 Pacific area	Missing aircraft
38. Brig. Gen. James A. Andersen	26 February 1945 Pacific area	Missing aircraft
39. Brig. Gen. Creswell Garlington	11 March 1945 Savannah, Ga.	Natural causes
40. Maj. Gen. W.H. Rupertus, USMC	25 March 1945 Washington, D.C.	Heart attack
41. Col. Henry W. Harms (former Brig. Gen.)	4 June 1945 Riverside, Cal.	Suicide
42. Rear Adm. Forrest B. Royal	18 June 1945 Philippines	Heart attack
43. Brig. Gen. Donald R. Goodrich	12 July 1945 Montgomery, Ala.	Heart attack
44. Gen. Malin Craig	25 July 1945 Washington, D.C.	Poor health

Korean War*

1. Lt. Gen. Walton H. Walker (posthumous Gen.)	23 December 1950 Seoul	Jeep accident
2. Maj. Gen. Bryant E. Moore	24 February 1951 Han River	Heart attack following helicopter crash
3. Brig. Gen. Laurence K. Ladue	24 May 1951 Korea	Heart attack
4. Brig. Gen. Aaron W. Tyer, USAF	28 May 1952 Komoki, Japan	Air crash

Vietnam War*

1. Brig. Gen. Alfred J.F. Moody	19 March 1967 Vietnam	Heart attack

*Deaths in the combat and support zones only

2. Maj. Gen. William J.   7 July 1967   Mid-air collision
   Crum, USAF   South China Sea

3. Maj. Gen. George W. Casey   1 July 1970   Helicopter crash
                                 Vietnam

4. Rear Adm. Rembrandt   8 May 1972   Helicopter crash
   Robinson   Tonkin Gulf

American General and Flag Officers Wounded in Action

Includes only officers serving in general or flag rank at time of wound. Does not include mortal wounds. Sequential numbers in second column indicate number of wounds for that officer. Rank in parentheses indicates wound in a higher grade.

NAME AND RANK   **DATE AND PLACE OF WOUND**

American Revolution

1. Maj. Gen. Benedict Arnold
   1. 27 April 1777, Danbury, Conn.
   2. 7 October 1777, Saratoga, N.Y.

2. Maj. Gen. Marquis de Lafayette
   11 September 1777, Brandywine, Pa.

3. Brig. Gen. Anthony Wayne
   1. 11 September 1777, Brandywine, Pa.
   2. 15 July 1779, Stony Point, N.Y.
   3. 2 September 1781, Virginia Peninsula

4. Brig. Gen. William Woodford
   11 September 1777, Brandywine, Pa.

5. Brig. Gen. James Clinton
   6 October 1777, Ft. Montgomery, N.Y.

6. Maj. Gen. Benjamin Lincoln
   7 October 1777, Saratoga, N.Y.

7. Brig. Gen. John Nixon
   7 October 1777, Saratoga, N.Y.

8. Brig. Gen. Isaac Huger
   1. 20 June 1779, Stono Ferry, S.C.
   2. 15 March 1781, Guilford Courthouse, N.C.

9. Brig. Gen. Thomas Sumter (South Carolina militia)
   20 November 1780, Blackstocks, S.C.

10. Brig. Gen. Andrew Pickens   8 September 1781, Eutaw Springs, S.C.
    (South Carolina militia)

War of 1812

1. Commo. John I. Rodgers   23 June 1812, aboard USS *President*
                                      off Nantucket Shoals
2. Maj. Gen. Jacob J. Brown   25 July 1814, Lundy's Lane, Canada
3. Brig. Gen. Winfield Scott   25 July 1814, Lundy's Lane, Canada
4. Brig. Gen. Edmund P. Gaines   1. 15 August 1814, Ft. Erie, Canada
5. Commo. Joshua Barney   24 August 1814, Bladensburg, Md.
6. Brig. Gen. Eleazer W. Ripley   17 September 1814, Ft. Erie, Canada

Indian Wars

1. Bvt. Maj. Gen. Edmund P. Gaines   2. 29 February 1836, Camp Izard, Fla.
2. Bvt. Maj. Gen. Thomas S. Jesup   24 January 1838, Lochahatchie, Fla.
3. Bvt. Maj. Gen. Ranald S.   19 October 1871, Brazos River, Tex.
   Mackenzie
4. Bvt. Maj. Gen. John Gibbon   3. 9 August 1877, Big Hole Basin,
                                      Mont.

Texas War for Independence

   Gen. Sam Houston   21 April 1836, San Jacinto, Tex.

Mexican War

1. Maj. Gen. William O. Butler   21 September 1846, Monterrey
2. Brig. Gen. Stephen W. Kearny   6 December 1846, San Pascual, Calif.
3. Brig. Gen. James Shields   1. 18 April 1847, Cerro Gordo
                                      2. 13 September 1847, Chapultepec
4. Maj. Gen. Gideon J. Pillow   1. 20 August 1847, Churubusco
                                      2. 13 September 1847, Chapultepec

Civil War, Union

1. Brig. Gen. Samuel P. Heintzelman   21 July 1861, Bull Run, Va.
2. Brig. Gen. David Hunter   21 July 1861, Bull Run, Va.
3. Brig. Gen. Thomas W. Sweeny   10 August 1861, Wilson's Creek, Mo.
   (Missouri volunteers)

4. Brig. Gen. Frederick W. Lander	22 October 1861, Edward's Ferry, Va.
5. Flag Officer Andrew H. Foote	14 February 1862, Ft. Donelson, Tenn.
6. Brig. Gen. Alexander S. Asboth	1. 7 March 1862, Pea Ridge, Ark. 2. 27 September 1864, Marianna, Fla.
7. Brig. Gen. James Shields	(3.) 23 March 1862, Kernstown, Va.
8. Brig. Gen. John McArthur	6 April 1862, Shiloh, Tenn.
9. Brig. Gen. William T. Sherman	6 April 1862, Shiloh, Tenn.
10. Brig. Gen. John J. Abercrombie	31 May 1862, Fair Oaks, Va.
11. Brig. Gen. Charles Devens	1. 31 May 1862, Fair Oaks, Va. 2. 3 May 1863, Chancellorsville, Va.
12. Brig. Gen. Oliver O. Howard (as Maj. Gen.)	1. 31 May 1862, Fair Oaks, Va. 2. 27 May 1864, Pickett's Mill, Ga.
13. Brig. Gen. Henry M. Naglee	31 May 1862, Fair Oaks, Va.
14. Brig. Gen. Henry W. Wessells	31 May 1862, Fair Oaks, Va.
15. Brig. Gen. Daniel Butterfield (as Maj. Gen.)	1. 27 June 1862, Gaines's Mill, Va. 2. 3 July 1863, Gettysburg, Pa.
16. Brig. Gen. William H.T. Brooks	1. 29 June 1862, Savage's Station, Va. 2. 17 September 1862, Antietam, Md.
17. Brig. Gen. William W. Burns	29 June 1862, Savage's Station, Va.
18. Brig. Gen. George G. Meade	30 June 1862, White Oak Swamp, Va.
19. Brig. Gen. John Sedgwick (as Maj. Gen.)	1. 30 June 1862, Glendale, Va. 2. 17 September 1862, Antietam, Md.
20. Brig. Gen. Edwin V. Sumner	wounded twice during the Seven Days battles in Virginia, June 1862
21. Brig. Gen. Christopher C. Augur	9 August 1862, Cedar Mountain, Va.
22. Brig. Gen. John W. Geary	9 August 1862, Cedar Mountain, Va.
23. Brig. Gen. John Buford	30 August 1862, Manassas, Va.
24. Brig. Gen. Abram Duryee	1. 30 August 1862, Manassas, Va. 2. 14 September 1862, South Mountain, Md. 3. 17 September 1862, Antietam, Md.
25. Brig. Gen. Washington L. Elliott	30 August 1862, Manassas, Va.
26. Brig. Gen. Alexander Hays	30 August 1862, Manassas, Va.
27. Brig. Gen. Robert C. Schenk	30 August 1862, Manassas, Va.
28. Brig. Gen. Zealous B. Tower	30 August 1862, Manassas, Va.

29. Brig. Gen. John P. Hatch
1. 30 August 1862, Manassas, Va.
2. 14 September 1862, South Mountain, Md.

30. Maj. Gen. William Nelson
30 August 1862, Richmond, Ky.

31. Brig. Gen. Mahlon D. Manson
1. 30 August 1862, Richmond, Ky.
2. 14 May 1864, Resaca, Ga.

32. Brig. Gen. John C. Caldwell
1. 17 September 1862, Antietam, Md.
2. 13 December 1862, Fredericksburg, Va.

33. Brig. Gen. Samuel W. Crawford
17 September 1862, Antietam, Md.

34. Brig. Gen. Napolean J.T. Dana
17 September 1862, Antietam, Md.

35. Brig. Gen. George L. Hartsuff
17 September 1862, Antietam, Md.

36. Maj. Gen. Joseph Hooker
17 September 1862, Antietam, Md.

37. Brig. Gen. James B. Ricketts (as Bvt. Maj. Gen.)
1. 17 September 1862, Antietam, Md.
2. 19 October 1864, Cedar Creek, Va.

38. Brig. Gen. Max Weber
17 September 1862, Antietam, Md.

39. Brig. Gen. Richard Oglesby
3 October 1862, Corinth, Miss.

40. Maj. Gen. Edward O.C. Ord
1. 5 October 1862, Hatchie, Miss.
2. 29 September 1864, Ft. Harrison, Va.

41. Brig. Gen. John Gibbon
1. 13 December 1862, Fredericksburg, Va.
2. 3 July 1863, Gettysburg, Pa.

42. Brig. Gen. Nathan Kimball
13 December 1862, Fredericksburg, Va.

43. Brig. Gen. Erastus B. Tyler
13 December 1862, Fredericksburg, Va.

44. Brig. Gen. Francis L. Vinton
13 December 1862, Fredericksburg, Va.

45. Brig. Gen. Morgan L. Smith
29 December 1862, Chickasaw Bluff, Miss.

46. Brig. Gen. Horatio P. Van Cleve
31 December 1862, Stone's River, Tenn.

47. Brig. Gen. Thomas J. Wood

(as Maj. Gen.)
1. 31 December 1862, Stone's River, Tenn.
2. 1 September 1864, Lovejoy, Ga.

48. Brig. Gen. Egbert B. Brown
8 January 1863, Springfield, Mo.

49. Brig. Gen. Charles E. Hovey
10 January 1863, Arkansas Post, Ark.

50.	Brig. Gen. William Hays	3 May 1863, Chancellorsville, Va.
51.	Brig. Gen. Gershom Mott	3 May 1863, Chancellorsville, Va.
52.	Brig. Gen. William P. Benton	14 May 1863, Jackson, Miss.
53.	Brig. Gen. Albert L. Lee	19 May 1863, Vicksburg, Miss.
54.	Brig. Gen. Peter J. Osterhous	19 May 1863, Vicksburg, Miss.
55.	Brig. Gen. Neal Dow	27 May 1863, Port Hudson, La.
56.	Brig. Gen. Thomas W. Sherman	27 May 1863, Port Hudson, La.
57.	Brig. Gen. Halbert E. Paine	27 May 1863, Port Hudson, La.
58.	Brig. Gen. Francis E. Barlow	1 July 1863, Gettysburg, Pa.
59.	Brig. Gen. Gabriel R. Paul	1 July 1863, Gettysburg, Pa.
60.	Brig. Gen. Alexander Schimmel-fennig	1 July 1863, Gettysburg, Pa.
61.	Maj. Gen. Daniel E. Sickles	2 July 1863, Gettysburg, Pa.
62.	Brig. Gen. James Barnes	2 July 1863, Gettysburg, Pa.
63.	Brig. Gen. David B. Birney	2 July 1863, Gettysburg, Pa.
64.	Brig. Gen. Charles K. Graham	2 July 1863, Gettysburg, Pa.
65.	Brig. Gen. Solomon Meredith	2 July 1863, Gettysburg, Pa.
66.	Brig. Gen. John H. Ward	1. 2 July 1863, Gettysburg, Pa. 2. 23 July 1863, Wapping Heights, Va. 3. 7 November 1863, Rappahannock Station, Va. 4. 12 May 1864, Spotsylvania, Va.
67.	Brig. Gen. Gouverneur K. Warren	2 July 1863, Gettysburg, Pa.
68.	Maj. Gen. Winfield S. Hancock	3 July 1863 Gettysburg, Pa.
69.	Brig. Gen. George Stannard	1. 3 July 1863, Gettysburg, Pa. 2. 20 June 1864, Cold Harbor, Va. 3. 31 July 1864, Petersburg, Va. 4. 29 September 1864, Ft. Harrison, Va.
70.	Brig. Gen. Alexander Webb	1. 3 July 1863, Gettysburg, Pa. 2. 12 May 1864, Spotsylvania, Va.
71.	Brig. Gen. Truman Seymour	18 July 1863, Ft. Wagner, S.C.
72.	Brig. Gen. Francis B. Spinola	23 July 1863, Wapping Heights, Va.
73.	Brig. Gen. George A. Custer	13 September 1863, Culpepper, Va.
74.	Brig. Gen. James S. Morton	19 September 1863, Chickamauga, Ga.
75.	Brig. Gen. John C. Starkweather	19 September 1863, Chickamauga, Ga.

76. Brig. Gen. George S. Greene	27 October 1863, Wauhatchie, Tenn.
77. Brig. Gen. David A. Russell	7 November 1863, Rappahannock Station, Va.
78. Brig. Gen. Walter C. Whitaker	24 November 1863, Lookout Mountain, Tenn.
79. Brig. Gen. John M. Corse	1. 25 November 1863, Chattanooga, Tenn.
	2. 5 October 1864, Allatoona, Ga.
80. Brig. Gen. Giles A. Smith	25 November 1863, Chattanooga, Tenn.
81. Brig. Gen. Charles L. Matthies	25 November 1863, Chattanooga, Tenn.
82. Maj. Gen. William B. Franklin	8 April 1864, Sabine Crossroads, La.
83. Brig. Gen. Thomas E.G. Ransom	8 April 1864, Sabine Crossroads, La.
84. Brig. Gen. Henry Baxter	5 May 1864, Wilderness, Va.
85. Brig. Gen. Joseph Hayes	5 May 1864, Wilderness, Va.
86. Brig. Gen. George W. Getty	6 May 1864, Wilderness, Va.
87. Brig. Gen. Charles A. Heckman	7 May 1864, Port Walthall, Va.
88. Brig. Gen. John C. Robinson	8 May 1864, Spotsylvania, Va.
89. Brig. Gen. Horatio G. Wright	9 May 1864, Spotsylvania, Va.
90. Brig. Gen. Judson Kilpatrick	9 May 1864, Dalton, Ga.
91. Brig. Gen. William H. Morris	9 May 1864, Spotsylvania, Va.
92. Brig. Gen. Charles G. Harker	13 May 1864, Resaca, Ga.
93. Brig. Gen. Joseph F. Knipe	13 May 1864, Resaca, Ga.
94. Brig. Gen. William T. Ward	15 May 1864, Resaca, Ga.
95. Brig. Gen. August Willich	15 May 1864, Resaca, Ga.
96. Maj. Gen. John A. Logan	27 May 1864, Dallas, Ga.
97. Brig. Gen. Richard W. Johnson	27 May 1864, New Hope Church, Ga.
98. Brig. Gen. John R. Brooke	3 June 1864, Cold Harbor, Va.
99. Brig. Gen. Julius Stahel	5 June 1864, Piedmont, Va.
100. Brig. Gen. Robert O. Tyler	7 June 1864, Cold Harbor, Va.
101. Brig. Gen. Edward H. Hobson	11 June 1864, Cynthiana, Ky.
102. Brig. Gen. Byron R. Pierce	18 June 1864, Petersburg, Va.
103. Brig. Gen. Romeyn B. Ayres	20 June 1864, Petersburg, Va.
104. Brig. Gen. Walter Q. Gresham	22 July 1864, Atlanta, Ga.
105. Brig. Gen. Manning F. Force	22 July 1864, Atlanta, Ga.

106. Brig. Gen. William F. Bartlett	30 July 1864, Petersburg, Va.
107. Brig. Gen. Nelson A. Miles	wounded once at Petersburg, Va.
108. Brig. Gen. Grenville M. Dodge	19 August 1864, Atlanta, Ga.
109. Brig. Gen. Lysander Cutler	21 August 1864, Globe Tavern, Va.
110. Brig. Gen. Joseph A.J. Lightburn	24 August 1864, Atlanta, Ga.
111. Maj. Gen. David S. Stanley	1. 1 September 1864, Jonesboro, Va. 2. 30 November 1864, Franklin, Tenn.
112. Brig. Gen. George H. Chapman	19 September 1864, Winchester, Va.
113. Brig. Gen. John B. McIntosh	19 September 1864, Winchester, Va.
114. Brig. Gen. Emory Upton	19 September 1864, Opequon, Va.
115. Brig. Gen. Cuvier Grover	19 October 1864, Cedar Creek, Va.
116. Maj. Gen. Edward R.S. Canby	4 November 1864, White River, Ark.
117. Brig. Gen. Thomas W. Egan	15 November 1864, Petersburg, Va.
118. Brig. Gen. Charles C. Walcutt	22 November 1864, Griswoldville, Ga.
119. Brig. Gen. Luther P. Bradley	30 November 1864, Franklin, Tenn.
120. Brig. Gen. Henry E. Davies	6 February 1865, Hatcher's Run, Va.
121. Brig. Gen. Lewis A. Grant	2 April 1865, Petersburg, Va.
122. Brig. Gen. Robert B. Potter	2 April 1865, Petersburg, Va.
123. Brig. Gen. Eli K. Long	2 April 1865, Selma, Ala.

Civil War, Confederate

1. Brig. Gen. Thomas J. Jackson	21 July 1861, Bull Run, Va.
2. Brig. Gen. Edmund Kirby Smith	21 July 1861, Bull Run, Va.
3. Maj. Gen. Sterling Price (Missouri State Guard) (as Maj. Gen. CSA)	1. 10 August 1861, Wilson's Creek, Mo. 2. 7 March 1862, Pea Ridge, Ark.
4. Brig. Gen. William Y. Slack (Missouri State Guard)	10 August 1861, Wilson's Creek, Mo.
5. Brig. Gen. Samuel J. Gholson (Mississippi state troops) (as Brig. Gen. CSA)	1. 14 February 1862, Ft. Donelson, Tenn. 2. 28 December 1864, Egypt, Miss.
6. Flag Officer Franklin Buchanan (as Admiral CSN)	1. 9 March 1862, aboard CSS *Virginia*, Hampton Roads, Va. 2. 5 August 1864, aboard CSS *Tennessee*, Mobile Bay, Ala.
7. Brig. Gen. John C. Bowen	6 April 1862, Shiloh, Tenn.

8. Maj. Gen. William J. Hardee   6 April 1862, Shiloh, Tenn.
9. Brig. Gen. Benjamin F. Cheatham   6 April 1862, Shiloh, Tenn.
10. Brig. Gen. Charles Clark   1. 6 April 1862, Shiloh, Tenn.
                                      2. 5 August 1862, Baton Rouge, La.

11. Brig. Gen. Bushrod R. Johnson   6 April 1862, Shiloh, Tenn.
12. Maj. Gen. Jubal A. Early   1. 5 May 1862, Williamsburg, Va.
                                      2. 27 June 1862, Cold Harbor, Va.

13. Brig. Gen. Edward Johnson   8 May 1862, McDowell, Va.
14. Gen. Joseph E. Johnston   31 May 1862, Seven Pines, Va.
15. Brig. Gen. Wade Hampton   1. 31 May 1862, Seven Pines, Va.
                                      2. 3 July 1863, Gettysburg, Pa.

16. Brig. Gen. James J. Pettigrew   1. 31 May 1862, Seven Pines, Va.
                                      2. 3 July 1863, Gettysburg, Va.

17. Brig. Gen. Robert E. Rodes   1. 31 May 1862, Seven Pines, Va.
                                      2. 17 September 1862, Antietam, Md.

18. Brig. Gen. Arnold Elzey   1. 9 June 1862, Port Republic, Va.
                                      2. 27 June 1862, Cold Harbor, Va.

19. Brig. Gen. George E. Steuart   9 June 1862, Cross Keys, Va.
20. Brig. Gen. George E. Pickett   27 June 1862, Gaines's Mill, Va.
21. Brig. Gen. Joseph R. Anderson   30 June 1862, Frayser's Farm, Va.
22. Brig. Gen. Winfield S. Featherston 30 June 1862, Frayser's Farm, Va.
23. Brig. Gen. George B. Anderson   1 July 1862, Malvern Hill, Va.
24. Brig. Gen. William D. Pender   1. 1 July 1862, Malvern Hill, Va.
                                      2. 13 December 1862, Fredericks-
                                         burg, Va.
                                      3. 3 May 1863, Chancellorsville, Va.

25. Brig. Gen. John R. Jones   1. 1 July 1862, Malvern Hill, Va.
                                      2. 30 August 1862, Manassas, Va.
                                      3. 17 September 1862, Antietam,
                                         Md.

26. Brig. Gen. Benjamin H. Helm   5 August 1862, Baton Rouge, La.
27. Maj. Gen. Richard S. Ewell   1. 29 August 1862, Groveton, Va.
                                      2. 7 November 1863, Kelly's Ford,
                                         Va.

28. Brig. Gen. Charles W. Field   29 August 1862, Groveton, Va.
29. Brig. Gen. William B. Taliaferro 29 August 1862, Groveton, Va.
30. Brig. Gen. Isaac R. Trimble   1. 29 August 1862, Groveton, Va.
    (as Maj. Gen.)   2. 3 July 1863, Gettysburg, Pa.

31. Brig. Gen. Micah Jenkins	30 August 1862, Manassas, Va.
32. Brig. Gen. William Mahone	30 August 1862, Manassas, Va.
33. Brig. Gen. Patrick R. Cleburne	30 August 1862, Richmond, Ky.
34. Maj. Gen. Richard H. Anderson	17 September 1862, Antietam, Md.
35. Brig. Gen. Maxcy Gregg	17 September 1862, Antietam, Md.
36. Brig. Gen. Alexander R. Lawton	17 September 1862, Antietam, Md.
37. Brig. Gen. Roswell S. Ripley	17 September 1862, Antietam, Md.
38. Brig. Gen. Robert A. Toombs	17 September 1862, Antietam, Md.
39. Brig. Gen. Ambrose R. Wright	17 September 1862, Antietam, Md.
40. Brig. Gen. John C. Brown	1. 8 October 1862, Perryville, Ky.
	2. 20 September 1863, Chickamauga, Ga.
(as Maj. Gen.)	3. 30 November 1864, Franklin, Tenn.
41. Brig. Gen. Sterling A.M. Wood	8 October 1862, Perryville, Ky.
42. Brig. Gen. Joseph Wheeler	1. 27 November 1862, LaVergne, Tenn.
(as Maj. Gen.)	2. 27 November 1863, Ringgold, Ga.
43. Brig. Gen. John R. Cooke	1. 13 December 1862, Fredericksburg, Va.
	2. 14 October 1863, Bristoe Station, Va.
	3. May 1864, Wilderness, Va.
44. Brig. Gen. Daniel W. Adams	1. 31 December 1862, Stone's River, Tenn.
	2. 20 September 1863, Chickamauga, Ga.
45. Brig. Gen. John R. Chalmers	31 December 1862, Stone's River, Tenn.
46. Brig. Gen. Francis R.T. Nicholls	2 May 1863, Chancellorsville, Va.
47. Maj. Gen. Ambrose P. Hill	3 May 1863, Chancellorsville, Va.
48. Brig. Gen. Robert F. Hoke	3 May 1863, Chancellorsville, Va.
49. Brig. Gen. Samuel McGowan	3 May 1863, Chancellorsville, Va.
50. Brig. Gen. Stephen D. Ramseur	1. 3 May 1863, Chancellorsville, Va.
	2. 12 May 1864, Spotsylvania, Va.
51. Brig. Gen. Harry Heth (as Maj. Gen.)	1. 4 May 1863, Chancellorsville, Va.
	2. 1 July 1863, Gettysburg, Pa.
52. Brig. Gen. William H.F. Lee	9 June 1863, Brandy Station, Va.
53. Brig. Gen. Martin E. Green	25 June 1863, Vicksburg, Miss.

54. Brig. Gen. Alfred M. Scales	1 July 1863, Gettysburg, Pa.
55. Maj. Gen. John B. Hood	1. 2 July 1863, Gettysburg, Pa.
	2. 20 September 1863, Chicka-mauga, Ga.
56. Brig. Gen. George T. Anderson	2 July 1863, Gettysburg, Pa.
57. Brig. Gen. John M. Jones	1. 2 July 1863, Gettysburg, Pa.
	2. 7 November 1863, Payne's Farm, Va.
58. Brig. Gen. Albert G. Jenkins	2 July 1863, Gettysburg, Pa.
59. Brig. Gen. Jerome B. Robertson	2 July 1863, Gettysburg, Pa.
60. Brig. Gen. James L. Kemper	3 July 1863, Gettysburg, Pa.
61. Brig. Gen. Laurence S. Baker	1. 1 August 1863, Rappahannock Station, Va.
	2. 22 September 1864, North Carolina
62. Maj. Gen. Thomas C. Hindman	1. 20 September 1863, Chicka-mauga, Ga.
	2. 27 June 1864, Kenesaw Mountain, Ga.
63. Brig. Gen. Henry D. Clayton	20 September 1863, Chickamauga, Ga.
64. Brig. Gen. John Gregg	20 September 1863, Chickamauga, Ga.
65. Brig. Gen. Evander McNair	20 September 1863, Chickamauga, Ga.
66. Brig. Gen. James B. Gordon	14 October 1863, Auburn, Va.
67. Brig. Gen. William W. Kirkland	1. 14 October 1863, Bristoe Station, Va.
	2. 2 June 1864, Cold Harbor, Va.
68. Brig. Gen. James A. Smith	1. 24 November 1863, Chattanooga, Tenn.
	2. 22 July 1864, Atlanta, Ga.
69. Brig. Gen. George E. Maney	25 November 1863, Chattanooga, Tenn.
70. Brig. Gen. Edward C. Walthall	25 November 1863, Chattanooga, Tenn.
71. Brig. Gen. Archibald Gracie	15 December 1863, Bean's Station, Tenn.
72. Brig. Gen. John Pegram	5 May 1864, Wilderness, Va.
73. Lt. Gen. James Longstreet	6 May 1864, Wilderness, Va.
74. Brig. Gen. Henry L. Benning	6 May 1864, Wilderness, Va.
75. Brig. Gen. Edward A. Perry	May 1864, Wilderness Va.

76.	Brig. Gen. William T. Wofford	1. May 1864, Wilderness, Va.
		2. May 1864, Spotsylvania, Va.
77.	Brig. Gen. Harry T. Hays	10 May 1864, Spotsylvania, Va.
78.	Brig. Gen. Henry H. Walker	10 May 1864, Spotsylvania, Va.
79.	Brig. Gen. Robert D. Johnston	12 May 1864, Spotsylvania, Va.
80.	Brig. Gen. James A. Walker	12 May 1864, Spotsylvania, Va.
81.	Brig. Gen. Jesse J. Finley	1. 14 May 1864, Resaca, Ga.
		2. 31 August 1864, Jonesboro, Ga.
82.	Brig. Gen. Arthur M. Manigault	1. 14 May 1864, Resaca, Ga.
		2. 30 November 1864, Franklin, Tenn.
83.	Brig. Gen. William F. Tucker	14 May 1864, Resaca, Ga.
84.	Brig. Gen. Matt W. Ransom	16 May 1864, Drewry's Bluff, Va.
85.	Brig. Gen. William S. Walker	20 May 1864, Petersburg, Va.
86.	Brig. Gen. Pierce M.B. Young	30 May 1864, Ashland, Va.
87.	Brig. Gen. Thomas L. Clingman	1. 1 June 1864, Cold Harbor, Va.
		2. 19 August 1864, Weldon Railroad, Va.
88.	Brig. Gen. James H. Lane	2 June 1864, Cold Harbor, Va.
89.	Brig. Gen. Evander M. Law	3 June 1864, Cold Harbor, Va.
90.	Brig. Gen. Francis M. Cockrell	1. 27 June 1864, Lost Mountain, Ga.
		2. 30 November 1864, Franklin, Tenn.
91.	Brig. Gen. Lucius E. Polk	27 June 1864, Kenesaw Mountain, Ga.
92.	Brig.Gen. Edward P. Alexander	30 June 1864, Petersburg, Va.
93.	Brig. Gen. Alfred J. Vaughan	9 July 1864, Vining's Station, Ga.
94.	Brig. Gen. Clement A. Evans	9 July 1864, Monocacy, Md.
95.	Brig. Gen. States R. Gist	22 July 1864, Atlanta, Ga.
96.	Brig. Gen. Robert D. Lilley	23 July 1864, Winchester, Va.
97.	Brig. Gen. Matthew D. Ector	27 July 1864, Atlanta, Ga.
98.	Lt. Gen. Alexander P. Stewart	28 July 1864, Ezra Church, Ga.
99.	Maj. Gen. William W. Loring	28 July 1864, Ezra Church, Ga.
100.	Brig. Gen. Alpheus Baker	28 July 1864, Ezra Church, Ga.
101.	Brig. Gen. George D. Johnston	28 July 1864, Ezra Church, Ga.
102.	Brig. Gen. David A. Weisiger	30 July 1864, Petersburg, Va.
103.	Maj. Gen. William B. Bate	10 August 1864, Atlanta, Ga.
104.	Brig. Gen. John D. Barry	about 15 August 1864, Petersburg, Va.

105. Brig. Gen. Adam R. Johnson   21 August 1864, Grubb's Crossroads, Ky.

106. Maj. Gen. J. Patton Anderson   31 August 1864, Jonesboro, Ga.

107. Brig. Gen. Alfred Cumming   31 August 1864, Jonesboro, Ga.

108. Brig. Gen. Benjamin G. Humphreys   4 September 1864, Berryville, Va.

109. Brig. Gen. John Vaughn   18 September 1864, Martinsburg, W. Va.

110. Maj. Gen. Fitzhugh Lee   19 September 1864, Winchester, Va.

111. Brig. Gen. William Terry
1. 19 September 1864, Winchester, Va.
2. 25 March 1865, Ft. Stedman, Va.

112. Brig. Gen. Zebulon York   19 September 1864, Winchester, Va.

113. Brig. Gen. William H. Young   5 October 1864, Allatoona, Ga.

114. Brig. Gen. James Conner   13 October 1864, Fisher's Hill, Va.

115. Brig. Gen. Cullen A. Battle   19 October 1864, Cedar Creek, Va.

116. Brig. Gen. Robert H. Anderson
1. 22 November 1864, Griswoldville, Ga.
2. 11 March 1865, Fayetteville, N.C.

117. Brig. Gen. William W. Allen
1. 28 November 1864, Waynesboro, Ga.
2. Carolinas campaign 1865

118. Brig. Gen. Felix H. Robertson   29 November 1864, Buckhead Creek, Ga.

119. Brig. Gen. George W. Gordon   30 November 1864, Franklin, Tenn.

120. Brig. Gen. William A. Quarles   30 November 1864, Franklin, Tenn.

121. Brig. Gen. Thomas M. Scott   30 November 1864, Franklin, Tenn.

122. Brig. Gen. Lucius J. Gartrell   9 December 1864, Coosawhatchie, S.C.

123. Lt. Gen. Stephen D. Lee   15 December 1864, Nashville, Tenn.

124. Brig. Gen. Claudius W. Sears   15 December 1864, Nashville, Tenn.

125. Brig. Gen. Thomas B. Smith*   15 December 1864, Nashville, Tenn.

126. Brig. Gen. Abraham Buford   28 December 1864, Lindville, Tenn.

127. Brig. Gen. Gilbert M. Sorrel
1. January 1865, Petersburg, Va.
2. 7 February 1865, Hatcher's Run, Va.

128. Brig. Gen. William Y.C. Humes
1. Carolinas campaign 1865
2. 10 March 1865, Monroe Crossroads, N.C.

129. Brig. Gen. Edmund W. Pettus	19 March 1865, Bentonville, N.C.
130. Brig. Gen. Daniel H. Reynolds	19 March 1865, Bentonville, N.C.
131. Brig. Gen. Philip Cook	25 March 1865, Ft. Stedman, Va.
132. Brig. Gen. James H. Clanton	25 March 1865, Ft. Stedman, Va.
133. Brig. Gen. William R. Terry	31 March 1865, Dinwiddie Courthouse, Va.
134. Brig. Gen. William H.F. Payne	1 April 1865, Five Forks, Va.
135. Brig. Gen. William G. Lewis	7 April 1865, Farmville, Va.

*General Smith was captured unharmed at Nashville but sustained life-threatening injuries from a beating at the hands of his captors before being carried off the field.

Spanish-American War

| Brig. Gen. Hamilton S. Hawkins | 2 July 1898, San Juan Hill, Cuba |

Philippine Insurrection

| Brig. Gen. Frederick Funston | 4 May 1899, San Tomas, Luzon |

World War I (all in France)

1. Maj. Gen. Leonard Wood	27 January 1918, Fère-en-Tardenois (training accident)
2. Brig. Gen. Evan M. Johnson	1. 10 September 1918, Petite Logette 2. 6 October 1918, Binarville
3. Maj. Gen. Peter E. Traub	wounded twice, Meuse-Argonne, September-November 1918
4. Brig. Gen. Douglas MacArthur	11 October 1918, Exermont
5. Brig. Gen. Henry F. Todd	30 October 1918, Bois de Bantheville
6. Maj. Gen. Robert Alexander	9 November 1918, Raucourt

World War II

1. Adm. Husband E. Kimmel	7 December 1941, Pearl Harbor, Hawaii
2. Brig. Gen. Clinton A. Pierce	January 1942, Bataan, Luzon, P.I.
3. Vice Adm. Frank J. Fletcher	31 August 1942, aboard USS *Saratoga* Solomon Islands
4. Brig. Gen. Hanford MacNider	23 November 1942, Buna, New Guinea

5. Brig. Gen. Albert W. Waldron — 5 December 1942, Buna, New Guinea

6. Brig. Gen. Clovis E. Byers — 16 December 1942, Buna, New Guinea

7. Brig. Gen. Robert L. Spragins — 18 January 1943, Guadalcanal

8. Maj. Gen. Orlando Ward — 24 March 1943, Maknassy, Tunisia

9. Brig. Gen. Edgar E. Glenn — 3 April 1943, Kunming, China

10. Lt. Gen. Lesley J. McNair — 23 April 1943, near Beja, Tunisia

11. Brig. Gen. Paul M. Robinett — 5 May 1943, Mateur, Tunisia

12. Brig. Gen. Thomas E. Lewis — 1. 9 September 1943, Salerno, Italy
2. 22 April 1945, Panaro River, Italy

13. Brig. Gen. Paul W. Kendall — 22 January 1944, Rapido River, Italy

14. Brig. Gen. Frederic B. Butler — 1 June 1944, near Rome, Italy

15. Brig. Gen. Robert T. Frederick (as Maj. Gen.) — 1. 4 June 1944, Rome, Italy
2. Wounded twice in the south of France, August-September 1944

16. Brig. Gen. Norman D. Cota — 18 July 1944, St. Lô, France

17. Brig. Gen. James A. Van Fleet — August (?) 1944, near Brest (?) France

18. Brig. Gen. William K. Harrison — 2 September 1944, near Mons, Belgium

19. Maj. Gen. Paul W. Baade — 1 October 1944, Fôret de Grémecy, France

20. Brig. Gen. Thomas K. Betts — 4 October 1944, France

21. Brig. Gen. William F. Heavy — October 1944 (?), Leyte, P.I.

22. Brig. Gen. Claudius M. Easley — 4 November 1944, Dagami, Leyte, P.I.

23. Maj. Gen. Maxwell D. Taylor — 9 November 1944, near Arnhem, Holland

24. Maj. Gen. William W. Eagles — 30 November 1944, Moder River, Germany

25. Brig. Gen. William C. Dunckel — 13 December 1944, aboard USS *Nashville*, Mindanao Straits, Philippines

26. Maj. Gen. Alan W. Jones — 26 December 1944, Liege, Belgium

27. Brig. Gen. John H. Church — 27 February 1945, near Wegberg, Germany

28. Maj. Gen. Verne D. Mudge — 28 February 1945, Antipolo, Luzon, P.I.

29. Maj. Gen. Matthew B. Ridgway — 25 March 1945, Diersfordterwald, Germany

30. Maj. Gen. John B. Wogan	15 April 1945, near Opladen, Germany
31. Brig. Gen. Edwin W. Piburn	17 April 1945, Schwaebisch-Hall, Germany
32. Brig. Gen. Robinson E. Duff	23 April 1945, near San Benedetto, Italy
33. Maj. Gen. Vernon E. Prichard	27April 1945, near Bergamo, Italy
34. Brig. Gen. Robert O. Shoe	10 May 1945, Negros Island, P.I.
35. Maj. Gen. Lemuel C. Shepherd, USMC	16 May 1945, Okinawa
36. Brig. Gen. William Spence	25 May 1945, Wawa Dam, Luzon, P.I.
37. Vice Adm. Jesse B. Olendorf	12 August 1945, aboard USS *Pennsylvania* off Okinawa

Korean War

Brig. Gen. Charles L. Dasher	16 August 1952, Chokko-ri, Korea

Vietnam War*

1. Brig. Gen. Joseph W. Stilwell, Jr.	30 December 1963, Mekong Delta
2. Lt. Gen. Lewis W. Walt, USMC	4 October 1966, near the Demilitarized Zone (DMZ)
3. Brig. Gen. John F. Freund	8 August 1967, near Saigon
4. Brig. Gen. Franklin M. Davis	5 August 1968, Nha Be
5. Brig. Gen. William A. Burke	23 April 1970, near the DMZ

*Incomplete list. News reports on the wounding of General Franklin Davis indicated, without naming the others, that he was the sixth American general wounded in Vietnam up to that date.

APPENDIX E

American General and Flag Officers Captured by Hostile Forces

Includes those serving in general or flag rank when captured or promoted while prisoners.

NAME AND RANK	DATE AND PLACE OF CAPTURE AND DISPOSITION
American Revolution	
1. Brig. Gen. William Thompson	8 June 1776, Canada Paroled August, 1776
2. Maj. Gen. John Sullivan	27 August 1776, Brooklyn, N.Y. Exchanged September 1776
3. Brig. Gen. William Alexander	27 August 1776, Brooklyn, N.Y. Exchanged September 1776
4. Brig. Gen. Nathaniel Woodhull	28 August 1776, Jamaica, N.Y. Died of wounds 20 September 1776
5. Maj. Gen. Charles Lee	13 December 1776, Basking Ridge, N.J. Exchanged April 1778
6. Maj. Gen. Benjamin Lincoln	12 May 1780, Charleston, S.C. Exchanged November 1780
7. Brig. Gen. Louis Duportail	12 May 1780, Charleston, S.C. Exchanged October 1780
8. Brig. Gen. Christopher Gadsden	12 May 1780, Charleston, S.C. Exchanged March 1781

9. Brig. Gen. James Hogun — 12 May 1780, Charleston, S.C.
Died in captivity 4 January 1781

10. Brig. Gen. Lachlan McIntosh — 12 May 1780, Charleston, S.C.
Exchanged February 1782

11. Brig. Gen. William Moultrie — 12 May 1780, Charleston, S.C.
Exchanged February 1782

12. Brig. Gen. Charles Scott — 12 May 1780, Charleston, S.C.
Paroled May 1780

13. Brig. Gen. William Woodford — 12 May 1780, Charleston, S.C.
Died in captivity 13 November 1780

14. Brig. Gen. Andrew Williamson (South Carolina militia) — May 1780, Ninety-six, S.C.
Paroled May 1780

15. Maj. Gen. Johann Kalb — 16 August 1780, Camden, S.C.
Died of wounds 19 August 1780

16. Brig. Gen. Peleg Wadsworth (Massachusetts militia) — 18 February 1781, Thomaston, Me.
Escaped June 1781

17. Brig. Gen. John Ashe (North Carolina militia) — 1781, North Carolina
Paroled 1781

War of 1812

1. Brig. Gen. William Hull — 16 August 1812, Detroit, Mich.
Exchanged 1812

2. Brig. Gen. William Wadsworth (New York militia) — 13 October 1812, Queenstown, Canada
Exchanged 1813

3. Brig. Gen. James Winchester — 22 January 1813, Frenchtown, Mich.
Exchanged 1814

4. Brig. Gen. John Chandler — 6 June 1813, Stoney Creek, Canada
Exchanged April 1814

5. Brig. Gen. William H. Winder — 6 June 1813, Stoney Creek, Canada
Exchanged 1814

6. Commo. Joshua Barney — 24 August 1814, Bladensburg, Md.
Paroled August 1814

Civil War, Union

1. Bvt. Maj. Gen. David E. Twiggs — 16 February 1861, San Antonio, Tex.
Paroled February 1861

2. Brig. Gen. Benjamin M. Prentiss — 6 April 1862, Shiloh, Tenn.
Exchanged October 1862

3. Brig. Gen. John F. Reynolds   28 June 1862, Glendale, Va. Exchanged August 1862

4. Brig. Gen. George A. McCall   30 June 1862, New Market Crossroads, Va. Exchanged August 1862

5. Brig. Gen. Thomas T. Crittenden   13 July 1862, Murfreesboro, Tenn. Exchanged October 1862

6. Brig. Gen. Richard W. Johnson   24 July 1862, Gallatin, Tenn. Exchanged September 1862

7. Brig. Gen. Henry Prince   9 August 1862, Cedar Mountain, Va. Exchanged September 1862

8. Brig. Gen. Mahlon D. Manson   30 August 1862, Richmond, Ky. Exchanged September 1862

9. Brig. Gen. Julius White   15 September 1862, Harper's Ferry, Va. Exchanged January 1863

10. Brig. Gen. William H. Lytle (promoted while a prisoner)   8 October 1862, Perryville, Ky. Exchanged February 1863

11. Brig. Gen. August Willich   31 December 1862, Stone's River, Tenn. Exchanged May 1863

12. Brig. Gen. Edwin H. Stoughton   9 March 1863, Fairfax Courthouse, Va. Exchanged May 1863

13. Brig. Gen. William Hays   3 May 1863, Chancellorsville, Va. Exchanged May 1863

14. Brig. Gen. Neal Dow   31 May 1863, near Port Hudson, La. Exchanged March 1864

15. Brig. Gen. Francis C. Barlow   1 July 1863, Gettysburg, Pa. Exchanged July 1863

16. Brig. Gen. Charles K. Graham   2 July 1863, Gettysburg, Pa. Exchanged September 1863

17. Brig. Gen. Eliakim P. Scammon   1. 11 February 1864, Kanawha River, W. Va. Exchanged August 1864
2. 24 October 1864, Charleston, S.C. Exchanged November 1864

18. Brig. Gen. Henry W. Wessells   20 April 1864, Plymouth, N.C. Exchanged August 1864

19. Brig. Gen. James S. Wadsworth   6 May 1864, Wilderness, Va. Died of wounds 8 May 1864

20. Brig. Gen. Truman Seymour   6 May 1864, Wilderness, Va. Exchanged August 1864

21. Brig. Gen. Alexander Shaler   6 May 1864, Wilderness, Va.
                                           Exchanged December 1864

22. Brig. Gen. Charles A. Heckman   16 May 1864, Drewery's Bluff, Va.
                                           Exchanged September 1864

23. Brig. Gen. Edward H. Hobson   11 June 1864, Cynthiana, Ky.
                                           Paroled June 1864

24. Maj. Gen. William B. Franklin   11 July 1864, near Frederick, Md.
                                           Escaped July 1864

25. Brig. Gen. William F. Bartlett   30 July 1864, Petersburg, Va.
                                           Exchanged August 1864

26. Maj. Gen. George Stoneman   31 July 1864, Macon, Ga.
                                           Exchanged October 1864

27. Brig. Gen. Joseph Hayes   19 August 1864, Petersburg, Va.
                                           Exchanged February 1865

28. Brig. Gen. Alfred A.N. Duffie   20 October 1864, Bunker Hill,
                                           Va. Exchanged April 1865

29. Maj. Gen. George Crook   21 February 1865, Cumberland,
                                           Md. Exchanged March 1865

30. Bvt. Maj. Gen. Benjamin F. Kelley   21 February 1865, Cumberland, Md.
                                           Exchanged March 1865

Civil War, Confederate (excludes end-of-war surrenders)

1. Brig. Gen. Daniel M. Frost   10 May 1861, St. Louis, Mo.
    (Missouri militia)   Exchanged November 1861

2. Brig. Gen. Lloyd Tilghman   6 February 1862, Ft. Henry, Tenn.
                                           Exchanged August 1862

3. Brig. Gen. Simon B. Buckner   16 February 1862, Ft. Donelson,
                                           Tenn. Exchanged August 1862

4. Brig. Gen. Samuel J. Gholson   16 February 1862, Ft. Donelson, Tenn.
    (Mississippi state troops)   Exchanged 1862

5. Brig. Gen. Bushrod R. Johnson   16 February 1862, Ft. Donelson, Tenn.
                                           Escaped same day

6. Brig. Gen. Edwin M. Price   February 1862, Arkansas
    (Missouri State Guard)   Exchanged October 1862

7. Brig. Gen. William W. Mackall   8 April 1862, Island No. 10, Tenn.
                                           Exchanged August 1862

8. Brig. Gen. Johnson K. Duncan   28 April 1862, Fts. Jackson & St.
                                           Philip, La. Exchanged August 1862

9. Brig. Gen. James J. Pettigrew   31 May 1862, Seven Pines, Va.
                                           Exchanged August 1862

10. Brig. Gen. Charles Clark   5 August 1862, Baton Rouge, La.
                                    Exchanged February 1863

11. Brig. Gen. Thomas J. Churchill 11 January 1863, Arkansas Post, Ark.
                                    Exchanged 1863

12. Brig. Gen. William H. F. Lee   26 June 1863, Hickory Hill, Va.
                                    Exchanged March 1864

13. Brig. Gen. James J. Archer   1 July 1863, Gettysburg, Pa.
                                    Exchanged August 1864

14. Brig. Gen. William Barksdale   2 July 1863, Gettysburg, Pa.
                                    Died of wounds 3 July 1863

15. Maj. Gen. Isaac R. Trimble   3 July 1863, Gettysburg, Pa.
                                    Exchanged February 1865

16. Brig. Gen. Lewis A. Armistead   3 July 1863, Gettysburg, Pa.
                                    Died of wounds 5 July 1863

17. Brig. Gen. James L. Kemper   3 July 1863, Gettysburg, Pa.
                                    Exchanged September 1863

18. Lt. Gen. John C. Pemberton   4 July 1863, Vicksburg, Miss.
                                    Declared exchanged July 1863*

19. Maj. Gen. John S. Bowen   4 July 1863, Vicksburg, Miss.
                                    Died on parole 13 July 1863

20. Maj. Gen. John H. Forney   4 July 1863, Vicksburg, Miss.
                                    Declared exchanged July 1863

21. Maj. Gen. Martin L. Smith   4 July 1863, Vicksburg, Miss.
                                    Declared exchanged July 1863

22. Maj. Gen. Carter L. Stevenson   4 July 1863, Vicksburg, Miss.
                                    Declared exchanged July 1863

23. Brig. Gen. William E. Baldwin   4 July 1863, Vicksburg, Miss.
                                    Declared exchanged July 1863

24. Brig. Gen. Seth Barton   1. 4 July 1863, Vicksburg, Miss.
                                       Declared exchanged July 1863
                                    2. 6 April 1865, Sayler's Creek, Va.
                                       Released July 1865

25. Brig Gen. Alfred Cumming   4 July 1863, Vicksburg, Miss.
                                    Declared exchanged July 1863

26. Brig. Gen. Louis Hebert   4 July 1863, Vicksburg, Miss.
                                    Declared exchanged July 1863

*On 13 July 1863, the Confederate agent for prisoner exchange unilaterally declared exchanged, over the protests of the Union commissioner for exchanges, all general officers, as well as colonels commanding brigades, captured at Vicksburg.

27. Brig. Gen. Stephen D. Lee	4 July 1863, Vicksburg, Miss. Declared exchanged July 1863
28. Brig. Gen. John C. Moore	4 July 1863, Vicksburg, Miss. Declared exchanged July 1863
29. Brig. Gen. Francis A. Shoup	4 July 1863, Vicksburg, Miss. Declared exchanged July 1863
30. Brig. Gen. John C. Vaughn	4 July 1863, Vicksburg, Miss. Declared exchanged July 1863
31. Brig. Gen. John V. Harris (Mississippi state troops)	4 July 1863, Vicksburg, Miss. Declared exchanged July 1863
32. Brig. Gen. John R. Jones	4 July 1863, Smithburg, Tenn. Released July 1865
33. Maj. Gen. Franklin Gardner	9 July 1863, Port Hudson, La. Exchanged August 1864
34. Brig. Gen. William N.R. Beall	9 July 1863, Port Hudson, La. Paroled December 1864; released August 1865**
35. Brig. Gen. John H. Morgan	26 July 1863, New Lisbon, Ohio Escaped November 1863
36. Brig. Gen. Daniel W. Adams	20 September 1863, Chickamauga, Ga. Exchanged 1863
37. Brig. Gen. Lunsford L. Lomax	23 September 1863, Woodstock, Va. Escaped same day
38. Brig. Gen. Harry T. Hays	7 November 1863, Rappahannock Station, Va. Escaped same day
39. Brig. Gen. John W. Frazer	9 November 1863, Cumberland Gap, Tenn. Released July 1865
40. Brig. Gen. Albert G. Jenkins	9 May 1864, Cloyd's Mountain, Va. Died of wounds 21 May 1864
41. Maj. Gen. Edward Johnson	1. 10 May 1864, Spotsylvania, Va. Exchanged September 1864 2. 15 December 1864, Nashville, Tenn. Released July 1865
42. Brig. Gen. George H. Steuart	12 May 1864, Spotsylvania, Va. Exchanged February 1865 (?)

**In December 1864 General Beall was released on parole to go to New York City to trade captured Southern cotton for commodities to aid Confederate prisoners. He was released with other CSA prisoners in the summer of 1865.

43. Brig. Gen. William S. Walker   20 May 1864, Petersburg, Va.
Exchanged October 1864

44. Brig. Gen. Robert D. Lilley   20 July 1864, Winchester, Va.
Recaptured July 1864

45. Adm. Franklin Buchanan   5 August 1864, Mobile Bay, Ala.
Exchanged February 1865

46. Brig. Gen. Richard L. Page   23 August 1864, Ft. Morgan, Ala.
Released July 1865

47. Brig. Gen. Daniel C. Govan   1 September 1864, Jonesboro, Ga.
Exchanged c. October 1864

48. Brig. Gen. William H. Young   5 October 1864, Allatoona, Ga.
Released July 1865

49. Maj. Gen. Stephen D. Ramseur   19 October 1864, Cedar Creek, Va.
Died of wounds 20 October 1864

50. Brig. Gen. John S. Marmaduke (promoted Maj. Gen. while imprisoned)   25 October 1864, Mine Creek, Mo.
Released July 1865

51. Brig. Gen. William L. Cabell   25 October 1864, Mine Creek, Mo.
Released July 1865

52. Brig. Gen. George W. Gordon   30 November 1864, Franklin, Tenn.
Released July 1865

53. Brig. Gen. William A Quarles   30 November 1864, Franklin, Tenn.
Released May 1865

54. Brig. Gen. Robert Bullock (promoted while imprisoned)   16 December 1864, Nashville, Tenn.
Released July 1865 (?)

55. Brig. Gen. Henry R. Jackson   16 December 1864, Nashville, Tenn.
Released July 1865

56. Brig. Gen. Thomas B. Smith   16 December 1864, Nashville, Tenn.
Released July 1865

57. Brig. Gen. Claudius W. Sears   21 December 1864, Pulaski, Tenn.
Released June 1865

58. Brig. Gen. Robert B. Vance   14 January 1865, Crosby Creek, N.C.
Exchanged March 1865

59. Maj. Gen. William H.C Whiting   15 January 1865, Ft. Fisher, N.C.
Died of wounds 10 March 1865

60. Brig. Gen. Philip Cook   2 April 1865, Petersburg, Va.
Released July 1865

61. Brig. Gen. Rufus Barringer   3 April 1865, Richmond, Va.
Released July 1865

62. Lt. Gen. Richard S. Ewell	6 April 1865, Sayler's Creek, Va. Released August 1865
63. Maj. Gen. Joseph B. Kershaw	6 April 1865, Sayler's Creek, Va. Released July 1865
64. Maj. Gen. George W.C. Lee	6 April 1865, Sayler's Creek, Va. Paroled April 1865
65. Brig. Gen. Theodore W. Brevard	6 April 1865, Sayler's Creek, Va. Released August 1865
66. Brig. Gen. Montgomery D. Corse	6 April 1865, Sayler's Creek, Va. Released August 1865
67. Brig. Gen. Dudley M. DuBose	6 April 1865, Sayler's Creek, Va. Released July 1865
68. Brig. Gen. Eppa Hunton	6 April 1865, Sayler's Creek, Va. Released July 1865
69. Brig. Gen. James P. Simms	6 April 1865, Sayler's Creek, Va. Released July 1865
70. Commo. John R. Tucker	6 April 1865, Sayler's Creek, Va. Released July 1865
71. Brig. Gen. William G. Lewis	7 April 1865, Farmville, Va. Paroled April 1865
72. Brig. Gen. Francis M. Cockrell	9 April 1865, Mobile, Ala. Released May 1865
73. Brig. Gen. St. John R. Liddell	9 April 1865, Ft. Blakely, Ala. Released May 1865
74. Brig. Gen. Bryan M. Thomas	9 April 1865, Ft. Blakely, Ala. Released May 1865

World War II

1. Brig. Gen. Mateo Capinpin (Philippine Army)	5 April 1942, Bataan, P.I. Paroled May 1942 (?)
2. Maj. Gen. Edward P. King, Jr.	9 April 1942, Bataan, P.I. Released August 1945
3. Maj. Gen. Albert M. Jones	9 April 1942, Bataan, P.I. Released August 1945
4. Maj. Gen. George M. Parker	9 April 1942, Bataan, P.I. Released August 1945
5. Maj. Gen. Guillermo Francisco (Philippine Constabulary)	9 April 1942, Bataan, P.I. Paroled May 1942 (?)

6. Brig. Gen. Clifford Bluemel   9 April 1942, Bataan, P.I.
                                      Released August 1945

7. Brig. Gen. William E. Brougher   9 April 1942, Bataan, P.I.
                                      Released August 1945

8. Brig. Gen. Vicente Lim   9 April 1942, Bataan, P.I.
   (Philippine Army)   Executed 6 January 1945

9. Brig. Gen. Simeon DeJesus   9 April 1942, Bataan, P.I.
   (Philippine Constabulary)   Paroled May 1942 (?)

10. Brig. Gen. Maxon S. Lough   9 April 1942, Bataan, P.I.
                                      Released August 1945

11. Brig. Gen. Allan C. McBride   9 April 1942, Bataan, P.I.
                                      Died in captivity 9 May 1944

12. Brig. Gen. Clinton A. Pierce   9 April 1942, Bataan, P.I.
                                      Released August 1945

13. Brig. Gen. Carl H. Seals   9 April 1942, Bataan, P.I.
                                      Released August 1945

14. Brig. Gen. Fidel Segundo   9 April 1942, Bataan, P.I.
    (Philippine Army)   Executed 6 January 1945

15. Brig. Gen. Luther R. Stevens   9 April 1942, Bataan, P.I.
                                      Released August 1945

16. Brig. Gen. James R.N. Weaver   9 April 1942, Bataan, P.I.
                                      Released August 1945

17. Lt. Gen. Jonathan M. Wainwright   6 May 1942, Corregidor, P.I.
                                      Released August 1945

18. Maj. Gen. George F. Moore   6 May 1942, Corregidor, P.I.
                                      Released August 1945

19. Brig. Gen. Lewis C. Beebe   6 May 1942, Corregidor, P.I.
                                      Released August 1945

20. Brig. Gen. Charles C. Drake   6 May 1942, Corregidor, P.I.
                                      Released August 1945

21. Brig. Gen. Arnold J. Funk   6 May 1942, Corregidor, P.I.
                                      Released August 1945

22. Maj. Gen. William F. Sharp   10 May 1942, Visayas, P.I.
                                      Released August 1945

23. Brig. Gen. Joseph P. Vachon   10 May 1942, Mindanao, P.I.
                                      Released August 1945

24. Brig. Gen. Bradford G.   16 May 1942, Visayas, P.I.
    Chynoweth   Released August 1945

25. Brig. Gen. Guy O. Fort   27 May 1942, Mindanao, P.I.
    (Philippine Army)   Executed 9 or 13 November 1942
26. Brig. Gen. Arthur W. Vanaman   27 June 1944, St. Martin L'Hortier,
                                    France. Liberated April 1945

Korean War

1. Maj. Gen. William F. Dean   25 August 1950, near Taegu
                                    Released July 1953

2. Brig. Gen. Francis T. Dodd   7 May 1952, Koje-do (by North
                                    Korean POWs)
                                    Released 4 days later

Vietnam War

1. Brig. Gen. John P. Flynn USAF   27 October 1967, North Vietnam
   (selected for promotion while a Released March 1973
   prisoner)
2. Brig. Gen. Edward B. Burdett   18 November 1967, North Vietnam
   USAF (promoted posthumously)   Died of wounds 18 November 1967
3. Brig. Gen. David W. Winn USAF   9 August 1968, North Vietnam
   (selected for promotion while a Released March 1973
   prisoner)

War Against Terrorism

   Brig. Gen. James L. Dozier   17 December 1981, Verona, Italy
   (kidnapped by terrorists)   Freed by police January 1982

APPENDIX F

Facts and Superlatives About Those Who Fell in Battle

Highest Ranking	General Albert Sidney Johnston, CSA
Highest Ranking in U.S. Army	Lt. Gen. Lesley J. McNair Lt. Gen. Simon B. Buckner, Jr. (both posthumous Generals)
First	Maj. Gen. Joseph Warren (Massachusetts Army)
First U.S. Army	Brig. Gen. Zebulon M. Pike (1813)
First While Commanding Troops	Maj. Gen. Richard Montgomery (Continental Army)
First U.S. Navy	Rear Adm. Isaac C. Kidd (1941)
First U.S. Air Force	Maj. Gen. Robert Worley (1968)
Only U.S. Marine Corps	Maj. Gen. Bruno A. Hochmuth (1967)
First Aerial	Maj. Gen. Clarence L. Tinker (1942)
Most Recent	Brig. Gen. Richard J. Tallman, USA (1972)
Oldest	Maj. Gen. David Wooster (66)
Youngest	Bvt. Brig. Gen. William N. Green (21)
Longest Service as General	Bvt. Maj. Gen. Edward R.S. Canby (11 years)
Shortest Service as General (excluding posthumous or deathbed promotions)	Brig. Gen. Elon J. Farnsworth (5 days)

First Outside the United States	Maj. Gen. Richard Montgomery (1775)
First U.S. Army Outside the United States	Brig. Gen. Zebulon M. Pike
Only Officer to Hold General Rank in Three Armies	Albert Sidney Johnston (Republic of Texas, U.S. Army, C.S. Army)
Only Officer to Hold General Rank in Two Armies	Johann Kalb (French Army, Continental Army)
Only Clergyman	Lt. Gen. Leonidas Polk, CSA
Family Members	Brig. Gens. Robert and Daniel McCook (USV), brothers Bvt. Maj. Gen. (USA) James B. and Brig. Gen. (CSA) William R. Terrill, brothers Lt. Gen. A. P. Hill and Brig. Gen. John Hunt Morgan (CSA), brothers-in-law Brig. Gens. Barnard E. Bee and Clement H. Stevens (CSA) brothers-in-law Brig. Gens. (CSA) Richard B. and Robert S. Garnett, cousins
Medal of Honor Recipients	Maj. Gen. Henry W. Lawton (as Captain, 1864) Rear Adm. Isaac C. Kidd (1941) Rear Adm. Daniel J. Callaghan (1942) Rear Adm. Norman Scott (1942) Brig. Gen. Kenneth N. Walker (1943) Brig. Gen. Frederick W. Castle (1944) Maj. Gen. Keith L. Ware (as Lieutenant Colonel, 1944)
Foreign Born	Maj. Gen. Richard Montgomery, Ireland Brig. Gen. Hugh Mercer, Scotland Brig. Gen. Casimir Pulaski, Poland Maj. Gen. Johann Kalb, Germany Brig. Gen. James Hogun, Ireland Maj. Gen. Richard Butler, Ireland Maj. Gen. Edward D. Baker, England Brig. Gen. Henry Bohlen, Germany Bvt. Brig. Gen. George A. Cobham, England

(Foreign Born, cont.)	Bvt. Maj. Gen. Thomas A. Smyth, Ireland Maj. Gen. Patrick R. Cleburne, Ireland Brig. Gen. Victor J. B. Girardey, France Brig. Gen. Frederick W. Castle, Philippines Brig. Gen. Vicente Lim, Philippines Brig. Gen. Fidel Segundo, Philippines
Non-Caucasian	Brig. Gen. Vicente Lim, Chinese-Filipino Brig. Gen. Fidel Segundo, Filipino
Never Actually Commissioned	Maj. Gen. Joseph Warren Maj. Gen. Edward D. Baker, USV Brig. Gen. Horace Randal, CSA
Single Unit with Highest Number of Fatalities	20th Massachusetts Volunteers lost three successive commanders all of whom became brevet brigadier generals: Paul J. Revere, Henry L. Abbott, Henry L. Patten

APPENDIX G

General Officer Fatalities in
Selected Battles and Campaigns

	Union	Confederate	Total
Gettysburg (July 1863)	9	6	15
Petersburg–Richmond (June 1864–March 1865)	8	7	15
Wilderness–Spotsylvania (May 1864)	6	7	13
Shenandoah Valley (July–October 1864)	9	3	12
Atlanta (May–August 1864)	6	4	10
Antietam (September 1862)	4	4	8
Vietnam (1965–1973)			8
Franklin–Nashville (November–December 1864)	1	6	7
Retreat to Appomattox (April 1865)	5	2	7
Northwest Europe (1944–1945)			7
Second Manassas (August–September 1862)	5	1	6
Chancellorsville (May 1863)	3	2	5
Vicksburg–Port Hudson (May–July 1863)	1	4	5
Central Pacific (1941–1945)			5
Fredericksburg (December 1862)	2	2	4

Stone's River (December 1862– January 1863)	2	2	4
Chickamauga (September 1863)	1	3	4
Red River (March–April 1864)	2	2	4
South Pacific (1942–1943)			4
Sicily–Italy (1943–1945)			4
Pea Ridge (March 1862)		3	3
Shiloh (April 1862)	1	2	3
Virginia Peninsula (March–June 1862)	1	2	3
Jenkins's Ferry (April 1864)	1	2	3
Strategic Air Offensive, Germany (1942–1945)			
Philippines (1944–1945)			3

Bibliography

Abbott, Steve. "Uncommon Soldier, Keith L. Ware," *Soldiers*, Vol. 34, No. 5 (May 1979).

Adjutant General of Illinois. *The Adjutant General Report, 1916–17.* Springfield: 1917.

Adler, Julius O. *History of the 77th Division, August 25, 1917–November 11, 1918.* New York: Wynkoop, Hallenbeck, Crawford Company, 1919.

Appleton's Cyclopedia of American Biography. 6 volumes. New York: D. Appleton, 1888.

Army Register: 1900, 1916, 1918–1920, 1942–1946, 1951–1954, 1966–1973.

Babcock, Willoughby M., Jr. *Selections from the Letters and Diaries of Brevet Brigadier General Willoughby Babcock of the 75th New York Volunteers.* Albany: The University of the State of New York, 1922.

Bauer, K. Jack. *The Mexican War, 1846–1848.* New York: The Macmillan Company, 1974.

BDAC-Congress of the United States. *Biographical Directory of the American Congress, 1774–1968.* Washington, D.C.: Government Printing Office, 1969.

Beck, Alfred M., Abe Bortz, Charles W. Lynch, Lida Mayo, and Ralph F. Weld. *The Corps of Engineers: The War Against Germany (U.S. Army in World War II, The Technical Services).* Washington D.C.: Center for Military History, 1985.

Beirne, Francis F. *The War of 1812.* New York: E.P. Dutton, 1949.

Belote, James H., and William M. Belote. *Typhoon of Steel, the Battle for Okinawa.* New York: Harper & Row, 1970.

Berton, Pierre. *Flames Across the Border: The Canadian-American Tragedy, 1813–1814.* Boston, Mass.: Little Brown, 1981.

Bevier, R.S. *History of the 1st and 2nd Missouri Confederate Brigades, 1861–1865.* St. Louis: Bryant, Brand and Company, 1879.

B&L-Johnson, Robert U., and Clarence C. Buel, eds. *Battles and Leaders of the Civil War.* New edition, 4 volumes. New York: Thomas P. Yoseloff, 1956.

Blair, Clay. *Ridgeway's Paratroopers, The American Airborne in World War II*. Garden City, N.Y.: Doubleday, 1985.

Blumenson, Martin. *Breakout and Pursuit (U.S. Army in World War II, The European Theater of Operations)*. Washington, D.C.: Office of the Chief of Military History, 1961.

Boatner, Mark M. *The Civil War Dictionary*. New York: David McKay Company, 1959.
————. *Encyclopedia of the American Revolution*. New York: David McKay Company, 1966.

Boone County—The Past and Present of Boone County, Illinois. Chicago: H.F. Kett & Company, 1877.

Bowen, James L. *Massachusetts in the War, 1861–1865*. Springfield, Mass.: Clark W. Bryant & Company, 1889.

Boyd, Thomas. *Mad Anthony Wayne*. New York: Charles Scribner's Sons, 1929.

Boyle, John R. *Soldiers True, The Story of the 111th Pennsylvania*. New York: Eaton & Mains, 1903.

Bradley, Omar N. *A Soldier's Story*. New York: Henry Holt, 1951.

Brown, Fred R. *History of the 9th U.S. Infantry, 1799–1909*. Chicago: R.R. Donnelly Sons, 1909.

Brown, Russell K. "Fallen Stars," *Military Affairs*, Vol. 45, No. 1 (February 1981).
————. "An Old Woman With a Broomstick, General David E. Twiggs and the U.S. Surrender in Texas, 1861," *Military Affairs*, Vol. 48, No. 1 (February 1984).

Calderon, Alfonso A., and Marciano C. Sicot. *Golden Book of the Philippine Constabulary*. Manila: 1951.

Campbell, Archibald. *Journal of an Expedition Against the Rebels of Georgia in North America*. Colin Campbell, ed. Darien, Ga.: The Ashantilly Press, 1981.

Carter, Kit C., and Robert Mueller, comps. *The Army Air Forces in World War II, Combat Chronology*. Washington, D.C.: Office of Air Force History, 1973.

Catton, Bruce. *Glory Road*. Garden City, N.Y.: Doubleday, 1952.
————. *Grant Moves South*. Boston: Little, Brown, 1960.
————. *Mister Lincoln's Army*. Garden City, N.Y.: Doubleday, 1951.
————. *A Stillness at Appomattox*. Garden City, N.Y.: Doubleday, 1953.

Chynoweth, Bradford G. *Out of Slavery*. Draft history in the Military History Research Collection, Carlisle, Pa.

Clark, Walter. "Career of General James Hogun: One of North Carolina's Revolutionary Officers," *Magazine of American History*, Vol. 28 (1892).

CMH, DSC, DSM-U.S. War Department. *Congressional Medals of Honor, Distinguished Service Crosses and Distinguished Service Medals issued by the War Department since 6 April 1917 up to . . . 11 November 1919*. Washington, D.C.: The Adjutant General's Office, 1920.

CMH-Evans, Clement A., ed. *Confederate Military History*. 12 volumes. Atlanta: Confederate Publishing Company, 1899.

Coddington, Edwin B. *The Gettysburg Campaign*. New York: Charles Scribner's Sons, 1968.

Coffman, Edward M. *The War to End All Wars*. New York: Oxford University Press, 1968.

Cole, H. M. *The Lorraine Campaign (U.S. Army in World War II, The European Theater of Operations)*. Washington, D.C.: Historical Division, Department of the Army, 1950.

Congressional Record-U.S. Congress. *The Congressional Record.* 1943 (78th Congress, 1st Session), 1970 (91st Congress, 2nd Session), 1974 (93rd Congress, 2nd Session).

Connecticut Men-Connecticut General Assembly. *Record of Service of Connecticut Men in the Army and Navy of the United States During the War of the Rebellion.* Hartford: 1889.

Connelly, Thomas L. *Army of the Heartland, The Army of Tennessee, 1861–1862.* Baton Rouge: Louisiana State University Press, 1967.

————. *Autumn of Glory, The Army of Tennessee, 1862–1865.* Baton Rouge: Louisiana State University Press, 1971.

Craven, Wesley F., and James L. Cate, eds. *The Army Air Forces in World War II.* 7 volumes. Chicago: University of Chicago Press, 1948–1958.

Croffut, W. A., and John M. Morris. *The Military and Civil History of Connecticut During the War of 1861–1865.* New York: Ledyard Bell, 1868.

Crookenden, Napier. *Drop Zone Normandy.* New York: Charles Scribner's Sons, 1976.

Cullum, George W. *Biographical Register of the Officers and Graduates of the United States Military Academy.* 2 volumes. Boston: Houghton Mifflin, 1891, with decennial supplements through 1950.

Current Biography, 1942. Maxine Block, ed. New York: H.W. Wilson Company, 1943.

DAB-Dictionary of American Biography. 10 volumes. New York: Charles Scribner's Sons, 1943.

Darke County-Biographical History of Darke County, Ohio. Chicago: The Lewis Publishing Company, 1900.

Davidson, Chalmers G. *Piedmont Partisan: The Life and Times of Brigadier General William Lee Davidson.* Davidson, N.C.: 1968.

Davidson, Orlando R., J. Carl Willems, and Joseph A. Kahl. *The Deadeyes, History of the 96th Infantry Division.* Washington, D.C.: Infantry Journal Press, 1947.

Devlin, Gerard M. *Paratrooper.* New York: St. Martin's Press, 1979.

DeWeerd, Harvey A. *President Wilson Fights His War.* New York: The Macmillan Company, 1968.

DNB-Dictionary of National Biography. 22 volumes. London: Oxford University Press, 1950.

Dyer, Frederick, H. *A Compendium of the War of the Rebellion.* 3 volumes. Reprint, New York: Thomas P. Yoseloff, 1959.

Dyer, John P. *"Fighting Joe" Wheeler.* Baton Rouge: Louisiana State University Press, 1941.

Elbert County-Records of Elbert County, Georgia, Volume III, Historical Collections of the Georgia Chapters, Daughters of the American Revolution. Atlanta: Stein Printing Company, 1930.

Fleming, Thomas J. *Now We Are Enemies.* New York: The Macmillan Company, 1960.

Ford, Andrew E. *The 15th Massachusetts Infantry in the War of the Rebellion.* Clinton, Mass: W.J. Coulter Press, 1898.

Forward, 80th! Orientation Section, Information and Education Division, European Theater of Operations. No publisher, no date.

Francine, Albert P. *Louis Raymond Francine.* Privately printed.

Freeman, Douglas Southall. *Lee's Lieutenants, A Study in Command.* 3 volumes. New York: Charles Scribner's Sons, 1943.

_____. *George Washington*. 7 volumes. New York: Charles Scribner's Sons, 1948–1957.

Freeman, Roger A. *The Mighty Eighth, A History of the U.S. Eighth Army Air Force*. Garden City, N.Y.: Doubleday, 1970.

_____. *Mighty Eighth War Diary*. New York: Jane's Publishing, 1981.

Fry, James B. *The History and Legal Effects of Brevets in the Armies of Great Britain and the United States*. New York: D. Van Nostrand, 1877.

Funston, Frederick. *Memories of Two Wars*. New York: Charles Scribner's Sons, 1911.

Gabriel, Richard A., and Paul L. Savage. *Crisis in Command*. New York: Hill & Wang, 1978.

Gallagher, Gary W. *Stephen Dodson Ramseur, Lee's Gallant General*. Chapel Hill: University of North Carolina Press, 1985.

Garfield, Bryan. *The Thousand Mile War, World War II in Alaska and the Aleutians*. Garden City, N.Y.: Doubleday, 1969.

Garland, Albert N., and Howard M. Smith. *Sicily and the Surrender of Italy (U.S. Army in World War II, The Mediterranean Theater of Operations)*. Washington, D.C.: Office of the Chief of Military History, 1965.

Godfrey, Edward S. "Custer's Last Battle." *Century Magazine*, Vol. 43 (1882).

Gordon, William W. "Count Casimir Pulaski," *Georgia Historical Quarterly*, Vol. 13 (1929).

Gould, Joseph. *The Story of the 48th*. Philadelphia: Alfred M. Slocum, 1908.

Graham, William A. *The Story of the Little Big Horn*. Harrisburg, Pa.: The Military Service Publishing Company, 1941.

Griesbach, Mark F., ed. *Combat History of the 8th Infantry Division in World War II*. Baton Rouge, La.: Army-Navy Publishing Company, 1946.

Guthman, William H. *March to Massacre, A History of the First Seven Years of the United States Army*. New York: McGraw-Hill, 1970.

Handbook of Augusta. Augusta, Ga.: Chronicle Job Printing Establishment, 1878.

Harmon, Ernest N. *Combat Commander*. Englewood Cliffs, N.J.: Prentice-Hall, 1970.

Harper's Encyclopedia of United States History. 10 volumes. New York: Harper & Brothers, 1907.

Heinl, Robert D. *Soldiers of the Sea, The U.S. Marine Corps, 1775–1962*. Annapolis, Md.: U.S. Naval Institute, 1962.

_____. "They Died with Their Boots On," *Armed Forces Journal*, April 11, 1970.

Heitman, Francis B. *Historical Register and Dictionary of the Continental Army*. Washington, D.C.: National Tribune, 1914.

_____. *Historical Register and Dictionary of the United States Army*. 2 volumes. Washington, D.C.: Government Printing Office, 1903. Reprint, Urbana: University of Illinois Press, 1965.

Henderson, G.F.R. *Stonewall Jackson and the American Civil War*. New York: Longmans, Green, 1936.

Intelligence Activities-U.S. Armed Forces Pacific, General Headquarters. *Intelligence Activities in the Philippines During the Japanese Occupation*. Tokyo: 1948.

Iowa Soldiers-Iowa General Assembly. *Roster and Record of Iowa Soldiers in the War of the Rebellion*. 6 volumes. DesMoines: E.H. English, State Printer, 1908–1911.

Irving, Theodore. *More than Conqueror or Memorials of Colonel J. Howard Kitching*. New York: Hurd and Houghton, 1873.

James, D. Clayton, ed. *South to Bataan, North to Mukden, The Prison Diary of Brigadier General William E. Brougher*. Athens: The University of Georgia Press, 1971.

Johnson, Stedman and Allied Families. New York: The American Historical Company, 1962.

Johnston, Richard W. *Follow Me! The Story of the Second Marine Division in World War II*. New York: Random House, 1948.

Kahn, Ely J. *McNair, Educator of an Army*. Washington, D.C.: Infantry Journal Press, 1945.

Kohn, Richard H. *Eagle and Sword*. New York: The Free Press, 1975.

Kuder, Edward M. "The Philippines Never Surrendered." *The Saturday Evening Post*, February 10, 1945.

Kurtz, Wilbur. "Civil War Days in Georgia, Major General W.H.T Walker," *The Atlanta Constitution*, July 27, 1930.

Lumpkin, Henry. *From Savannah to Yorktown, The American Revolution in the South*. Charleston: University of South Carolina Press, 1981.

MacArthur, Douglas. *Reminiscences*. New York: McGraw-Hill, 1964.

Mahon, John K. *History of the Militia and the National Guard*. New York: The Macmillan Company, 1983.

————. *History of the Second Seminole War*. Gainesville: The University of Florida Press, 1967.

Martin, Edward, ed. *The 28th Division in the World War*. 5 volumes. Pittsburgh, Pa: The 28th Division Publishing Company, 1924.

Maryland in the World War, 1917–1919. 2 volumes. Baltimore: Maryland War Records Commission, 1933.

McDonald, Charles B. *The Last Offensive (U.S. Army in World War II, The European Theater of Operations)*. Washington, D.C.: Office of the Chief of Military History, 1973.

McDonough, James L., and Thomas L. Connelly. *Five Tragic Hours: The Battle of Franklin*. Knoxville: The University of Tennessee Press, 1984.

McWhiney, Grady, and Perry D. Jamieson. *Attack and Die, Civil War Military Tactics and the Southern Heritage*. University: The University of Alabama Press, 1982.

Miles, Nelson. *Serving the Republic*. New York: Charles Scribner's Sons, 1911.

Miller, Francis T., ed. *The Photographic History of the Civil War*. 10 volumes. New York: The Review of Reviews Company, 1911.

MOH-U.S. Senate. *Medal of Honor, 1863–1978*. Prepared for the Subcommittee on Veterans Affairs of the Committee on Labor and Public Welfare. Washington, D.C.: Government Printing Office, 1978.

Moore, Samuel T. "The General Died a Major." *The American Legion Magazine*, Vol. 25, No. 3 (September 1938).

Morison, Samuel Eliot. *History of U.S. Naval Operations in World War II*. 15 volumes. Boston: Little, Brown, 1947–1962.

————. *The Two Ocean Navy, A Short History of the U.S. Navy in World War II*. Boston: Little, Brown, 1963.

Morton, J. Sterling. *Illustrated History of Nebraska*. 2 volumes. Lincoln: Jacob North and Company, 1907.

Morton, Louis. *The Fall of the Philippines (U.S. Army in World War II, The War in the Pacific)*. Washington, D.C.: Historical Division, Department of the Army, 1953.

Muller, William G. *The 24th Infantry, Past and Present*. No publisher, 1923.

Muscatine County-Portrait and Biographical Album of Muscatine County, Iowa. Chicago: Acme Publishing Company, 1889.

The Navy and Marine Corps Register, 1899, 1918, 1919.

New York at Gettysburg-New York Monuments Commission. *Final Report on the Battlefield at Gettysburg*. 3 volumes. Albany, N.Y.: J.B. Lyon Company, 1900.

Nivens, John. *Connecticut for the Union*. New Haven: Yale University Press, 1965.

Officers Register-Register of the Commissioned and Warrant Officers of the U.S. Navy and Marine Corps, 1942-1946, 1951-1954, 1970-1973.

Official Army Register of the Volunteers Forces of the U.S. Army. 8 volumes. Washington, D.C.: The Adjutant General's Office, 1867.

OR—The War of the Rebellion, Official Records of the Union and Confederate Armies. 128 volumes. Washington, D.C.: Government Printing Office, 1880-1901.

Palfrey, Francis W. *In Memoriam, Henry Livermore Abbott*. Boston: Privately printed, 1864.

Peithmann, Irvin M. *The Unconquered Seminole Indians*. St. Petersburg, Fla.: The Great Outdoors Association, no date.

Phisterer, Frederick. *New York in the War of the Rebellion*. 3rd ed. 6 volumes. Albany, N.Y.: J.B. Lyon Company, 1912.

————. *Statistical Record of the Armies of the United States*. New York: Charles Scribner's Sons, 1883. Reprint, New York: The Blue and the Gray Press, no date.

Prange, Gordon W. *Miracle at Midway*. New York: McGraw-Hill, 1982.

Rapport, Leonard, and Arthur Norwood, Jr. *Rendezvous with Destiny, History of the 101st Airborne Division*. Washington, D.C.: Infantry Journal Press, 1948.

Rice, Thomas E. "The Bright and Particular Star." *Civil War Times Illustrated*, Vol. 26, No. 3 (May 1987).

Ridgeway, Matthew B. *Soldier: The Memoirs of Matthew B. Ridgeway*. New York: Harper & Brothers, 1956.

Robertson, James I. *General A.P. Hill, The Story of a Confederate Warrior*. New York: Random House, 1987.

Robertson, John, comp. *Michigan in the War*. Lansing, Mich. W.S. George & Company, 1880.

ROS Henry R. Hill-U.S. Army National Guard Personnel Center. "Record of Service, Henry Root Hill."

Ruppenthal, Roland G. *Logistical Support of the Armies (U.S. Army in World War II, The European Theater of Operations)*. Vol. I. Washington, D.C.: Office of the Chief of Military History, 1953.

Rutherford, William D. *165 Days, The Story of the 25th Division on Luzon*. Manila: 1945.

Sabine, W.H.W. *Suppressed History of General Nathaniel Woodhull*. New York: 1954.

Schnapper, M. *Who's Who in the Army*. Washington, D.C.: American Council on Public Affairs, 1948.

Sellers, Charles C. *Benedict Arnold, The Proud Warrior*. New York: Minton, Balch, 1930.

Shaw, Horace H. *The First Maine Heavy Artillery, 1862-1865*. Portland, Me.: 1903.

Sixth Infantry Division Public Relations Staff. *The Sixth Infantry Division in World War II*. Washington, D.C.: Infantry Journal Press, 1947.

69th Division—Pictorial History of the 69th Infantry Division, 15 May 1943–15 May 1945. Munich, Germany: F. Bruckmann KG, 1945.

Smith, Robert R. *Triumph in the Philippines (U.S. Army in World War II, The War in the Pacific)*. Washington, D.C.: Office of the Chief of Military History, 1963.

SMS, Guy O. Fort-Headquarters, Philippine Constabulary. "Statement of Military Service, Guy O. Fort."

Spiller, Roger J., ed. *Dictionary of American Military Biography*. 3 volumes. Westport, Conn.: Greenwood Press, 1984.

Stallings, Laurence. *The Doughboys, The Story of the AEF, 1917–1918*. New York: Harper & Row, 1963.

Starr, Stephen Z. *The Union Cavalry in the Civil War*. 3 volumes. Baton Rouge: Louisiana State University Press, 1979–1985.

Stewart, Mrs. Catesby Willis. *The Life of Brigadier General William Woodford of the American Revolution*. 2 volumes. Richmond, Va.: Whitett & Shepperson, 1973.

Templeton, Kenneth S. *Tenth Mountain Division, America's Ski Troops*. Chicago: 1945.

34th Division—The Story of the 34th Infantry Division, Louisiana to Pisa. No publisher, 1945.

32nd Division—Wisconsin War Historical Division. The 32nd Division in the World War. Milwaukee: The Wisconsin Printing Company, 1920.

Thomason, John W. *Jeb Stuart*. New York: Charles Scribner's Sons, 1930.

Twentieth Century Biographic Dictionary of Notable Americans. 10 volumes. Boston: The Biographic Society, 1904. Reprint, Detroit: Gale Research Company, 1968.

28th Division in World War II-History and Pictorial Review of the 28th Infantry Division in World War II. Atlanta: Albert Love Enterprises, 1948.

28th, Roll On (GI Stories). Paris, France: 1945.

U.S. Air Force Register, 1951–1954, 1968–1974.

U.S. Armed Forces Information School. *The Army Almanac*. 2nd Ed. Harrisburg, Pa.: The Stackpole Company, 1959.

U.S. Army. Army Battle Casualties and Non-Battle Deaths in World War II, 7 December 1941–31 December 1946. Washington, D.C.: 1947.

————. Battle Casualties of the Army. Office of the Assistant Chief of Staff, G-1: 1954.

U.S. Navy. *Civil War Chronology, 1861–1865*. Washington, D.C.: Government Printing Office, 1971.

U.S. War Department. *Report of the Secretary of War to the President, 1926*. Washington, D.C.: Government Printing Office, 1926.

————. U.S. Army General Officer Casualties, 7 December 1941–2 September 1945. Washington, D.C.: War Department Public Relations Division, 1946.

Utley, Robert M. *Frontier Regulars, The U.S. Army and the Indian, 1866–1890*. New York: The Macmillan Company, 1973.

Wailes, Benjamin L.C. *Memoir of Leonard Covington*. Natchez, Miss. Privately printed, 1928.

Waite, Otis F.R. *Claremont War History*. Concord, N.H.: McFarland & Jenks, 1868.

————. *History of the Town of Claremont*. Manchester, N.H.: John B. Clarke Company, 1895.

Warner, Ezra J. *Generals in Blue*. Baton Rouge: Louisiana State University Press, 1964.

_____. *Generals in Gray*. Baton Rouge: Louisiana State University Press, 1959.

Weigley, Russell F. *Eisenhower's Lieutenants*. Bloomington: University of Indiana Press, 1981.

Werstein, Irving. *The Lost Battalion*. New York: W.W. Norton, 1966.

Weygant, Charles H. *The Sacketts of America*. Newburgh, N.Y.: Journal Printers, 1907.

Who's Who in America, Vol. 23 (1944–45). Chicago: A.N. Marquis Company, 1944.

The World Almanac and Book of Facts, 1983. New York: Newspapers Enterprise Association, 1982.

Wright, Robert K. *The Continental Army*. Washington, D.C.: Center for Military History, 1983.

Periodicals

Albany (New York) *Evening Journal*
Assembly (U.S. Military Academy, West Point, N.Y.)
Augusta (Georgia) *Chronicle*
Belvidere (Illinois) *Standard*
Berkshire (Massachusetts) *Eagle*
Boston Globe
Burlington (Vermont) *Free Press*
Charlotte (North Carolina) *Observer*
Chicago Tribune
Frederick (Maryland) *News-Post*
Greenville (Ohio) *Democrat*
Kootenai County (Idaho) *Leader*
Macon (Georgia) *Telegraph*
Marion (Illinois) *Republican*
Nebraska Republican
Newsweek
New York Times
Official U.S. Bulletin (World War I daily publication of the Committee on Public Information)
Omaha (Nebraska) *World-Herald*
Portland (Maine) *Press-Herald*
Riverside (California) *Press-Enterprise*
St. Augustine (Florida) *Record*
San Francisco Chronicle
Staunton (Virginia) *Leader*
Time
Washington Post
Wayne (Pennsylvania) *Independent*

Archives and Manuscript Collections

Boston University, Mugar Memorial Library, Special Collections
Cherry Valley, N.Y. Historical Society
Missouri Historical Society
Missouri National Guard, Adjutant General's Office

Musser Public Library, Muscatine, Iowa

National Archives, Records of the Adjutant General's Office, 1780s–1917 (RG 94), Records of the Record and Pension Office, 1784–1917, Military Service and Pension Application Records.

National Archives, Records of the Adjutant General's Office, 1917–(RG 407), Report, Files 1941–1954.

National Archives, Records of the Army Air Forces (Record Group 18), Other General Records, Civilian and Military Personnel Records, 1919–1947.

National Archives, Records of the Post Office Department (RG 28), Records of the Office of the Postmaster General, 1773–1953.

National Archives, Records of U.S. Air Force Commands, Activities and Organizations (RG 342), Records 1934–1955, Unit Histories.

New Jersey State Library, Bureau of Archives and History, Trenton

New York Division of Military and Naval Affairs, Albany

Ohio Historical Society

Orange County, N.Y. Historical Society

Pennsylvania Department of Military Affairs, Harrisburg

Pennsylvania Historical and Museum Commission, Bureau of Archives and History, Harrisburg

Don F. Pratt Museum, 101st Airborne Division, Fort Campbell, Kentucky

Southern Historical Collection, University of North Carolina, Chapel Hill

U.S. Air Force Office of History, Washington, D.C.

U.S. Air Force Records Center, St. Louis

U.S. Army Center for Military History, Washington, D.C.

U.S. Army Military History Research Institute, Carlisle, Pennsylvania

U.S. Army Service Center for the Armed Forces Library (formerly The Army Library), Military Documents Section, The Pentagon, Washington, D.C.

U.S. Marine Corps Historical Division, Washington, D.C.

U.S. Military Academy, West Point, New York

U.S. Navy Office of Information, Washington, D.C.

Western Historical Manuscript Collection, University of Missouri, Columbia

Index

Entries in this index refer to names which are the subjects of the biographical entries or are in the introduction or the appendices. Names are not cross-indexed from entry to entry. Names of officers who were not casualties are not indexed.

ABOUT THE AUTHOR

RUSSELL K. BROWN is a retired U.S. Army officer who is now employed by the Georgia Power Company. He is a graduate of the University of Maryland and other schools and holds a doctorate in U.S. military history from Columbia Pacific University. His published articles have appeared in a variety of military and historical journals. Dr. Brown also teaches history part time as an avocation. He is married and lives in Grovetown, Georgia.